D1429494

FROM WAR TO COLD WAR, 1942–48

FROM WAR TO COLD WAR, 1942–48

Roy Douglas

First published 1981 by
THE MACMILLAN PRESS LTD
London and Basingstoke
Companies and representatives
throughout the world

ISBN 0 333 25346 9

Typeset by Computacomp (UK) Ltd,
Fort William, Scotland
Printed in Hong Kong

Contents

List of Plates

Acknowledgements

The author wishes to thank many people for their help with this book: his wife, who has read and criticised all the manuscript, and Mr Bertram Pockney of the University of Surrey, who has read and criticised much of it; Lord Home, Lord Gladwyn, Count Raczynski and Sir Frank Roberts who have kindly granted interviews relating to their own important experiences of events in the period described. He is also very grateful to many of his colleagues at Surrey who have helped with very useful discussions on aspects of the work. It is perhaps invidious to mention particular names in this connection, but he would like to express particular gratitude to Dr Michael Burstall, Dr Teresa Poole and J. W. J. Wielogorski Esq., who have helped crystallise many of the ideas discussed in this book.

Thanks are also due to the librarians and archivists of the various institutions listed in the Appendix as sources of original manuscripts, and to the following copyright owners for permission to quote from material: British Library of Political and Economic Science for the extracts from the *Dalton Diaries*; Cassell Limited for the extracts from vols. VII, X, and XII of *The Second World War* by Sir Winston Churchill; The Controller of Her Majesty's Stationery Office for the extracts from Crown copyright documents in the Public Record Office; The Executors for the Harry S. Truman Estate for the extracts from *Memoirs* published by Doubleday & Co. Inc. 1955; University of Iowa Library for the extracts from the Henry A. Wallace Papers; University of Virginia Library, Manuscripts Department, for the extracts from the Edward R. Stettinius Papers; and Viking Penguin Inc. and Knox Burger Associates for the extracts from *Henry Wallace, Henry Truman and the Cold War* by Richard J. Walton, Copyright © 1976 by Richard J. Walton.

If other copyrights have been inadvertently infringed, the author expresses his sincere regrets. Finally, the author wishes to thank the custodians of the Surrey University Research Fund, the Vice-Chancellor's special fund, and the funds of the General Studies

Department, for their financial assistance with travelling and other expenses incurred in this work.

ROY DOUGLAS

General Studies Department
University of Surrey
October 1979

1

Appeasement

'En conséquence sera reconnu, comme agresseur dans un conflit international ... l'État qui, le premier, aura commis ... invahision par ses forces armées, même sans déclaration de guerre, du territoire d'un autre État.... Aucune considération d'ordre politique, militaire, économique ou autre ne pourra servir d'excuse ou de justification à l'agression....' (Convention for the definition of aggression. Signed 3 July 1933 by representatives of Poland, Estonia, Latvia, Romania, Turkey, USSR, Persia and Afghanistan.)

In the middle phase of the Second World War, official propaganda in Allied countries was full of statements designed to persuade people that the 'Big Three' – Britain, the United States and the Soviet Union – were united not merely in their determination to defeat the enemy, but also in their intention to cooperate closely in the post-war period. Yet, within a year or two of victory, terms like 'Cold War' and 'Iron Curtain' were in general use, and many people believed that full-scale military conflict between the erstwhile Allies was likely within a short time. What had happened to destroy the idyllic cooperation; or was that cooperation never very real or idyllic in the first place? The present study is designed to try to find out.

Ever since 1917, Soviet Russia had been the topic of extreme controversy in the West: controversy not merely about motives but about facts. During the middle and late 1930s, however, there seemed little doubt that the Soviet Union passionately desired the destruction of Nazi Germany, and was prepared to cooperate with others who were like-minded. Russia took all the 'correct' international attitudes. She joined the League of Nations; she opposed the Italian attack on Abyssinia; she did what she could to defeat Franco in Spain; she sounded the alarm when Germany invaded Austria, and bound herself to go to war in defence of Czechoslovakia, if France would do likewise.

Russia's vigorous opposition to Nazi Germany appealed to a wide range of British and American opinion. People with very disparate political views applauded Russia as Hitler's most implacable enemy, and contrasted her attitude favourably with that of the 'appeasing' democracies.

Few people are disposed to be over-critical about possible Allies when they are themselves gravely threatened; and one of the most characteristic features of attitudes in the late 1930s was the steadfast refusal of most of the virulent opponents of Nazi Germany in democratic countries to give serious attention to the possibility that Soviet Russia might conceivably possess an internal régime as oppressive as that of Nazi Germany, and international designs no less alarming. Some people were disposed to dismiss any evidence for this view as a wicked calumny on the Soviet system; others, who suspected that the criticisms might contain a grain of truth, extenuated Russian behaviour as an essentially defensive response to the evil machinations of enemies. Most people probably dismissed the whole question from their minds. Russia was a long way off; they did not know what was going on there, or why; but they did know that Hitler's Germany was a great deal nearer, and was behaving in a very unpleasant and dangerous manner. The enemy of my enemy is my friend.

The Russo-German Non-aggression Pact of August 1939 – followed swiftly by invasion of Poland from both Germany and Russia – caused a profound shock to many who had taken a very sympathetic attitude to the Soviet Union. When the 'fourth partition of Poland' was followed by Russian invasion of Finland, disillusion was complete. Many of Russia's most ardent advocates became her bitterest enemies. The useful word 'communazi' was coined; and nowhere was criticism of Russia sharper than among democratic socialists. People suddenly recollected the obvious similarities between the Nazi and Communist régimes. When the Finns made a spectacular defence against the vastly more numerous Red Army, then even Russia's most convinced apologists found it difficult to explain why the morale of the Red Army was so incredibly low. If the Russians thought they were fighting for something worthwhile – then why did they not fight a lot harder?

The period of German Blitzkrieg in the west was accompanied by further Russian aggression. The three Baltic States – Estonia, Latvia and Lithuania – had broken free from Russia at the time of the Revolution. While both Germany and the Western countries were preoccupied elsewhere, Soviet troops crossed the frontiers in large numbers, deposed the governments of the three Republics, and replaced them with their own nominees. 'Elections' were then held; but only candidates on the new pro-communist Government lists were allowed to stand. The new Assemblies called for incorporation in the Soviet Union, and the three countries were duly annexed. Simultaneously, Russia compelled Romania to return Bessarabia – which had formed part of the empire of the Tsars, but whose population was overwhelmingly Romanian – and also to cede northern Bukovina, which in the past had never been Russian.

On 22 June 1941, Germany attacked the Soviet Union. There was a very powerful argument for Britain withdrawing to the sidelines; but instead, Winston Churchill promptly offered Britain's full assistance to the Soviet Union. As the Prime Minister said, if a devil came out of hell and offered to fight the Nazis, he would grasp it by the hand.

At this stage, the United States was not at war, although she had far exceeded the strict limits of neutrality in the assistance offered to the Allies. In August 1941, Churchill and President Roosevelt met at sea to conclude the famous Atlantic Charter. The two statesmen promulgated elevated principles which, they believed, should actuate international behaviour: 'no territorial changes which do not accord with the freely-expressed wishes of the peoples concerned'; 'right of all peoples to choose the form of government under which they will live'; 'sovereign rights and self-government restored to those who have been forcibly deprived of them': access of all states 'on equal terms to the trade and to the raw materials of the world'; all this, and much more in the same spirit. No doubt cynics thought that it was little more than a propaganda exercise. That was not the case; the two men who concluded the Atlantic Charter demonstrably believed what they said. Next month, representatives of the Soviet Union, and of all the Allied governments in exile, acceded in general terms to the Charter. When the United States formally entered the war in December 1941, the Atlantic Charter really looked like an authoritative declaration of war aims which, if put into effect, would truly justify the misery and destruction of the war, and make future war impossible.

About the time of the German invasion of Russia, a 'groundswell' of political and social awareness became apparent in the West. With little or no encouragement from orthodox political figures in any party, people were coming to question the economic inequalities which had existed in the past, and showed growing determination that these should be radically reduced in the future. If the Soviet Union was indeed a 'workers' state' – and no official propagandists in Britain were saying otherwise – then might not those actions which had received so much attention from Russia's critics be excused on the grounds that you can't make omelettes without breaking eggs? Was it not possible to synthesise the British ideals of parliamentary democracy, freedom of expression and rule of law with the supposed Soviet ideal of a 'classless society'? All this was heady stuff; and in that atmosphere many of the best and most idealistic people in Britain were unwilling to listen to criticisms of the Soviet state. Those who suspected that Soviet Russia was not merely no paradise, but a hell without equal outside Nazi Germany, had all the emotional dice, as well as all the official propaganda, loaded against them.

When the United States was brought into the war, American opinion underwent a similar shift in Russia's favour. The American diplomat Charles Bohlen, who was his country's leading Soviet expert and in close contact with policy-making procedures, has written that there was 'a guilt complex in our relations. American officials and British too were always trying to reassure the Soviets about Allied intentions. Often this effort was overdone and had a counter effect'.[1] The Americans had – or thought they had – a special bond to the Russians in a common dislike for European empires. It will later be necessary to consider whether this affinity was really an American illusion. Nevertheless, there was a very strong current of American thought which considered that it was possible to bring together on a world-wide scale the best real, or imagined, features of Soviet and of Western society.

Even before the United States entered the war, there were signs that the Russians were by no means prepared to abide by the spirit of the Atlantic Charter. In September 1941, Lord Beaverbrook – proprietor of the 'off-beat' Conservative *Daily Express* and various other newspapers, and also a member of the War Cabinet – was visiting Moscow. Stalin suggested to Beaverbrook that the British and Russian Governments might enter into a far-reaching political agreement.[2] In November, Stalin evinced irritation that this proposal had not been followed up. Early in December – just before Pearl Harbor – the British Government agreed that Foreign Secretary Anthony Eden should go to Moscow to explore the matter. The Americans were informed of this, and almost immediately after their entry to the war, Eden departed for Moscow.

The American State Department was convinced that the Russian approach was

'part of a maneuver the purpose of which was to place the British Government in such a position that it would be embarrassing for it to reject Soviet demands that it recognize certain Soviet territorial claims and that it promise to agree to certain territorial adjustments on the European continent, and to other arrangements which would make the Soviet Union the dominating Power of eastern Europe if not of the whole continent'.[3]

A despatch was accordingly prepared by the American Secretary of State, Cordell Hull, and approved by Roosevelt, declaring that

Britain would thereby be set in a 'difficult position to resist additional Soviet demands relating to frontiers, territory or spheres of influence which would almost certainly follow whenever the Soviet Government would find itself in a favorable bargaining position'. The Ambassador in London was instructed to make representations to that effect.

When Eden arrived in Moscow, it soon became apparent that American apprehensions were justified to the hilt. On 17 December, Stalin indicated that he wished Britain to sign two Treaties, 'one dealing with military cooperation during the war and the other with cooperation in the Peace Settlement and during the post-war period'.[4] Drafts were handed to Eden. The following day, Stalin proposed amendments to his own drafts. One of these, 'though its meaning was somewhat obscure, would appear to involve recognition of the 1941 frontiers, and, in reply to a direct question, M. Stalin admitted frankly that it did'.[5] It was apparently intended by Stalin that British acknowledgement of Russia's '1941 frontiers' – that is, her acquisition of at least the Baltic States, and the parts of Finland and Romania which she seized in 1940 – should be contained in a secret protocol. This would also contain acknowledgement of other territorial changes effecting the frontiers of other European states.[6]

The Foreign Secretary reported all this to his Cabinet colleagues, who unanimously decided that they could not sign an agreement on the lines proposed by Russia.[7] Stalin 'displayed considerable irritation'[8] but was somewhat mollified when Eden promised to discuss matters, on his return, with the British, American and Dominion Governments, and endeavour to obtain a decision favourable to Stalin. The Prime Minister delivered a sharp and unwonted reproof to his Foreign Secretary:

> Your [cable] surprised me. . . . We have never recognised the 1941 frontiers of Russia except *de facto*. They were acquired by acts of aggression in shameful collusion with Hitler. The transfer of peoples of the Baltic States to Soviet Russia against their will would be contrary to all the principles for which we are fighting this war and would dishonour our Cause . . . There must be no mistake about the opinion [of] any British Government of which I am the head, namely, that it adheres to those principles of freedom and democracy set forth in the Atlantic Charter, and that these principles must become especially active whenever any question of transferring territory is raised.[9]

In other messages which Churchill sent to important people at the turn of 1941–2, the same points were made with equal emphasis.[10]

There followed swiftly a period of many calamities in the war: not least in the war against Japan. British policy towards the Soviet Union underwent a remarkable change. On 10 February 1942, Eden cabled Viscount Halifax, Ambassador to the United States and a former Foreign Secretary himself:

> Since my return from Moscow we have been considering ways and means of dealing with Stalin's demand for recognition of his 1941 frontiers in Finland, the Baltic States and Romania.[11]

This demand, in Eden's view, was

> put to us as a test of sincerity of our avowed desire to work with [Stalin] during and after the war. It is the fruit of a long period of suspicion and misunderstanding. A simple refusal to meet him would involve the risk that Anglo-Soviet relations will deteriorate, and that cooperation between Great Britain and Russia, and between the USA and Russia, both during and after the war, may be seriously endangered.[12]

Halifax was instructed to set this view before the American Government. The Ambassador required no persuasion to advance such arguments, for he had written to the Prime Minister long before, backing Eden's attitude.[13]

Halifax saw Sumner Welles, Acting Secretary of State. Welles could not speak with authority, but his own response was very similar to Churchill's first reaction. Endorsement of the Soviet position in the Baltic States would be 'a complete repudiation of the principles for which this Government stood'.[14] Russian demands for security against future attack were reasonable; but these must not be pleaded as an excuse for placing millions of unwilling people under Soviet domination.

Roosevelt was no more impressed than Welles: 'Only one word had come into the President's mind, and that was the word "provincial".'[15] He was particularly shocked at the idea that Russia's position in the Baltic States should be recognised by some kind of secret undertaking. Like Churchill, he perceived that the whole idea was incompatible with the Atlantic Charter.[16]

By this time, Churchill had abandoned his original stand, and after strong pressure from Eden[17] was persuaded to send a personal message to Roosevelt, urging that 'the principles of the Atlantic Charter ought not to be construed so as to deny Russia the frontiers she occupied when Germany attacked her'.[18] At Washington, Halifax stated the position even more bluntly. What Russia really wanted was a 'Second Front' – a major military invasion of Western Europe. As

Britain was in no immediate position to offer this, she tendered in lieu a Treaty, whose terms would include acknowledgement of Russian acquisition of the Baltic States. This, he explained, would be 'a political substitute for material military assistance'.[19] Eden – so Halifax went on to argue – considered that the situation would otherwise be 'catastrophic'. The Ambassador amplified this expression. Stalin might 'demonstrate marked hostility to Great Britain'. If that happened, 'Mr. Churchill's Government would probably fall'; whereafter it was likely that a 'frankly pro-communist, pro-Moscow policy would be pursued'.[20] Whatever Halifax may have thought about the substantive advantages of recognition, it is exceedingly difficult to see how he can possibly have believed anything so improbable. Roosevelt certainly did not believe it. Echoing the language of a closely-argued State Department memorandum he had received a couple of months earlier,[21] the President pointed out that 'concessions on the frontier question would only encourage further demands'.[22] Eventually the President suggested a compromise which was not very creditable from the standpoint of principles, but at least suggested some sense of humanity. Perhaps Britain could persuade the Russians to agree to a term in the Treaty which would authorise people from the annexed territories to emigrate if they wished, and take their property with them? An important American diplomat noted in his diary that – if the President's suggestion were accepted – 'I think this would be construed as a recognition by us of a pressure deal which condemns about three million people to death'.[23] It soon became apparent, however, that the Russians would not make even that small concession. Eden and Halifax were now in a condition of panic, and hinted strongly to the Americans that they might go ahead with the Russian Treaty even in the teeth of American disapproval.

American official opinion remained most unhappy about the proposed Anglo-Russian understanding. 'The attitude of the British Government,' wrote Sumner Welles, 'is not only indefensible from every moral standpoint, but likewise extraordinarily stupid. I am confident that no sooner will this Treaty have been signed than Great Britain will be confronted with new additional demands for the recognition of the right of the Soviet Union to occupy Bukovina, Bessarabia and very likely eastern Poland and northern Norway.'[24] Roosevelt, however, had now retreated from the stand he took earlier, into a Pilate-like attitude. Eden was thus able to assure the Russian Ambassador that 'the President would not . . . approve our act, but he did not wish to oppose the negotiations'.[25]

Meanwhile, a considerable political crisis had developed in Britain. This did not follow predictable party lines. Lord Beaverbrook pressed with great vigour for Britain formally to recognise Russia's acquisition of the Baltic States.[26] His most resolute opponent was Clement Attlee, leader of the Labour party, who threatened resignation if Russia's position in the Baltic States were acknowledged.[27] During the course of the negotiations, Attlee was made Deputy Prime Minister. That precipitated Beaverbrook's resignation.[28] Nevertheless, Churchill indicated that he and Beaverbrook 'remain[ed] close friends and intimate political associates'.[29] Altercations between pro-Russian and anti-Russian members of the British Government continued on a considerable scale. Ernest Bevin, the great Trade Union leader and currently Minister of Labour, took the same line as his party leader. R. A. Butler, the Conservative in charge of Education, took the opposite view – writing to Eden, strongly urging acceptance of the 1941 frontiers.[30] A great deal of information about the proposed Treaty leaked out long before the Government intended. Many well-known Conservatives and associates took a far more principled stand than most of their leaders. Victor Cazalet, Harold Nicolson and the Lord Chancellor, Viscount Simon, evinced great concern about the developments.[31] Criticisms from such quarters were perhaps predictable; but by far the most pungent of all came from Duff Cooper. He had a special *locus standi*, for he was the only member of Chamberlain's Cabinet who had resigned over Munich. This fact gave great weight to his argument:

> 'There was no more brutal, and indefensible, act of aggression than Russia's occupation of [the Baltic States.] ... Germany's interference with Czechoslovakia, where there was a large German population, and with Poland, where a corridor created an extremely difficult position, were far more excusable actions than that of Russia against the Baltic States.'[32]

If Britain were now to endorse that Russian aggression, declared Duff Cooper, that action 'would tear into ribbons the Atlantic Charter and brand us as the arch-hypocrites of the world'.

The argument raged fast and furious. Churchill's Parliamentary Private Secretary reported that there was great concern among MPs, who argued for a variety of reasons that it would be both immoral and foolish. 'We are acquiescing in aggression,' they contended. 'This is Munich over again, but worse.' They correctly guessed that America did not favour the Treaty. Even from the most cynical point of view this was hardly the moment; military events might soon place Russia in a much weaker bargaining position.[33] The Prime Minister's informant went on to add that 'this is a matter which may develop into a major crisis'.

The Foreign Office, who had been the active agents from the start, prepared two drafts of possible Treaties between Britain and the Soviet Union. Stalin was not satisfied with these proposals, and decided to send his Foreign Minister, Molotov, to London to negotiate. When Molotov arrived, Churchill at once warned him of both American and domestic opposition. At the second meeting of the British with Molotov, Churchill was not present, but Eden spoke for the Government:

> When he was in Moscow he had no authority to agree to the Soviet proposals concerning the Baltic States. Now on that point H.M. Government were prepared to agree; they had made this concession and they were prepared to agree to the phrase proposed by the Soviet Government.[34]

This view was plainly in flat contradiction to the War Cabinet decision reached five months earlier.

Another even more difficult question was raised by Molotov: the Soviet claim to eastern Poland. These representations were premature. Eden and Churchill decided that the political repercussions of acknowledging Russia's conquests even in the Baltic States through a formal instrument would be too embarrassing. Accordingly, Eden put forward a new suggestion. Instead of the Treaty under discussion, let Britain and Russia execute a completely different instrument – a Twenty Year Treaty, which would provide not only for collaboration in wartime but for cooperation thereafter. This might please the Russians and prove politically innocuous at home.[35] The Russians accepted this proposal, even though it made no mention of the vexed frontier question, and the Twenty Year Treaty was eventually signed.

This might seem like a satisfactory arrangement for all concerned; but it was really nothing of the kind. The record of the Eden–Molotov discussions – to which, of course, neither the British MPs nor the Americans had access – made it absolutely clear that Eden acknowledged Russian possession of the Baltic States.[36] This made it impossible for Britain later to support any more determined stand which the Americans might wish to take.

British discussions with Molotov were concerned with military as well as diplomatic matters. The Russian demand for a Second Front in 1942 was pressed strongly. Churchill listened with sympathy, but gave an *aide-memoire* which stated expressly that 'we can . . . give no promise in the matter'.[37] Molotov proceeded to the United States, and on 11 June a White House statement was issued declaring that the Soviet Foreign Minister and American President had reached 'full understanding . . . with regard to the urgent tasks of creating a

Second Front in Europe in 1942'.[38] The circumstances of the discussion between the President and Molotov, and of the announcement which followed, were – to put it mildly – no very good example of inter-Allied cooperation. An informed British observer fulminated that 'Roosevelt had calmly told Molotov he would be prepared to contemplate a sacrifice of 120,000 men – *our* men!'[39] Nor were the British the only people aggrieved. Cordell Hull, American Secretary of State, seems to have been allowed no part in phrasing the communiqué.[40] The Russians were rather better served, for they were given to understand that the 'promise' must not be taken at face value. In any case, this proposed operation was conceived as a device for relieving pressure on the Russians, not as one which would eventually lead to the invading forces from the West joining hands with the Russians across a prostrate Germany. Further examination made it plain that it would involve vast sacrifices of British lives, and the likely result would be a major disaster for all the Allies – not least for the Russians. In the end, the whole idea was abandoned in favour of a different strategy.

The inability of the Western Allies to launch a Second Front was bound to distress and infuriate the Russians; but another irritant arose from a different source. Considerable supplies had been sent to Russia from Britain by the northern route to Archangel and Murmansk. In the course of 1942 the German U-boats became increasingly active, and in July only four vessels out of a convoy of thirty-three reached the destined Russian port, with five more 'precariously in the ice' off Novaya Zemlya.[41] Churchill explained all this to Roosevelt: 'If half had got through we should have persevered, but with only about a quarter arriving, the operation was not good enough.' The two men agreed that it was imperative to stop Arctic convoys for the time being.

The thankless task of explaining all this to the Russians fell upon Churchill. In August he flew to Moscow to unfold the plans devised by Britain and the United States. There was much plain – not to say brutal – speaking; but eventually understanding was reached on the essential strategy. In lieu of the limited Second Front of 1942, there was to be a much grander affair the following year. Twenty-seven American and twenty-one British divisions would assemble in the United Kingdom, ready for an assault in the spring of 1943.[42] This invasion would be heralded by 'Operation Torch', which would be launched against French North-west Africa in Autumn 1942. .

Many of the aspects of Operation Torch will be considered in a later chapter. From a military point of view it was a success; and in January 1943 Churchill and Roosevelt met at Casablanca, in Morocco. The main, but by no means the exclusive, function of the conference was to discuss revised strategic plans for 1943. These would include an attack on Sicily, and an assault on France – which would take place in September at the latest. Stalin was informed of the main conclusions, and objected vigorously to the decision to postpone the Second Front. The 'first charge on the resources of the United Nations' proclaimed at Casablanca, however, was defeat of the German U-boats.

The U-boats were crucial in all military operations which involved the Americans. At one point in the autumn of 1942, the Western Allies were budgeting together 'for a balance of shipping on the basis of 700,000 tons a month loss'.[43] 'True,' added Churchill, 'it is not yet as bad as that.' In the spring of 1943, the Prime Minister reported to some of his leading colleagues that 'the Americans had planned to have thirty divisions in England by now, but in fact they only have one, and in North Africa seven or eight. This is due to the U-boats.'[44] The idea of launching a Second Front in 1943 was not readily abandoned, but eventually Churchill and Roosevelt were compelled to report to Stalin that the Second Front must be postponed again – this time until 1944. The news was transmitted at the beginning of June 1943, and produced further recriminations from Stalin. Thus the leaders of the Western Allies were still morally on the defensive in all dealings with Russia.

Although the Western Allies were unable to satisfy the Russian demand for a major attack on the Atlantic coast, they were soon able to assault what Churchill called the 'soft underbelly of the Axis', by an attack on Sicily, followed swiftly by landings on the Italian mainland. These gains were important, but were not of a kind likely to offer significant relief to the Red Army. Meanwhile, however, the Russians were in the process of turning the tide on the eastern front. In the winter of 1942–3, the great battle of Stalingrad was fought. The Russian triumph did not yet establish that the Allies would eventually win an outright victory; but from that point forward it became most unlikely that the Germans would do so. During the course of 1943 it became increasingly clear that the conflict was likely to result in a complete victory for the Allies; and the public in Britain and America thrilled to the Russian successes. The Western Allies might indeed point to substantial progress in the war against Japan; but to British opinion, and to a large bulk of opinion in the United States, the Japanese conflict was very much a side show.

Winston Churchill's emotional reactions were very similar to those of the man in the street. Thus he wrote to Anthony Eden at the beginning of 1944, with particular reference to the Baltic States:

I ask myself, how do all these matters stand now? Undoubtedly my own feelings have changed in the two years that have passed since the topic was first raised ... The tremendous victories of the

Russian armies, the deep-seated changes which have taken place in the character of the Russian state and Government, the new confidence which has grown in our hearts towards Stalin – these have all had their effect . . .[45]

Averell Harriman, American Ambassador to the Soviet Union, wrote in similar terms to President Roosevelt in the summer of 1943:

. . . As you know, I am a confirmed optimist in our relations with Russia because of my conviction that Stalin wants, if obtainable, a firm understanding with you and America more than anything else. He sees Russia's reconstruction and security more soundly based on it than on any alternative. He is a man of simple purposes and, although he may use devious means in order to accomplish them, he does not deviate from his big main objectives.[46]

Stalin was no doubt aware of this developing sympathy in Britain and America, and was anxious to encourage it. The lingering fear that Russia aimed at internal subversion within all other countries was largely allayed in May 1943 when the 'Communist International' or 'Comintern' was dissolved. This decision was more symbolic than real. As an American State Department official observed, 'for over fifteen years the Comintern has been . . . used primarily as an instrument of Soviet foreign policy and not as an instrument for the attainment of world revolution'.[47] Nevertheless, there was a substantial body of opinion in the United States, and some in Britain too, which felt that the Comintern had not abandoned its original objectives, and heard the news with considerable relief. Henceforth, it would seem, Russia would be treated as a Great Power with the ordinary aspirations of Great Powers, not as the nerve-centre of world-wide subversion.

By the spring of 1943, when the Comintern was dissolved, Stalin could look back on a period of vast diplomatic triumphs in relation to Britain and America. The Soviet claim to the Baltic States had been conceded for all practical purposes, and notice had been served to the effect that Atlantic Charter principles would not be construed in a manner inimical to the interests of the Soviet Union. Other considerations of even more immediate and practical importance had been established. Despite the close personal relations subsisting between Churchill and Roosevelt, wedges could be driven between Britain and the United States, from either angle, to the advantage of the Soviet Union. Finally, it was possible to obtain diplomatic concessions piecemeal. This was much more convenient than waiting for the final reckoning and then presenting the West with a formidable list of demands. Hitler had reached a similar conclusion some years earlier.

2

Tehran

'The Poles tell me, not unreasonably, that they know a great deal more about Russia than we do, and that we are wrong in expecting any response in action to efforts on our part to conciliate the Soviet Government and get its confidence.' Sir Owen O'Malley to Anthony Eden, 27 February 1943. FO 371/34564, fo. 198.

Against the background of pro-Russian euphoria which characterised the Western Democracies in 1943 must be set the story of Poland. That story, one of the great tragedies in world history, must itself be seen in a much deeper historical and ethnic context.

Between the area of Europe which is overwhelmingly Polish in race and the area which is overwhelmingly Russian, there lie the vast, but ill-defined, regions known as the Ukraine and White Russia (Byelorussia). The name 'White Russia' is unfortunate, for hardly any real Russians lived in the western part of that country. The old name, 'White Ruthenia', would be a better one, but it is now obsolete. Both the Ukraine and White Russia were of profoundly mixed population. Most of both formed part of Poland from the fourteenth century to the eighteenth. Then, in three 'Partitions', the whole of Poland – the ethnically Polish area as well as the racially mixed eastern provinces – was divided between Russia, Austria and Prussia. The three predatory empires collapsed almost simultaneously in 1917–18, and a Polish state was restored.

It was exceedingly difficult to decide what were proper boundaries for the new Poland, especially in the East; and the situation was complicated further by the revolutionary and national wars which continued to rage in the territory of the former Russian Empire. Towards the end of 1919, and in two separate stages, the Allied Supreme Council defined a line in eastern Europe. What lay to the west of that line was definitely Polish; there was no implication or suggestion that territory to the east of it might not also be Polish.[1] There were many large and important Polish communities east of the line, although these were mostly embedded in non-Polish countryside. There was certainly no implication that territory east of the line should go to Russia. The large, important and overwhelmingly Polish town of Lwow (Lemberg, Lvov), for example, lay a little to the east of the southern extension of the Curzon Line. It had not belonged to Russia at any point in its history, and it was obviously not intended by the Supreme Council that it should now become Russian.

The Supreme Council Line acquired new importance in the following year. War was raging between the Russians and the Poles. In July 1920, the Russians were on the offensive. The British Foreign Secretary, Lord Curzon, proposed that the Supreme Council Line should constitute an armistice line – again with no implication whatever that it should form a permanent frontier. Thereafter the Supreme Council Line was usually known as the Curzon Line. The Russians ignored the suggestion, and advanced to the environs of Warsaw, where they were soundly defeated by Marshal Pilsudski. Eventually, at the Treaty of Riga in March 1921, the Russians and Poles agreed on a permanent frontier. The 'Riga Line', which followed approximately the Russo-Polish frontier after the Second Partition of Poland in 1793, was not wholly satisfactory, for a strict ethnic line was impossible. Many 'ethnic Poles' lived well to the east of the Riga Line; while, conversely, the eleven or twelve million people lying between the Curzon Line and the Riga Line were profoundly mixed. In many cases it was impossible to give any satisfactory designation to a particular individual; but, at a rough estimate, there were between four and five million 'ethnic Poles', and a rather smaller number of Ukrainians; while the remainder were divided into White Russians, Lithuanians and 'unassimilated' Jews.

When Russia and Germany partitioned Poland again in 1939, the new line of demarcation – the 'Ribbentrop–Molotov Line' – followed roughly the Curzon Line, but in places bulged a little to the west. Wilno (Vilna) was given initially to Lithuania, but was incorporated in the Soviet Union along with all the Baltic States a few months later. 'Plebiscites' were held in eastern Poland in conditions redolent of similar ventures under Hitler,[2] and the predictable vast majorities declared for incorporation in the Soviet Union – a boon promptly granted to them. Nobody outside the range of Communist propaganda took these results seriously as an expression of local opinion. Britain and France were left to face Germany alone, with Russia malevolently neutral.

Many Poles escaped to the West, and a Polish 'Government in Exile' was formed under Allied tutelage. This was very different from the pre-war Polish Government, most of whose members had been killed, captured or interned during the invasions. The new government contained members from all substantial parties, and was 'thoroughly democratic in personnel and ideas'.[3] The leading figure was General Wladyslaw Sikorski, who combined the offices of Prime Minister, and Commander in Chief of the Polish forces.

When Germany invaded Russia, arrangements were rapidly made to settle the current differences between Russia and Poland. A treaty was concluded in July 1941 between the two governments, under which they made common cause against Germany. Polish prisoners in the USSR would be released, and an army of Polish nationals organised on Soviet soil. Difficulties arose later about the equipment of this army, and it was eventually agreed that they should move to the Middle East, and be set under British command. In the course of 1942, some 77,000 Polish troops and 26,000 civilians left the Soviet Union.

The 1941 Treaty deliberately left open the whole question of the frontier between Poland and the Soviet Union. At the time, this appeared a highly theoretical question; for the whole of Poland (however defined) and a large part of the Soviet Union was in German occupation. The Russians, however, did not resile from their designs on Eastern Poland. As already noted, the matter was touched on at the time of Eden's 1941 visit to Moscow, and mentioned more explicitly during Molotov's visit to London in 1942. The Russian request for recognition of these conquests was not granted, although records of the 1942 meeting do not suggest that the Foreign Secretary felt any deep objection on principle. When Molotov told him that a recent Order of the Day by Stalin 'had claimed the restoration of all frontiers violated by Hitler and this point could not be abandoned', no protest seems to have been made about frontiers which Russia herself had acquired such a short time before. Eden, like a lot of people, had double standards on international aggression. The Russians had double standards of a somewhat different kind. When they had been pressing the British for the full 1941 frontiers for a long time, they told the Americans 'that what they claimed in the west was Petsamo, an adjustment in Karelia, Estonia, Latvia and Bessarabia. They made no mention of either Lithuania or Bukovina.'[4] Nor do they seem to have mentioned their claims for Eastern Poland.

As the battle around Stalingrad swung strongly in favour of the Russians, so also did Soviet diplomacy begin to tighten the screw against the Poles. On 16 January 1943, a Note was given to their Chargé in the Soviet Union. Hitherto, the Soviet Government had treated 'ethnic' White Russians and Ukrainians from eastern Poland as Soviet citizens, but ethnic Poles as Polish citizens. Now, the Note declared, all alike would be treated as Soviet citizens.[5] This was an announcement of profound significance in more ways than one. Some 200,000 Poles who had fled into the Soviet Union ahead of the advancing Germans were apparently being held as hostages for the pliant behaviour of their compatriots, 'virtually under threat of death'.[6] Those who were, or who became, of military age would be liable for service in the Red Army. Even more serious than these grave matters was the territorial implication, for it very clearly suggested that Russia intended to hold Eastern Poland for herself once the Germans had been removed. Then, on 19 February, a press item appeared in a local Soviet newspaper, and was reproduced a day or two later in *Pravda*.

The theme of the article was indicated by the title, 'Ukraine is indivisible'. The author bitterly criticised former Polish rule in the eastern provinces, indicating that post-war arrangements would keep the area within the Soviet Union. The publication was obviously an inspired statement of the official Soviet view. On 6 March, a British diplomat elicited from the Russian Ambassador to Poland the information that Russia intended the post-war delimitation between the two countries to follow closely the Curzon Line. There was some doubt whether the Curzon Line, strictly understood, ran through the old Austrian territories; but for purposes of these and future discussions the Line was 'so prolonged as to leave Lwow to Russia'.[7] In vain did Jan Ciechanowski, Polish Ambassador to the United States, attempt to explain 'that the Curzon Line had never been a frontier. It was a suggested line of demarcation between the Polish and Soviet armies to be accepted while the parties should negotiate; it had been rejected by both sides and had never had any standing.'[8]

All exiled Poles regarded any Russian claim to the eastern half of their country with deepest disapproval. Not least emphatic on the matter was the Polish Socialist Party, a body whose ideology resembled that of the British Labour Party, and whose support was drawn from similar social quarters.[9] Of all eastern Poland, the city of Lwow had the highest significance, both economic and emotional, to the Poles.

The overriding concern of Anthony Eden was to damp down discussion of the matter. He could have no influence on the Russians who had first raised it; but he could exert pressure to stop the Poles replying. On 3 March he pleaded with representatives of the Polish Government for cessation of 'public polemics'.

'General Sikorski said that it was impossible to do as the Foreign Secretary wished . . . his authority with his own people, particularly with the Polish Army, would be undermined unless he publicly and emphatically contradicted Russian statements . . . he thought that the Soviet Government were trying to see how far they could go and that silence would lead them to increase the brutality of their language to and treatment of Poland.'[10]

During March, the 'public polemics' became a good deal sharper. On 10 March, *The Times* carried a leading article written by E. H. Carr – a Russophile, to say the least. This averred that Russia's frontier was 'on the Oder'. The crucial passage could be read in a slightly less offensive way than the words seemed to imply; but the Poles not unnaturally took considerable alarm. Another strongly anti-Polish article, 'Cadavers in the Carpathians', soon appeared in *Pravda*, and was then syndicated all over the Soviet Union. A Polish language newspaper, *Wolna Polska*, made its first appearance in Moscow, with strong official encouragement. The Polish Acting Foreign Minister complained that 'almost all Polish "men of trust" in the USSR have been arrested and the entire Polish welfare organisation has been taken over by the Soviet authorities'.[11] Sir Owen O'Malley, British Ambassador to the exiled Polish Government, became increasingly disturbed. 'Never since June 1941 have Polish-Soviet relations been worse than they are at present,' he wrote to Eden. 'At any moment the decorous official drapery which conceals the real state of things may be torn away.'[12]

Roosevelt also began to feel concern on the matter of Russo-Polish relations. The President resolved to send a special representative to Stalin 'to do what might be possible on behalf of the Polish refugees and in the interest of an improvement of Soviet-Polish relations'.[13] Soon Roosevelt was able to suggest to Eden a possible line of solution – although it was one which he would later qualify in an important respect. Let Russia take all up to the Curzon Line, and let Poland receive in compensation the German lands of East Prussia, 'and perhaps some concessions in Silesia'.[14] What if the Poles demurred? '[Britain], the United States and Russia should decide at the appropriate moment what was a just and reasonable solution and if we were agreed Poland would have to accept.'[15] So much for the Atlantic Charter and the rights of small nations. In any event, nobody could at that point state in public the nature of the disreputable deal proposed: 'it would be too good for Goebbels,' as Eden wrote.[16] The idea was by no means new; Stalin had in fact discussed it with the Foreign Secretary in Moscow in December 1941.[17]

On 12 April 1943, Eden was compelled to tell the Cabinet that 'differences between the Russians and the Poles were now acute'.[18] They were even more acute than he realised; for the Germans had just launched a new line of propaganda, which was pressed with great force in the next few days. According to the German story, a mass grave of Polish officers had been discovered by the occupying forces in Katyn Forest, near Smolensk. The Germans contended that these officers had been prisoners-of-war captured by the Russians in 1939, who had been massacred in the following year – that is, long before the German attack on the Soviet Union.

Shortly after these revelations, Churchill and Sikorski lunched together. Roosevelt's boundary proposal was bruited, but rejected by Sikorski. The question of the Katyn graves was also raised. The Polish Prime Minister then gave Churchill a memorandum on the subject, which seems to have persuaded the latter that the evidence against Russia was compelling. Sikorski explained that in December 1941 he had personally handed Stalin a list which (with later additions) included 4664 names of missing officers – comprising exclusively those whose sojourn in three named camps near Smolensk could be established beyond doubt.[19] Yet, according to Soviet officials, 'all Polish officers, without exception, had been released'. Apart from the officers specifically listed, and many others whose location in the prison camps had not been conclusively proved, Sikorski recorded that 'several thousands of officers and men of the Polish Police Force, also a large number of lawyers and judges, up to approximately 8000 men in all, were deported . . . into the Soviet Union and have disappeared beyond trace'.

A great deal more is now known about the Katyn massacre. The German figure, variously given at 8000 or 10,000 bodies, was a large exaggeration: half these numbers is nearer the mark. On the other hand, there were about 5000 officers who were not at Katyn, but at two other camps in the Soviet Union, and these men – who remain unaccounted for to this day – must be presumed to have suffered a similar fate. So also must 6000 other ranks, policemen and civil officials who vanished around the same time.[20]

Soviet spokesmen, predictably, repudiated the German story with the greatest possible indignation. As Sir Archibald Clark-Kerr, British Ambassador in Moscow, noted, 'the anger and unconvincing terms of Russian denials suggests a sense of guilt'.[21] American reactions were similar to the British. Halifax reported that State Department officials 'do not, to put it mildly, give the impression that they are thoroughly convinced by the Soviet story'.[22] The Polish Government itself reacted to the dispute by requesting the International Red Cross to investigate the conflicting accusations. More embarrassing still, the Germans promptly took up the Polish request with enthusiasm.

Russia now acted at the highest possible level. On 21 April, Stalin addressed a message to Churchill in which he proclaimed that the Polish request was 'a treacherous blow to the Soviet Union to serve the cause of Hitler's tyranny'. The message concluded with information that 'in view of the foregoing, the Soviet Government came to the conclusion that it is necessary to interrupt relations' with the Polish Government.[23]

Churchill was placed in a very difficult position. As we have seen, he had dark suspicions that the German story might be based on fact. Whether for this reason or for others, he wrote to Stalin promising to 'oppose vigorously any "investigation" by the International Red Cross or any other body in any territory under German authority'.[24] He also promised to intervene with Sikorski to try to persuade the Poles to withdraw their request to the Red Cross. Meanwhile, he urged Stalin not to publicise the rupture of relations 'at any rate till every other plan has been tried'. On 25 April, the Prime Minister again wrote to Stalin, this time giving the encouraging news that 'as a result of Eden's strong representations Sikorski has undertaken not to press request for Red Cross investigation and will so inform the Red Cross authorities in Berne'.[25] Stalin, however, was not to be mollified merely because the Poles had withdrawn the request which was the nominal cause of the proposed diplomatic rupture. He told Churchill brusquely that 'an interruption of relations with the Polish Government is already decided'.[26] On the same day, 25 April, the Soviet Commissar for Foreign Affairs, Molotov, informed the Poles that relations had been broken.

The British and American Ambassadors both urged Molotov to delay publication of the Soviet Note to the Poles, in order to give their own governments time to make further proposals 'and so to avert a disaster'.[27] Roosevelt telegraphed Stalin promising his own good offices, and warning him of the damage which a diplomatic rupture would do in the United States;[28] all in vain. Meanwhile, enormous pressure was again exerted on the Poles to prevent them replying in kind to the Russians; while the British Ministry of Information did what it could to persuade the press to damp down the issue – and at all events not to take sides.

Obviously the Polish request to the Red Cross had been used by Russia as no more than a pretext to break off relations. Eden told the War Cabinet of his own fears 'that the Russians might seek to set up an alternative Polish government under their influence',[29] and Churchill wrote to Stalin, indicating that Britain would not recognise such a government. Stalin eventually replied that no such thought was in his mind;[30] but nothing was done about restoring diplomatic relations. The territorial claim was unabated, and Russia pressed for reconstruction of the Polish government to remove those members whom she regarded as most hostile to herself. At this point matters rested for eight weeks.

On 4 July 1943 there occurred a most unexpected catastrophe: the death of General Sikorski in an air crash near Gibraltar. German propaganda immediately alleged that this was a murder which lay at

Britain's door, and some Poles suspected the same. This seems most unlikely, for Britain had nothing to gain and much to lose thereby. Sikorski had been prepared to take British advice on most matters, and possessed far more authority over his compatriots than anyone with a similar disposition was likely to acquire. Stanislaw Mikolajczyk, leader of the Peasant Party, succeeded Sikorski as Prime Minister; but the General's other office as Commander-in-Chief went to different hands; and from that appointment much trouble would later flow.

Official opinion both in Britain and in the United States remained seriously disturbed by the continuing disagreement between the Polish and Russian Governments. In August, Stalin was presented with a joint statement on the matter – but without effect. The following month found Viscount Halifax arguing privately that 'they should settle ... the question of Russia's post-war frontiers'. Otherwise, when the Russians arrived in the 'debatable districts ... there might well be risings and bloodshed, e.g. as between Russians and Poles. This would produce the most shocking impression.'[31] This was exactly the frame of mind the Russians sought to encourage. They had everything to gain by piecemeal – but final – solutions at a time when their military and moral prestige was high. They became eager for a top-level conference at which some of the advantages they sought might be formally conceded.

Meanwhile, Russia developed some further plans by contact with another 'minor Ally', Czechoslovakia. Although the Czechs had not fought the Germans, their moral prestige as Hitler's pre-war victims was high, and a 'government in exile' was set up under the pre-Munich President Beneš, and was formally recognised as a belligerent Ally. When the tide of war began to turn, and men could think of possible post-war alignments, the Czechs contemplated setting up a defensive alliance with Poland. The Russians, however, vetoed that suggestion, and the Czechs promptly dropped it.[32] Sikorski was furious – concluding that Beneš 'has tried to play both sides against the middle and sacrifice the rest of the small Powers in order to be a favorite little brother of the Soviets'. 'Regrettably,' commented the American Assistant Secretary of State, 'there is a good deal of evidence to suggest this.'[33]

In June 1943, the British Government learnt that Beneš proposed shortly to visit Russia, to conclude a treaty between his own country and the Soviet Union 'on the general lines of the Anglo-Russian Treaty'[34] – that is, the twenty-year alliance which had been established a year or two earlier. This sounded innocuous enough; yet it posed serious problems. Eden and Molotov had previously agreed that 'both Governments should refrain from concluding treaties concerning the post-war period with minor Allies'.[35] The vital point, however, was no mere question of international propriety. The original vision of British, Poles and Czechs alike had been that some kind of confederation should emerge after the war, which would include Poland, Czechoslovakia and perhaps other countries as well. As far back as June 1942, Sikorski began to see signs of Beneš backing out of these plans.[36] The Czech President later explained 'that he was under an obligation to consult the Soviet Government' on the matter.[37] The moves made in 1943 towards a Czech-Soviet Treaty appear to have commenced very soon after the rupture of relations between Russia and Poland,[38] and there is some evidence that the initiative came from Beneš. A mild complaint was made to Russia about the proposed Treaty; but Eden later agreed that 'if the Soviet Government still insisted on a Treaty, we might agree that the proposed Soviet-Czech Treaty should be concluded in the form of an instalment of a Three-Power Treaty which could include Poland at a later date'.[39] On this understanding, Beneš proceeded to Moscow and concluded a treaty which satisfied the British conditions.[40] Ostensibly, that treaty was designed merely to prevent a recrudescence of German power after the war. The enigma was, why should either the Russians or the Czechs think it worthwhile stirring up suspicions, if the only result intended was such an apparently harmless agreement? The Russians manifestly sought to drive a wedge between the Poles and the Czechs; while perhaps Beneš sought some implied ratification from Russia that his country would be restored after the war. If so, he was successful, for the Russians were 'quite agreeable to Beneš having his old pre-Munich frontier back with slight military adjustments along the northern crests of the mountains and a little territory to the eastward linking them with Russia'.[41]

The general implications, however, were profound. What Russia evidently sought was not merely security against possible future German aggression – for that could have been provided readily enough by a strong federation of states lying between the two great countries – but rather domination over the smaller states of central and eastern Europe. One senior British official observed – tartly, but not unjustly – that Beneš had judged that Russia would be dominant in the area after the war, and had therefore thrown in his lot with the Soviets – 'with the mental reservation, of course, that in the unlikely event of the Western Powers showing that they were going to have a say in central Europe he will be ready to rat back again'.[42]

The Americans were concerned not only with individual European countries but with the general drift of events. In May, Maxim Litvinov, Soviet Ambassador to Washington, was recalled to Moscow – ostensibly for conversations, but in the event permanently. Litvinov – always regarded as a particular friend to the West – had an exceptionally frank off-the-record conversation with an American official just before departure.[43] The Ambassador complained of 'insuperable difficulties'. He had been 'completely bereft of any information as to the policy and plans of his own government'. Litvinov 'explained in very clear-cut and blunt terms that Stalin was entirely unaware of the fact that public opinion in the United States was a determining factor in the creation of Government policy'. He 'did not believe that his messages were received by Stalin – in any event none of his recommendations had been adopted'. Another important figure in international diplomacy must have felt similar frustrations. Cordell Hull considered that 'if we are to make considerable concessions to the Soviet Government we must ask something in return'.[44] Hull's chief seemed equally indifferent to good advice. Perhaps Roosevelt was frightened because rumours of a possible separate Russo-German peace were again being circulated about this time.[45]

There were certainly many matters which needed top-level decisions between the 'Big Three' Allies. Military operations against Germany required coordination, and the Russians could not unreasonably demand an explicit agreement about the Second Front. On the other side of the medal – should Russia enter the war against Japan? If so, how, and when – and what bribe would be required? As an American diplomat had sagely observed, as far back as 1941, 'it may be taken for granted . . . until the Soviet Government can be convinced of the advantages of entering the war against Japan no other considerations (such as the help that would thereby be rendered us or the British) will affect its decision'.[46] There was need for at least preliminary discussion about how the Allies would treat Germany in the aftermath of victory. There was also the immensely important and unresolved question of Poland's future. It was eventually decided to take discussion in two stages. The three Foreign Ministers should meet at Moscow in October, the Heads of Government at some other venue at the end of the year.

Poland was likely to prove the most difficult question of all at the Foreign Ministers' Conference. On 5 October, Anthony Eden circulated a Memorandum to the British War Cabinet, indicating his own preliminary views on the matter. British policy, he recommended, 'should be not to oppose the Soviet claim that the Curzon Line should form the basis of the new Soviet-Polish frontier, but to make every effort to secure a modification whereby the City of Lwow would be included in Poland. The further Polish claim to Vilna ... would be unrealistic ... Poland should receive as compensation in the West Danzig, East Prussia and Upper Silesia.'[47]

When Eden met Count Raczynski, the Polish Ambassador, a couple of days later, however, he discovered that the Poles were not willing to have their country's destiny dealt with on the basis of arrangements between the major Allies. The British Foreign Secretary was urged to press for resumption of diplomatic relations between Poland and Russia 'without entering any discussion on frontier differences between the two countries'.[48] If Eden were given virtual plenipotentiary powers to negotiate on the matter, then no doubt the three Great Powers would reach some kind of package deal in which a great many considerations – territorial, military and economic – would be bargained together. Poland would be one counter in the deal, not necessarily the most important. What the Poles demanded was the right of their country to be treated as a full Ally, with authority to negotiate for her own destiny on her own behalf. Mikolajczyk made a similar point to the Americans.[49] Eden and Hull were therefore constrained to tell Molotov of their 'anxiety to see normal relations between Soviet Russia and Poland restored at the earliest moment possible'.[50] 'M. Molotov,' the Foreign Secretary reported later to his Department, 'was non-committal.'

Averell Harriman, American Ambassador in Moscow, sent the President a revealing and comprehensive account of proceedings at the Conference on these and other matters. 'Our whole permanent relations' with Russia, the Ambassador recorded, 'depend in a large measure on their satisfaction in the future with our military operations. It is impossible to overemphasise the importance they place strategically on the initiation of the so-called "Second Front" next spring.'[51] Incredibly, 'Soviet territorial questions were never raised at the Conference', but Harriman decided that the Russians considered their desideratum of the 1941 frontiers 'has been tacitly accepted by the British and the fact that we did not bring up the issue may have given them the impression that we would not raise serious objection in the future'. The Polish question, the Ambassador decided, was 'even tougher than we believed. [The Russians] regard the present Polish Government-in-Exile as hostile and therefore completely unacceptable to them ... On the other hand Molotov told me definitely that they were willing to have a strong, independent Poland, giving expression to whatever social and political system the Polish people wanted.' Harriman was inclined to treat this kind of assurance 'with some reservations'.

In the immediate aftermath of the Moscow Conference, the Poles felt a great deal more than 'some reservations' about Soviet designs on their own country. Both British and American diplomats were warned that the Russians were developing propaganda which was preparing the ground for shooting Polish partisans as soon as Soviet troops entered Poland. Raczynski told Eden that the Moscow Conference had been a 'disaster'. Poles feared not merely loss of eastern Poland, but the 'growing danger that as soon as the Soviet armies entered Polish territories the Soviet Government might present all concerned with a *fait accompli* which *inter alia* might take the form of the setting up of a puppet government in Poland'.[52] Mikolajczyk warned Cordell Hull 'that as far west as the Russian armies marched, just so far would Russia's western frontier develop'.[53]

Plans continued for the 'Summit Conference' which was to follow the meeting of the Foreign Ministers. Arrangements were complex, and bore many signs of improvisation, compromise and perhaps at times objectives of a more sinister kind. The first part of the eventual meeting took place in Cairo in the late autumn of 1943. The main participants were Roosevelt, Churchill and Chiang Kai-Shek of China. The presence of Chiang was regarded by the British with feelings of irritation. For reasons we shall consider later, China's military contribution in the war against Japan was at this stage minimal; yet presence of a Chinese representative made it inevitable that the main discussions at Cairo should concern the Far Eastern war. Running true to form in committing others without their consent, Roosevelt blithely promised Chiang an amphibious 'Operation Buccaneer' in the Indian Ocean – where Britain was to play the major part. The Americans also showed their draft about post-war arrangements in the Pacific to the Chinese before consulting the British. 'It gave the Chinese everything, including Formosa and the Pescadores,' wrote one British Minister, 'but it is very doubtful whether, on a strict reading, either we or the Dutch would get back anything of what the Japs had seized.'[54] Chiang's presence was annoying to Britain for another reason. There were a great many matters, both military and diplomatic, which Churchill and Roosevelt could profitably have discussed together before they met Stalin; but such conversations were, in the circumstances, impossible; for by the time Chiang left they were already almost due to depart for a rendezvous with Stalin at the unlikely venue of Tehran. Hair-raising security risks to the principal figures were disclosed almost immediately they arrived in the Iranian capital, and the main meetings were held at the Soviet embassy. In some circumstances, diplomatic risks of an equally grave character might have been incurred at such a venue; but on this occasion Britons and Americans had little to say to each other which the Russians would have resented.

Military matters were of overriding importance at Tehran. 'Buccaneer' was abandoned, and Roosevelt was left with the task of explaining matters to Chiang. The main Anglo-American 'Second Front' operation, known as 'Overlord', would take place in the spring of 1944. It was intended that this should be accompanied by a similar invasion – 'Anvil' – in the south of France. There is a persistent story that Churchill envisaged a totally different strategy. The alleged author of this strategy later castigated as 'nonsense' the 'legend in America that I strove to prevent the cross-Channel enterprise called "Overlord" and that I tried vainly to lure the Allies into some mass-invasion of the Balkans, or a large-scale campaign in the Eastern Mediterranean which would effectively kill it'.[55] It is not easy to decide how seriously the idea of an Anglo-American strategy aimed at striking up through the Balkans into Central Europe was ever taken. It was certainly under consideration in the middle of 1943,[56] and there has been much discussion as to whether Churchill visualised it as the primary operation. The Prime Minister did press for vigorous engagement in Italy, and some well-informed Americans were of the opinion that he only abandoned the idea of a major attack through the Balkans in response to irresistible pressure from Roosevelt and Stalin.[57] Those who have since perceived ulterior motives in the Balkan strategy have argued that the object of that strategy was to cut off the Russians from access to Germany. There is no reason for thinking that the political objectives underlying such a strategy were in the minds of anybody who mattered at the time. Indeed, if matters had been considered from that viewpoint, it is most doubtful whether such a plan would have been followed; for, if the plan in any way miscarried, the likely result would have been to tie down the Americans in southern Europe, while the Russians swept ahead to the Rhine – or to the Channel.

Predictably, the chief political question at Tehran was the future of Poland. Eden told British Ministers afterwards that 'the President, with his mind full of the elections, did not want to get involved in a discussion on Poland, and this, therefore, was entirely an Anglo-Russian affair, the President sitting in a corner and feigning sleep'.[58] American information suggests that Roosevelt was very far from somnolent. Charles Bohlen, who interpreted, reports that Roosevelt warned Stalin that 1944 would be a Presidential election year. Roosevelt might run for a fourth term; if so, he did not wish to lose six or seven million American-Polish votes. 'Therefore, while he personally agreed with Stalin's general view that Poland's frontiers should be moved to the west, he hoped that Stalin would understand why the President could not take part at Tehran ... in any such arrangements.'[59] Eden later reported to the British Cabinet that Stalin 'had taken a very hard line' on the question of Poland's eastern frontier – which, he declared, had been 'settled'. The British tried unsuccessfully to save Lwow for Poland. The Russians apparently allowed them to believe that it was British intervention which won for Poland the less important town of Bialystok – one of the few places of any significance which lay west of the Curzon Line but east of the Ribbentrop–Molotov Line.[60] This, however, was a delusion; Beneš already knew that the place was destined for Poland.[61]

Poland's western frontier was also discussed, though outside the main Tehran conference. Eden later reported that

> Stalin said that this should be on the Oder. This was, of course, a rather extreme step, and would bring Poland within sixty miles of Berlin. It was also clear that he was agreeable to the Poles getting the Oppeln area of Silesia. Further discussions had been directed to making it clear that the Russians agreed that Poland should have East Prussia. Marshal Stalin had agreed to this, but said that he wanted Königsberg as a free port.[62]

The effect of these changes would be enormous. Poland would lose her eastern half. Her claims in the west were qualified by the Russian demand for Königsberg, but in other respects were far exceeded. She would receive not only the areas to which she had laid claim, and which were reasonably necessary to her economy or her defence, but also a great part of Germany whose population was purely German, and which the Poles had never sought.

Churchill reacted to the proposals with great enthusiasm. 'This gives the Poles a magnificent piece of country three or four hundred miles across each way with over 150 miles of sealand, even on the assumption that they do not begin till west of Königsberg,' he wrote to Eden on 20 December 1943.[63] 'On the other hand, if they cast it all aside I do not see how H.M. Government can press for anything more for them.'

Warsaw

(Jan Ciechanowski, Polish Ambassador to the United States.) 'The Soviet Government in his opinion had the impression that the failure of Great Britain and the United States to intervene on behalf of Poland was indicative that those two countries had lost interest in Poland and were willing to allow the Soviet Government to do what it wished in Eastern Europe.' Memorandum of conversation ... with Polish Ambassador, 22 March 1943. FRUS 1943, III, p. 352 et seq.

Why indeed (one may fairly ask) should the Poles acquiesce in the loss of half of their country in order to gratify Stalin, to salve Churchill's uneasy conscience, and to facilitate Roosevelt's task with Polish electors in the United States? The German lands they would receive as the other side of this transaction were undeniably of greater natural value than eastern Poland; but they would prove a *hereditas damnosa*. Whatever happened to the indigenous population, Germany would feel a sense of bitter grievance for the whole foreseeable future; and the Poles could only be defended against German revanchism by becoming military satellites of the Soviet Union.

The developing situation was regarded with much concern in the United States. 'Very considerable and important elements in this country', wrote Hull to Harriman in January 1944, 'are viewing the attitude and actions of the Soviet Government with regard to the Polish boundary question as a test of the reality of international cooperation.'[1] Sir Owen O'Malley, British Ambassador to Poland, spelt out the matter in more detail in a confidential message to Eden. O'Malley argued that the arguments about frontiers and the composition of the Polish Government were 'relatively superficial'.[2]

The underlying questions at issue are: (1) whether Poland's independence is to be respected or not; (2) whether or not any change in her situation is to be the result of the Prime Minister's words of 'the free consent and goodwill of the parties concerned', or of force; (3) whether the basis of international law is to be law or whether an exhibition of power politics is to be covered with our approval; (4) whether England can be relied upon to act in what was understood to be the spirit of the Atlantic Charter.

O'Malley was very explicit about Britain's moral dilemma.

> The real choice before us seems to me, to put it brutally, to be between on the one hand selling the corpse of Poland to Russia and finding an alibi to be used in evidence when we are indicted in abetting a murder; or on the other hand putting the points of principle to Stalin in the clearest possible way and warning him that our position might have to be expressed publicly with equal clearness.

Churchill, a few days later, began to have his own doubts and fears. 'Did the Russians really want an independent Poland?' he asked the Cabinet rhetorically after return from Tehran. 'Or had they in view a puppet government under Russian control and a Soviet Republic?' Quoting Eden's view that 'there were increasing signs which pointed in the latter direction', the Prime Minister added, 'if there was any risk of this, His Majesty's Government should consider carefully how far they could now press the Poles to go to meet the Russian viewpoint.'[3] Yet – so Churchill continued –

> If no settlement were now reached between Russia and Poland the result would be a certain strain or even some degree of estrangement between Russia and the Western Powers. This would be calamitous, and might carry with it the seeds of future wars.

Here was the very language which Churchill had condemned so strongly when used by the defenders of Munich: but there was one important difference. No informed man doubted that the great majority of the Sudetendeutsch had desired to belong to Germany; but there was every reason for doubting whether the people of eastern Poland wished to belong to Russia.

Churchill was determined to take 'action to bridge the gap . . . as early as possible'. He very soon found that this task was a great deal more difficult than he had imagined. Messages sent by the Prime Minister in December show that he believed that the Poles would quickly snap up the bait so temptingly dangled before them by Stalin. The Prime Minister fell ill later that month, and Eden conducted the negotiations. When Churchill returned to full duties in January, he joined his colleague in the talks. The British were a good deal less than frank with the Poles. Cadogan, Permanent Under-Secretary of the Foreign Office, tried to avoid telling them of the Russian demand for Königsberg by a flat prevarication.[4] When all else failed to move the Poles, the Prime Minister turned to bullying. 'He proposed to press them very strongly indeed,' he told his colleagues. In the last resort he would inform the Russians that he would support their claim to the Curzon Line.[5]

At last Churchill brought the Poles to the point where he could send one of his many confidential 'personal messages' to Stalin. 'We have been wrestling continually with the Poles, and I am glad to say we have at last produced some results,'[6] he wrote. The Poles, he explained, were ready, with British participation, to discuss the question of a new eastern frontier – although no public declaration could be made of their willingness to cede claims to territory. As for the immediate future, districts west of the Curzon Line might be placed under Polish civil administration as soon as military conditions permitted.

By this time, the Red Army had already crossed the eastern frontier of pre-war Poland. As the Poles never tired of saying, their country had never produced a single 'Quisling', and they had a very strong 'underground' movement operating against the Nazis. That movement would probably have been a great deal stronger still if the larger Allies had been more generous in sending supplies of weapons.[7] Within eastern Poland there existed both Polish and Soviet partisans. The Polish Government learnt of instructions from the Russians to the Soviet partisans to disarm Polish detachments and shoot those who resisted.[8] A considerable number of Polish partisans had already been captured and shot by their Soviet opposite numbers. There was now the prospect of virtual guerrilla warfare against the Red Army in eastern Poland, unless something was done to prevent it.

At the beginning of February 1944, Churchill and Eden had a long discussion with the Polish Ministers on the partisan question. All agreed that 'the first essential was to avoid armed conflict between the Poles and the Russians'.[9] The Polish Government explained that it had already

> sent instructions to the leaders of the underground movement that, when the Russians entered Poland, they should disclose themselves to the Russian officers and offer to cooperate with them. In any case in which units of the Polish underground movement had previously been engaged in hostilities with Russian partisans, they had orders to withdraw.[10]

Would the exiled Polish Government return to its own country at

the earliest possible moment? First indications were favourable.
Early in February, the British Ambassador had an 'encouraging
interview' with Stalin, in which he asked whether the Russians would
allow this. Churchill reported to Roosevelt that 'U.J.' – 'Uncle Joe' –
had 'replied that of course ... the Polish Government would be
allowed to go back and to establish the broad-based kind of
government they had in mind'.[11] Churchill went on to explain that
Stalin continued to press for the expulsion of certain members of the
Polish Government, 'and I doubt very much whether he will deal
with the Poles while they remain in'. So much for the prospects of
independence for Poland. By the end of February, Eden's secretary
recorded the view that the Russians would eventually set up their
own Polish government 'and we shall have to recognise it'.[12]

In the spring of 1944, preparations for the 'Second Front' overrode
all other questions between the Allies. Once the invasion was
launched in France on 6 June, Churchill at any rate felt much easier
about his moral obligations to Russia. Meanwhile, there was a
deceptive lull in the Russo-Polish dispute. Mikolajczyk visited the
United States to plead his country's cause. The American election
year had begun, and Roosevelt gave the Poles a much less chilling
view of their prospects in eastern Poland than Churchill and Eden
had done. 'The President,' wrote Romer, the Polish Minister for
Foreign Affairs,

> indicated that the policy of the United States Government was
> contrary to the settlement of territorial problems before the end of
> the war. The President assured the Prime Minister that, at the
> appropriate time, he would help Poland to retain Lwow,
> Drohobyek and Tarnopol and to obtain East Prussia including
> Königsberg, as well as Silesia.[13]

The best American account of the interview suggests that Roosevelt
went even further.

> The President said he did not agree on the formula based on the
> Curzon Line. He did not feel the Russians would insist upon this.
> Further, the President stated, he did not feel that Stalin would insist
> on Königsberg.[14]

With this message ringing in their ears, it is not surprising that the
Poles were unwilling to reach a settlement on the sort of terms Stalin
was proposing and Churchill was urging them to accept. Roosevelt,
however, went on to recommend Mikolajczyk to see Stalin personally
about various points at issue between their two countries; and on
that point Churchill heartily endorsed the President's advice.[15]

Considerable delay followed; but eventually Churchill brought Mikolajczyk to a receptive mood. He did not wish to make a formal British approach to Russia on the matter, but sent a message to Stalin: 'Should Mikolajczyk ask to come to see you I hope you will consent.'[16] This message was despatched on 20 July. Two days later, before Stalin's reply had been delivered, came further news from Poland. The Red Army had recently pushed west of the Curzon Line, and Moscow Radio announced that a 'Committee of National Liberation' had been established at Chelm, the first large town to be captured. The Foreign Office reported that the Committee were 'mostly . . . Communists, either completely unknown to the Polish people or of secondary importance'.[17]

Stalin's reply to Churchill was despatched on the following day. The Red Army, he announced, had just occupied Lublin, and the 'question of administration of Polish territory' arose. He assured Churchill that 'we do not wish to have and shall not set up our administration on the territory of Poland, for we do not wish to interfere in the internal affairs of Poland'. Furthermore, added Stalin, 'I cannot consider the Polish Committee as the government of Poland'.[18] So far, so good. Stalin would be prepared to receive Mikolajczyk, but 'it would . . . be better if he were to address himself to the Polish National Committee whose attitude would be friendly towards Mikolajczyk'. Churchill immediately made contact with the Poles, and was soon able to tell Stalin that Mikolajczyk would depart for Moscow on the evening of 26 July.

No formal agreement was reached, but a number of matters were discussed in an amicable atmosphere, and the general view of both sides seemed to be that the visit had been worthwhile. Stalin gave a 'categorical assurance that he had no intention of Communising Poland'.[19] The frontier question was touched on. Both men had apparently been 'anxious to avoid pressing [it] to the point of deadlock' and eventually agreed to postpone it 'until a regular Polish Government should have been set up in Warsaw'.[20] Compensation in the west was offered: this time not merely the whole of Germany east of the Oder, save Königsberg, but even 'some territory on the west bank of the Oder. From all these lands Stalin undertook to expel all Germans.'[21] Romer told Harriman that the German territory proposed for Poland included 'even Stettin and Breslau which . . . was beyond what the Poles considered sensible'.[22] The Polish Foreign Minister 'got the impression that the question of Vilna was difficult but that there was some hope for Lwow'.

Contacts were also made between Mikolajczyk and the new Polish Committee for National Liberation – a body which was coming to be known as the 'Lublin Committee'. The Committee suggested that a new Polish Government should be established which he should head, but in which his London colleagues should receive only four out of sixteen seats.[23] This proposal was obviously unacceptable to Mikolajczyk – perhaps it had never been intended as more than the first stage in a bargaining process.

Mikolajczyk's visit to Moscow coincided with the first stages of one of the most heroic and tragic incidents of the whole war. On 29 July, the Russian offensive in central Poland had reached the approaches to Warsaw, and Moscow Radio broadcast an appeal to the population of the city to 'join battle with the Germans'.[24] This Soviet appeal was no piece of vague and general rhetoric. 'The hour of action, the broadcast stated, had already arrived for Warsaw. The Germans were planning to bring about the destruction of the city. Whatever could not be saved by direct effort would be lost.'[25] Two days later Mikolajczyk, who had just arrived in Moscow,

> told M. Molotov that, before leaving London, he had discussed with the Polish military authorities the details of the general rising which was to take place in Warsaw and the need of airborne supplies. No mention was made of the date of the rising, which had been left to the discretion of the Polish Commander in Warsaw.[26]

The following day, 1 August 1944, the Warsaw rising began. It was no mere riot or civil disturbance, but a carefully planned insurrection which for a long time pinned down large numbers of German troops, and cleared great areas of the city for several weeks. It was designed to drive the Germans from within the city, while the Russians assaulted it from without. Stalin himself later admitted that 'all Poles were united for resistance in Warsaw under the leadership of the commanding general of the underground forces'.[27]

Early indications suggested that this pattern would be followed. A few days later, however, difficulties began to appear. The Russians ran into heavy military opposition from the Germans. There were signs of political difficulties no less severe. On 4 August, Churchill telegraphed Stalin to inform him that Britain proposed to drop about sixty tons of equipment and ammunition into Warsaw. Stalin's reply, however, was contemptuous of the Polish Home Army, and concluded, 'I cannot see how such detachments can capture Warsaw'.[28] Cabinet Minutes of 9 August record a drop of supplies on Warsaw, but add – somewhat wistfully – 'It would clearly be much easier for help to be sent by the Russians instead of from Western Europe'.[29] On 12 August, Churchill sent Stalin a copy of a 'distressing message' which had come from the Poles in Warsaw, indicating that unless they received 'immediate support consisting of drops of arms and ammunition [and] bombing of objectives held by the enemy', their fight was likely to collapse in a few days.[30] The Prime Minister concluded with an impassioned appeal for the Russians to give help to Warsaw.

On the following day, 13 August,

> Moscow papers published articles placing the responsibility for the events in Warsaw on the Polish circles in London and blaming them for not coordinating the rising with the Soviet Command.[31]

If the Russians could not – or would not – actively assist the rising, then would they help others who sought to do so? Initially, supplies had been flown to Warsaw from Italy by Polish volunteers; but losses were fearful,[32] and the operation had been called off on advice from the RAF authorities. Now the Americans, who had new long-range aeroplanes based on Britain, wished to fill the gap; but it was essential that they should be allowed to land on Soviet-controlled territory after supplying the Polish insurgents. A formal request was lodged on 14 August, but on the following day was refused by the Russians.[33] Stalin delayed his answer to Churchill until 17 August. The reply, when it came, made it clear that the Soviet refusal either to help the insurgents or make facilities for others to land was based on a fundamental Soviet view of the rising: '... The Soviet Command has come to the conclusion that it must dissociate itself from the Warsaw adventure as it cannot take either direct or indirect responsibility for the Warsaw action.'[34] This message occasioned a joint appeal to Stalin from Churchill and Roosevelt, urging the Russians either to drop supplies and munitions immediately for the Poles – or at least to 'agree to help our planes in doing it'.[35]

Harriman began to suspect very sinister Russian motives. 'For the first time since coming to Moscow,' he wrote to the President,

> I am gravely concerned by the attitude of the Soviet Government in its refusal to permit us to assist the Poles in Warsaw [as] well as in its own policy of apparent inactivity. If Vyshinsky correctly reflects the position of the Soviet Government, its refusal is based not on operational difficulties or denial that the resistance exists but on ruthless political considerations.[36]

This judgement was soon supported by stronger evidence. On 23 August, Stalin not merely refused the Anglo-American appeal, but viciously castigated the insurgent leaders as 'the group of criminals who have embarked on the Warsaw adventure in order to seize power'.[37] Russian malice towards the insurgents was illustrated not merely in these major matters but even on a technical question which would have cost the Soviets nothing. Britain and America desired recognition of the Polish 'Home Army' as belligerents, with combatant rights in event of capture by the Germans. A demand of that kind would have much more force if the Russians participated as well; but they refused to join in representations.[38]

The inter-Allied dispute was steadily becoming more menacing. The Minister of Information, though not a member of the War Cabinet, was invited to their meeting on 28 August. As he explained to his superiors,

> . . . We could not reckon for long on the Press maintaining silence about the present difficulties between Poland and Russia, and, in particular, about the Russian refusal to allow the United States Air Force the use of airfields in Russia for the purpose of dropping supplies to the Polish Underground Army in Warsaw.[39]

While the Warsaw rising continued to rage, there was an extraordinary political crisis within the London Polish Government. Under the Polish constitution, the Commander-in-Chief possessed great executive power, and his appointment or dismissal was the prerogative of President Raczkiewicz. After Sikorski's death, General Sosnkowski had been appointed to that post. Sosnkowski was regarded with particular animus by the Soviet Government. Mikolajczyk began to exert pressure on Raczkiewicz to dismiss Sosnkowski, apparently in the belief that this might lead Russia to take a kindlier view of the Warsaw insurgents. British information suggested that the positions of Sosnkowski, Mikolajczyk and Raczkiewicz were all matters of heated debate within the Polish Government. Apparently, Mikolajczyk was under heavy attack from a combination of socialist members of the Government and generals, who

> mentioned that although Mikolajczyk had to a great extent followed [British] advice he had failed to get adequate assistance for Warsaw from the United Nations. A Polish Prime Minister was required who would explain to all Poles how the Polish Government had been deceived by the Russian Government.[40]

Churchill was most emphatic that Mikolajczyk must stay. Removal of the Polish Prime Minister would be 'an attack on His Majesty's Government removing the last chance of a solution'.[41] The unfortunate Pole was caught in the middle, between the British and his own compatriots. There is some evidence that the situation was eased, to a degree, by representations from Hugh Dalton, who in his dual capacity as a British Minister and a senior member of the Labour Party could speak with special authority to the Polish socialists.[42] Whatever actually happened, both Mikolajczyk and Sosnkowski remained in office for a little longer.

Meanwhile, the Western Allies exerted every pressure they could upon the Russians to relax their obstructiveness over Warsaw. On 13 September, Churchill informed Eden that the Russians had given clearance for the Americans to land after dropping supplies on the insurgents. The Prime Minister was overjoyed: 'This is really a great triumph for our persistence in hammering at the Russians when we had a good case.'[43] On the following day, the forty-fifth day of the rising, the Russians themselves dropped small supplies on Warsaw.[44]

These gestures cost Russia little. The Warsaw rising was already near its last gasp, and could no longer benefit from anything short of a major breakthrough by the Red Army. Yet they strengthened the hand of the more pro-Russian element among the Poles in London. Mikolajczyk tried to persuade the President to exert his prerogative and dismiss Sosnkowski. He was unsuccessful; but eventually Eden took that matter into his own hands, and prevailed upon Raczkiewicz to comply. The dismissal was reported on 28 September. It was followed by the announcement that General Bor-Komorowski, leader of the Warsaw rising, had been appointed *in absentia* to the vacant office. This drew a furious response from the Lublin Committee, who – as the British Cabinet was told – 'regarded General Bor as a criminal ... more hated than General Sosnkowski'.[45] After an interval, and still further British pressure, Bor-Komorowski's theoretical appointment was rescinded, and the office set into commission.

The day of Sosnkowski's removal brought grim news from Warsaw. The key position of Mokotow was menaced by the Germans, and urgent Allied action was required to preserve it. Frantic appeals were issued for help by land and air; but this time no useful assistance was rendered, and on 3 October Polish forces in the shattered city of Warsaw capitulated.

It is now worth reflecting what considerations lay behind the Warsaw rising. The Polish Home Army in Warsaw existed for one overriding purpose: to drive the Germans out of the city. They rose with this one object in view, in answer to a clear call from the Russians, and with every intention of assisting in a common cause. In the first few days of the rising, when the Russians still had reasonable grounds for thinking that the Red Army would soon break through to the city, there was little sign of animosity towards the Polish insurgents, although the Russians underestimated their strength and determination. When German resistance stiffened, and it became apparent that the Red Army would not be able to reach Warsaw for a long time, the Poles committed the unforgiveable sin – in Russian eyes – of not collapsing. The worst possible thing, from the Russian point of view, would be for the Polish Home Army to take Warsaw when the Red Army had failed. Everything was therefore done to obstruct the Western Allies when they tried to assist the Poles. It was only when the greatest possible pressure was set upon Stalin by Churchill and Roosevelt that the Russians relented – fearing, no doubt, that the story would otherwise become generally known and understood, and a great gulf set between Russia on one side and the Western Allies on the other. Having rendered perfunctory assistance at the last moment, Stalin no doubt witnessed with pleasure the collapse of the rising. The Polish Home Army was not dead; but there could never be another Warsaw. The prestige of the Polish Government in London was grievously undermined; which was exactly the result which Russia had desired.

4

Tolstoy

'βεβαρβάρωσαι, χρόνιος ὢν ἐν βαρβάροις.'

'In your time among savages, you have become a savage.'
Euripides, *Orestes*, 1.485

Although the problems of Poland were right at the centre of the developing dispute between the Soviet Union and her Western Allies, yet the fate of all central and eastern Europe was closely bound up with this dispute, and around 1943 and 1944 the issues at stake became increasingly clear. We have already seen something of Czechoslovakia's rôle. Six other countries were deeply involved: the 'minor Allies', Greece and Yugoslavia, and the 'minor enemies', Finland, Romania, Bulgaria and Hungary.

Yugoslavia had been invaded by the Axis countries in 1941. The Yugoslavs fought back, but the Government and the boy-King Peter II were driven into exile. A substantial body of the armed forces continued guerrilla warfare in the mountains. These were the Ćetniks, led by General Mihajlović. Later, another resistance organisation appeared – the 'partisans'. Until late 1942, these partisans were not taken very seriously: indeed, nobody seemed to know much about them at all. The Americans considered them to be 'small bands with local leadership', '70 per cent Communist', who had originally fought against the Ćetniks, but were currently attacking Germans and Italians as well.[1] The British were disposed to treat them rather more seriously; as early as December 1942, King Peter complained to Eden that Mihajlović was not receiving full British support. To this the Foreign Secretary replied 'that we had recently had some doubts about the General, who appeared to be devoting his energies ... against the "partisans" or Communists'.[2] These partisans, explained Eden, 'had been causing considerable embarrassment to the Axis'. No doubt the view was that any group of people who might tie down enemy forces or sap communications was useful – and if the Western Allies should later decide to make a major thrust through the Balkans in the direction of Central Europe, then those irregular forces could prove very useful indeed.

Evidence – such as it was – suggested a situation of almost incredible confusion in Yugoslavia. There were three bodies of armed Yugoslavs: the Croatian Ustashi, who fought on the side of the Axis and had an egregious reputation for savage and wanton atrocities; the Ćetniks; and the Partisans. Both Ćetniks and Partisans loathed and fought the Ustashi; but they also fought each other. There was apparently substantial collaboration between Ćetniks and Italians; but while that collaboration brought the Ćetniks under growing suspicion with the British, it also caused considerable ill-feeling between Germans and Italians: for the Ćetniks continued to fight Germans wherever they found them. At one point, there was a serious possibility of at least local conflict between Germans and Italians. There were other cross-currents too. When the Yugoslav state had been formed after the First World War, the ruling dynasty was Serbian, and there was much resentment among Croats and Slovenes against Serb domination throughout the inter-war period. The main resistance to the Axis invasion of 1941 came from Serbs; the other nationalities were at that time much more indulgent. Yet when the Partisan movement began to get under way, its support was largely Croat.[3] Thus conflicts which Axis and Allies alike tended to rationalise in terms of their 'own' war, or perhaps of social, political and ideological issues, were to no small extent ethnic, or even tribal, in their roots.

In the first three months of 1943, British official opinion underwent a very pronounced change in favour of active liaison with the Partisans: an attitude encouraged by the growing suspicion that Mihajlović was pulling his punches against the enemy.[4] By the end of June, the British Government had decided to cooperate with the Partisans 'on a fairly substantial scale'.[5] Support for Mihajlović continued; but by November, British information suggested that his activities against the Axis were negligible, while some Ćetnik units were by then even making agreements with the Germans.[6] American information indicated that the balance of blame between the two groups was much more even. 'In both Yugoslavia and Greece the guerrilla forces appear to be engaged largely in fighting each other and not the Germans,' wrote Roosevelt to Churchill.[7] An American diplomat went even further, observing that the Partisans were 'fighting everyone else they met, and even among themselves'.[8] The Russians, who might have been expected on ideological grounds to favour the Partisans, were also unwilling to set special blame upon Mihajlović: 'It is necessary to make efforts to find a basis for collaboration with both sides,'[9] declared the Soviet Ambassador in London, as late as December 1943.

In October 1943, Roosevelt proposed that an American officer be sent to Yugoslavia; but it was generally acknowledged at the time that initiative in the central Mediterranean should come from Britain, and Churchill decided in favour of a British Brigadier, Fitzroy Maclean, who duly made contact with the Partisans. At the end of 1943, the British Government decided, on the basis of information received, that the Partisans represented the future rulers of Yugoslavia, and that they should be fully supported – 'subordinating political considerations to military', as Eden wrote.[10] Early in the new year, Churchill assured Josip Broz Tito, who had now emerged as clear leader of the Partisans, 'that the British Government will give no further military support to Mihajlović and will only give help to you'.[11]

It is important to observe that the lead in securing support for Tito was wholly British. At the Cabinet meeting of 11 January 1944, Eden described the Russian attitude as 'reserved', adding that 'no indication had been received' regarding the United States.[12] With a decent show of hesitation, the other two major Allies soon followed that British lead, and by the end of February arrangements were more or less complete for establishing military missions with Tito and withdrawing missions from Mihajlović.[13] The Americans nevertheless retained some mental reservations about the whole matter, and later obtained information from their own sources, which tended to refute the charges of collaboration against the Ćetniks, but showed that the Partisans for their part were 'fighting the nationalists and otherwise establishing a supreme political hegemony in Yugoslavia'.[14] By that time, however, the Allies were too deeply committed to alter their policy again. The broad strategy of the Partisans was clear enough. As an American diplomat explained, they tried to face all other resistance units 'with the alternatives either to fight the Germans under [partisan] leadership or to collaborate with the enemy'.[15] They were glad enough to accept active support from non-Communists – always provided that the real leadership lay in Communist hands.

Not only was Mihajlović cast aside, but also the position of King Peter and his government-in-exile was steadily undermined. According to the King's own account, he was 'advised' by Eden in the middle of March 1944 to abandon Mihajlović, and was told soon afterwards by the British Ambassador that he 'did not need a government'.[16] When the King seemed reluctant to accept such advice, Churchill threatened Peter 'that he would accuse General Mihajlović of collaboration with the Germans and that he would treat all of us accordingly, myself as well as the Royal Government'.

Despite all this, there was no immediate denunciation of either the King or Mihajlović; but in June, Peter was prevailed upon to accept a new Prime Minister, Ivan Subasić, Ban of Croatia, who was commissioned to form an all-party government. A little later, the King was even persuaded to broadcast an appeal to all Yugoslavs to join Tito's 'National Liberation Army'.[17]

The pattern of events in the other Balkan Ally was in some ways similar to that in Yugoslavia, in others markedly different. In 1941, an essentially 'right wing' Greek Government resisted the Axis, but was later driven into exile. Two different groups of guerrillas appeared, one orientated towards the Greek Government, the other – EAM – Communist-inspired. Like its Yugoslav counterparts, EAM included many non-Communists within its ranks. Here the resemblances end. The two bodies of Greek guerrillas both appeared considerably later than their Yugoslav counterparts, and by the middle of 1943 serious quarrels had not yet occurred between them – partly, no doubt, because they tended to operate in different parts of the country. Unlike King Peter of Yugoslavia, who was personally popular even among people who had little respect for the government-in-exile which surrounded him, King George II of Greece was not popular at all, and the exiled Greek Government had a strongly republican flavour.[18] In the autumn of 1943, the British decided that the Allied cause would be best served if the King did not return to Greece until his country had decided on the future of the monarchy, and the King appeared to accept this advice. Then – apparently without warning either his Allies or his own State Department – Roosevelt suddenly advised the King to stand his ground, although the President gave no similar encouragement to Peter.

Just as the condition of the two monarchies contrasted, so also did that of the partisan forces. EAM was of little military value to the Allies. 'The Communists are not fighting the Germans,' wrote one British diplomat late in 1943. 'They are fighting the moderates, and they are accumulating the arms to seize Athens when the day comes and set up a communist dictatorship there.'[19] Churchill soon became alarmed at the prospect that 'EAM would work a reign of terror in Greece forcing the villagers and many other classes to form Security Battalions under German auspices to prevent utter anarchy'.[20] Eventually the major Allies gravitated towards a compromise. An uneasy Coalition government was set up, with Communist as well as non-Communist members. There was no clear break with the King, nor with either right-wing or left-wing guerillas.

Thus did most anomalous situations develop in Greece and Yugoslavia. For uncertain and probably marginal considerations of military advantage, first the Četniks and later King Peter were thrown to the wolves, while EAM was held at arm's length and King George of Greece was in process of being rescued. These decisions would have a profound effect on the whole political complexion of the Balkans, right to the present day. Russia's essentially passive role in both places may seem to contrast with her much more active part in Poland; yet perhaps in that matter there was real consistency. She felt herself strong enough to establish and maintain a military and political hegemony over Poland, while in both Greece and Yugoslavia this would strain her lines of communication too much. Thus in Poland she was prepared to make large sacrifices of the general military interest of the Allies in order to secure post-war political control, while in both Greece and Yugoslavia she was largely indifferent to the political system under which the people would eventually live. In those places, Russia's concern was immediate and military: to ensure that the maximum damage was done to the Germans. In Yugoslavia she would defer to British advice and back Tito; although if the British advice had been different she would have been equally content to support Mihajlović. The responsibility for setting Yugoslavia on a course towards Communism rests with Churchill and his advisers, not with the Russians.

Just as minor Allies posed problems for the Big Three, so also did the fate of minor enemies. None of them had much enthusiasm for the German cause, but all were more or less prisoners of circumstances. In the course of 1944, all were actively contemplating some kind of peace settlement with the advancing Allies.

The fate of Romania was the first to prove of importance in determining future relationships between major Allies. In the spring of 1944, she was ready to negotiate terms of capitulation. Russia would certainly reclaim Bessarabia and northern Bukovina, which Romania had temporarily recovered in 1941. There were other matters at stake beside territorial adjustments, and on 18 May 1944, Eden informed the British embassy in Moscow of recent conversations with Molotov:

> I have spoken to him about the possibility of our agreeing between ourselves as a functional matter that Romanian affairs would be the main concern of the Soviet Government while Greek affairs would be in the main our concern, each government giving the other help in the respective countries. The Soviet Government agreed with this suggestion, but before giving any final assurance on the matter they would like to know whether we had consulted the United States Government.[21]

The Foreign Secretary anticipated no difficulty with America, and Churchill sent an explanatory message to Roosevelt – assuring the

President that 'we do not of course wish to carve up the Balkans into spheres of influence and in agreeing to the arrangement we would make it clear that it applied only to war conditions'.[22]

There is nothing in life so permanent as a temporary expedient, and American suspicions were immediately aroused as to whether Britain and Russia were in fact engaged in the very operation Churchill had assured them was far from their thoughts. When the Secretary of State heard of the matter, he was 'nervous'.[23] Roosevelt was more emphatic. The American Government, he told Churchill, was 'unwilling to approve the proposed arrangement'.[24]

> Briefly, we acknowledge that the militarily responsible government in any given territory will inevitably make decisions required by military developments but are convinced that the natural tendency for such decisions to extend to other than military fields would be strengthened by an agreement of the type suggested.

Churchill was 'much concerned' at this reply, but suggested a compromise: the proposed arrangements in Greece and Romania 'may have a trial of three months, after which it may be revised by the three Powers'.[25] Roosevelt was prepared to accept this, but insisted that 'we must be careful to make it clear that we are not establishing any particular spheres of influence'.[26] When the Russians learned of the new stipulations about 'trial period', and of the American dislike for 'spheres of influence', they came to the conclusion that it was necessary to give 'further consideration' to the proposed bargain over Greece and Romania.[27]

This triangular correspondence was clearly of importance far wider than the two Balkan countries immediately considered. Roosevelt won the first battle in his opposition to 'spheres of influence'. He hoped to see post-war cooperation between the three Great Powers in all conquered and liberated territories. The Russians, who had no intention of opening their treatment of Romania to review in three months' time, retired to prepare for the next encounter. A Soviet mission was sent to the Greek partisans which – as Eden wrote to Churchill – 'speaks for itself'.[28] Perhaps we may elaborate these somewhat cryptic words. The Russians proposed to stir up the Greek partisans in a manner which would prove so embarrassing to the British military authorities in the area that the British Government would be willing to allow Russia a free hand in Romania, with no questions asked, in return for similar Soviet indulgence in Greece – and without reference to any scruples which Roosevelt might feel on the matter. Other countries in eastern and south-eastern Europe were likely to present similar problems. Unless some arrangement was reached, the situation might soon become dangerous.

In such circumstances, the natural solution might seem to be a meeting between leaders of the three major Allies, to hammer out some kind of mutually tolerable solution. What wrecked any such prospect for the immediate future was the American constitution. In the autumn of 1944, there would have to be a Presidential election. It was by no means certain that Roosevelt would run again, or that the Democrats would win even if he did. Ultimate responsibility for American foreign policy rests on the President, and the Republican nominee, Thomas Dewey, who eventually appeared against Roosevelt, was known to have markedly 'isolationist' opinions.

When it eventually became clear that Roosevelt would indeed seek a fourth term, a good deal of attention was focused on a matter which would eventually assume even greater importance: who should be Roosevelt's Vice-Presidential running-mate. In the event of the President's death, incapacity or retirement, the Vice President succeeds to the office. In 1944, there was a feeling among Roosevelt's political associates that 'the chances are strongly in favor of the next Vice President, if he is elected with Roosevelt, succeeding to the Presidency'.[29] In the current period, the Vice President was Henry Wallace, a man known to have strongly radical views on internal policies, and particularly strong sympathy for Russia to boot. The function of a Vice-Presidential candidate in United States politics is usually to attract a few votes to the 'ticket' which the Presidential candidate could not reach. Wallace would certainly not draw votes to the Democratic ticket which Roosevelt would not himself attract, and might well lose quite a lot; for not only *cognoscenti* but ordinary voters would scrutinise any Vice-Presidential candidate as a likely successor. If all this was a black mark against Wallace, then who should run? Several men were seriously considered. Perhaps the most impressive record of public service was held by the jurist James Byrnes. Yet Byrnes, and most of the others, were well into their sixties or even older, and Roosevelt was deeply conscious that a relatively youthful Republican must not be met by an elderly Democratic team. At the last moment, the Democratic choice lighted on an unexpected and relatively unknown figure, Harry S. Truman of Missouri.[30] Neither Byrnes nor Wallace could be expected to view this selection without a degree of pique, and both men would play an important part in events when Truman eventually succeeded to Roosevelt's office.

Until the election was over, nobody could speak with authority for the United States. Unfortunately, events would not wait as long as that. The rapid military advances of the Allies made some kind of working understanding about the immediate future imperative. Decisions were therefore left largely to Britain and Russia – both of whom were thinking on completely different lines from Roosevelt and his advisers.

So Churchill resolved to meet the Russians – intending (so he told Roosevelt) to clinch the question of Russian intervention against Japan, and to attempt a friendly settlement over Poland. America, the Prime Minister assured the President, would be kept informed at every point.

Roosevelt was at first inclined to let the British and the Russians dispose of matters as they chose. Later, Charles Bohlen, the leading State Department expert on Russia, approached Roosevelt's close associate, Harry Hopkins, and succeeded by that route in changing the President's mind.[31] There was a danger, explained Bohlen,

> that the Soviet Government would regard the absence of an American representative as a clear indication that the US Government has authorised the British Prime Minister to speak for both governments. . . . Any decisions reached between the Prime Minister and Stalin at the proposed meeting will set the picture, without American participation, for the future structure of Europe.[32]

Bohlen also foresaw that a meeting between Churchill and Stalin without United States participation would produce either 'a first class row' or 'the division of Europe into spheres of influence on a power political basis'. Eventually the President requested that the American Ambassador, Averell Harriman, should also be present at the main meetings – and further asked Stalin that these should be 'preliminary to a meeting of the three of us'.[33] In that atmosphere the 'Tolstoy' conference opened in Moscow.

Discussion about Japan could hardly proceed very far in the circumstances, and the extremely important talks about Poland which did take place will be considered in a later chapter. As for the matter which originally convinced the British and Russians that an early conference was imperative, it is difficult to escape the conclusion that both countries took advantage of the absence of a major American representative to reach a settlement of which they were both full well aware that Roosevelt would have strongly disapproved. The printed record of the meeting states Churchill's position with engaging candour:

> The Prime Minister said it was better to express these things in diplomatic terms and not to use the phrase 'dividing into spheres' because the Americans might be shocked. But as long as he and the Marshal understood each other he could explain matters to the President.[34]

The abortive deal over Romania and Greece was again considered. Romania, declared the Prime Minister,

> was very much a Russian affair, and the treaty the Soviet Government had proposed was reasonable . . . But in Greece it was different. Britain must be the leading Mediterranean Power and he hoped Marshal Stalin would let him have the first say about Greece . . . Marshal Stalin . . . agreed.[35]

Britain and Russia went a great deal further than that – so far, indeed, that even the British Foreign Office began to express qualms and apprehensions.[36] Churchill and Stalin resolved to express their respective concern for south-east European countries in percentages. 'The system,' wrote Churchill, was intended 'to express the interest and sentiment with which the British and Soviet Governments approach the problems of these countries and so that they might reveal their minds to each other in some way that could be comprehensible.'[37] The allocation of these percentages was not a casual, rule-of-thumb arrangement devised between Churchill and Stalin; their respective Foreign Ministers had some quite detailed preliminary discussions before agreement was reached. The eventual conclusion was that Russia should receive a 90 per cent interest in Romania, 80 per cent in Hungary and Bulgaria, 50 per cent in Yugoslavia and 10 per cent in Greece.[38] Some documents refer to the balance passing to Britain; while some, a trifle more diplomatically, declare that it should revert to 'the others'. The future destiny of most of the countries concerned followed closely the terms of that agreement. Whether by accident or design, Harriman was apparently absent when the crucial agreement was reached[39] – although he had already foretold the upshot with considerable accuracy.[40]

Whether or not the Americans liked the agreement, they were in no position to upset it. One important member of Roosevelt's Cabinet wrote to the President in considerable distress about the understandings which 'are being reached or pointed towards which look like a repetition of the things that occurred just previous to and during the Versailles Treaty'.[41] American diplomats as a body were disposed to accept the view that the British were compelled – by reason of their own weakness and in absence of any firm United States backing – to work out 'spheres of influence' with the Russians.

The fate of Yugoslavia under the '50–50' agreement was rather difficult to decide. The Yugoslav Government-in-Exile was under British patronage; while Tito, of his own volition, looked to Russia. He had long made it clear that King Peter would not be allowed to return to the country until a final decision had been taken on the future of the monarchy. Meetings were accordingly held betwen Tito and Ivan Subasić, the Prime Minister foisted on Peter not long before. On 1 November, what became known as the 'Tito-Subasić Agreement' was concluded.[42] Tito's main point was conceded: the King should not return before the popular decision had been taken. Meanwhile, Royal powers should be exercised by a Regency Council, on the proposal of a reconstituted Government, and in agreement with Tito and Subasić. The new government would emerge from an amalgamation of the old Subasić Government and Tito's 'National Committee'. A Partisan body would remain the supreme legislative body until elections could be held. These would be conducted in conditions of freedom, with a secret ballot, and with the right for all parties who had not collaborated with the enemy to participate. There was to be an express guarantee of 'personal freedom, freedom from fear, freedom of worship, liberty of conscience, freedom of speech, liberty of the press, freedom of assembly and association . . . and . . . the right of property and personal initiative'.

There were, however, several serious difficulties. In the first place, there had been no contact between the King and Subasić during the negotiations, and omission of the King from a government formed in such circumstances was either clumsy or sinister. As Peter observed to Churchill, it 'seemed to him to be a procedure to get rid of him more or less painlessly'.[43] For reasons quite unconnected with the Tito-Subasić agreement, Churchill's early enthusiasm for Tito was turning to profound mistrust,[44] and the British Prime Minister became increasingly suspicious of the proposed arrangements. Eden reminded him of doubts whether the eventual elections would be genuinely free.[45] In the next few weeks, however, various modifications were suggested, and by the middle of December it began to look as if the Tito-Subasić agreement would be accepted by most of the Yugoslavs affected, and also by Britain and Russia.

The King, however, persisted in his objections, and Churchill began to waver – writing to Eden on 1 January 1945 that 'the agreement is . . . hopelessly one-sided and can mean nothing but the dictatorship of Tito, that well-drilled Communist'.[46] The Prime Minister nevertheless decided a few days later that it

> should be accepted for what it is worth by King Peter. It must be understood that this gives him a very poor chance of ever seeing his native land again, whether as King or subject. All the same, it is the best chance he has, and the arrangement preserves the principle of the monarchy.[47]

Churchill spoke to King Peter bluntly. 'Military considerations make it necessary for us to continue to support Marshal Tito. There was no prospect of our intervening by force to replace the King on the throne.'[48]

The King was not prepared to disappear quietly without the world knowing the issues at stake. On 11 January 1945, he issued a press statement outlining his objections to the agreement, among which apprehensions that it would result in a Tito dictatorship ranked high.[49] The British Government, which was appalled at the possible consequences of the Russians, or Tito, or both, suspecting that the King was acting with British support, took action at the highest level and with considerable speed. The War Cabinet accepted the idea that Churchill should write to Stalin, declaring support for the Tito-Subasić agreement, and promising to recognise a government which might be constituted thereunder. By a rather dangerous fiction, they would 'take as granted the King's approval of the Agreement, and ... treat the views expressed by His Majesty ... as null and void'.[50] Eden, however, felt bound to intervene. It was, 'of course', necessary 'to consider the United States Government'. Here, too, there was no dissent. Nobody seems to have anticipated the slightest difficulty there.

The Americans, however, did not prove as compliant as the British Government had hoped, and refused to be stampeded into accepting the agreement while the King remained reluctant. Indeed, they began to feel growing doubts about the alleged iniquity of Mihajlović (whose Četniks had by no means disappeared from the scene), noting that 'Allied observers attached to the Partisans do not have the freedom of movement which would enable them to evaluate the real situation'.[51] The Americans were also aware that Mihajlović was anxious to place himself under command of the British General Wilson: a course of behaviour scarcely consistent with the myth that he had gone over to the enemy.

Meanwhile the Russians pressed hard for immediate action. Britain was caught in the middle. One unidentified member of the Cabinet stated the position with more frankness than tact: 'We had still some slight influence in Yugoslavia, though our position was far from strong. . . . Was it desirable to risk sacrificing what remained of our influence, solely because of United States delay?'[52] This 'slight influence' was all that remained of the 'Tolstoy' agreement that Britain's share of influence in Yugoslavia should be equal to that of Russia.

At this point King Peter announced the dismissal of Subasić's Government. This did not worry Churchill, who assured both Subasić and Stalin that 'the King's action does not affect HM Government's intention to see that the Tito-Subasić agreement is carried out'.[53] Regents would be appointed 'whatever the King may say'. Eden was even instructed by Churchill that 'if necessary you should tell Peter that futher obstruction on his part will result in our requesting him to leave this country'.[54] At last the King capitulated, and appointed the Regents.

In Greece, the apportionment between British and Russian interest was different from that in Yugoslavia, and so the struggle between Communists and anti-Communists wore a different aspect. The Russians more or less withdrew their backing to EAM for a considerable time, and allowed events to take their own course. In October 1944, British troops entered Athens, and there were soon clashes between EAM and the 'right-wing' EDES. At the beginning of December, six of the EAM ministers withdrew from the Government. A day or so later, a pro-EAM demonstration in Athens was dispersed by fire from the Greek police. As *The Times* commented, 'seeds of civil war were well and truly sown'.[55] The British Ambassador threw different light on the situation, claiming that 'the small but well-armed Communist party had been practising a reign of terror all over the country'.[56] He reported from Athens that 'men, women and children were murdered here in large numbers and thousands of hostages were taken, dragged along the roads, and many left to die'. There were similar reports from Salonika, and the Ambassador expressed fear that 'red terror' might easily lead to 'white terror'. The presence of large numbers of British troops, plus the relative moderation of the Greek authorities in the later stages of the disturbances, held matters somewhat in check; but the strain was considerable. 'I never knew EAM would be so powerful,' wrote Churchill wistfully. 'I only wish they had fought one tenth as well against the Germans.'[57]

Anyone reading much of the British press at the time of the Greek disturbances could be excused for thinking that a trigger-happy right-wing government, with support from British occupying forces, was brutally suppressing a popular rising which was spearheaded by the idealistic youth of the country. Many British politicians and others criticised the military action, much in the spirit of this interpretation. Early in the new year, however, a delegation from the Trades Union Congress, headed by Sir Walter Citrine, paid a visit to the country and presented a profoundly different picture of the situation. There was a 'great and universal resentment among the British troops at what they considered the inadequate and unfair manner in which recent events in Greece had been presented'[58] by a large section of the press. The delegation recorded a 'dread . . . among all kinds of people that the British Government might throw overboard its responsibility by a premature withdrawal of British troops'. The TUC report confirmed diplomatic views expressed a year or so earlier, to the effect that EAM and its military section ELAS had done little fighting against the Germans – but the arms with which the British had supplied them 'had been hoarded presumably for other purposes, and the weapons carried by ELAS during the German occupation consisted almost exclusively of arms captured from the Italians'. British troops moving northwards in pursuit of retreating Germans in the latter part of 1944 passed forces of ELAS moving in the opposite direction. 'That, in the view of our troops, showed undoubtedly that ELAS was more concerned with returning to Athens to seize power than with fighting the Germans.' The Trades Union delegation heard 'horrible stories of the atrocities committed by a section of ELAS named OPLA' and noted the 'universal opinion' of British troops that 'had they not been ordered into action against ELAS there would have been wholesale massacre in Athens'.

Thus were matters beginning to fall into place in much of south-eastern Europe at the very beginning of 1945, well before the famous Yalta Conference. The British had abdicated any claim to serious influence in Romania, Bulgaria and Hungary. This arrangement did not bind the Americans, but made it difficult for them to assert their own position. In Yugoslavia, thanks to British military assistance, Tito had already established himself as very much the dominant military force on the Allied side, while – thanks to British diplomatic assistance – his position in political matters was greatly facilitated. Only in Greece was Britain effectively allowed *carte-blanche* by the Russians; but there were well-armed forces operating in the country which were making matters exceedingly difficult for the occupying troops.

5

The Latin West

'1. The only bond of the victors is their common hate.
2. To make Britain safe she must be responsible for the safety of a cluster of feeble states.
We ought to think of something better than these.' Churchill to Eden, 8 February 1945. PREM 3/192/3, fo. 16.

The experience of the Latin lands in southern Europe during the Second World War is less closely and directly related to the genesis of the eventual 'Cold War' than is the experience of countries in the centre and east of Europe. Yet it has considerable pertinence to the main story, for the history of those Latin countries during the war played a considerable part in conditioning post-war attitudes, while the behaviour of the Great Powers towards them during the period throws important light on issues which later developed between Russia and her erstwhile Allies. For two or three years after the war, there were very serious doubts whether the Latin countries would go Communist; and if they had done so, the whole balance of world power would have been altered beyond recognition.

At the commencement of the war, France and Italy both ranked as 'Great Powers'. They stood on different sides in that war; but there had been nothing approaching unanimity in either country in favour of participation in the conflict. Neither country fought with particular vigour, even when invasion came; and in each case defeat was received without signs of universal distress – although in both countries substantial minorities continued to struggle against the original enemy.

When France fell in 1940, both the United States and the Soviet Union were at peace with Germany, and both countries maintained normal diplomatic relations with the government established at Vichy under Marshal Pétain. The government was not initially unpopular; Churchill later wrote that 'there is no doubt that three-quarters of France' accepted it.[1] Yet considerable numbers of

Frenchmen were not prepared to endorse the apparent verdict of war, and escaped to Britain to continue the struggle. Among these 'Free French', General Charles de Gaulle was soon accepted as leader. In September 1941, the 'Free French' set up the 'French National Committee', which had a more 'official' status – though it was not recognised even by Britain as the notional government of France. A large section of 'Vichyite' opinion regarded the Gaullists not as misguided patriots who were foolishly continuing to fight a war which was already lost, but rather as traitors, taking the view that France's military defeat imposed on all Frenchmen a special duty to rally behind the Government which was doing what it could to preserve a measure of French independence from the Germans. The French colonies, unlike metropolitan France, had some freedom of choice between rival claimants to their allegiance. Some opted for de Gaulle; most of them remained loyal to Vichy until Allied troops appeared in their immediate vicinity.

When the Americans entered the war at the end of 1941, they saw no reason to abandon their diplomatic relations with Vichy. The American Consul-General declared that

> Not all newly appointed by the Vichy Government, and not all who continued to serve under it, although appointed earlier, are pro-Nazi or anti-British or anti-American ... There were many high up in the Government itself at Vichy who quietly 'covered' their subordinates cooperating with the Americans.[2]

Cordell Hull later explained that the American policy towards Vichy was designed 'for such vital purposes as combatting Nazi designs, the preservation of the French fleet from German hands and the prevention of Nazi occupation of French Africa or the establishment of military bases there'.[3] Indeed, for a time the Americans were much more at loggerheads with de Gaulle than with Vichy. In the very month of American entry to the war, the Gaullists occupied the tiny islands of St. Pierre and Miquelon, off Newfoundland, which had hitherto owed allegiance to Vichy. The American Secretary of State was furious, for he considered that this action gravely endangered his policy of bringing the Vichyites towards a sympathetic relationship with the Allies.[4] Hull was angry with Churchill, who had encouraged the operation, and felt that Roosevelt had not given sufficient backing to the State Department view; but his most lasting resentment was reserved for de Gaulle.

What shifted the American attitude towards Vichy was the military situation which developed in 1942. When it became obvious that a 'Second Front' in western Europe was impossible that year, the British and Americans resolved to effect landings in French north-west Africa, a strategy of which Stalin had approved during Churchill's visit to Moscow in August. 'Operation Torch' was launched in November 1942 as a joint Anglo-American venture, under command of the American General Eisenhower.

The invasion precipitated several crises almost simultaneously. The first was predictable, and caused little regret in Britain: Pétain's Government broke off diplomatic relations with the United States. The second was almost equally predictable: the Germans decided to occupy that part of France which had been left unoccupied in 1940. The invasion of French Africa also produced a series of angry recriminations between the Free French and their Allies. On Roosevelt's insistence, Britain and America had no collusion with de Gaulle until the attack was almost ready. There were sound reasons for this – including a serious risk of information leakage to the enemy – but the effect when de Gaulle eventually heard of the expedition was explosive. His feelings were exacerbated when the Americans showed interest in winning support from the Vichyite Admiral Darlan. Darlan was removed from the scene by assassination, in circumstances which still carry an aura of mystery. The Americans now came to look with sympathy towards another French officer with better credentials, General Giraud. This attitude was motivated by a desire to secure a political counterpoise to de Gaulle rather than by any strong faith in Giraud's military capacity – though probably Giraud himself misunderstood this fact.[5] Roosevelt expressed his position clearly to a meeting of his Cabinet early in 1943: 'it was all right for Giraud to operate as Eisenhower's agent if Eisenhower had designated him as his agent' – but 'there was no chain of title running to either Darlan or Giraud or even de Gaulle'.[6] In the President's judgement, 'the British see some advantage for themselves in recognising de Gaulle and trying to ride on his coat-tails back into France'.

The Americans continued to reciprocate fully de Gaulle's hostility, and for a long time there was little dispute between Roosevelt and Hull on that score. Churchill leaned towards the same opinion. He was often infuriated by de Gaulle, and the aphorism that the heaviest cross he had to bear was the Cross of Lorraine will long be remembered. Yet the Prime Minister could never wholly forget that de Gaulle had continued the fight against Germany at a time when all seemed lost; and his anger and irritation against de Gaulle were qualified by admiration for a French patriot. The British Foreign Office and Eden were much more positively sympathetic with de Gaulle, but highly critical of the Americans – who, in Eden's view, 'dislike the growth of an independent spirit in any French administration anywhere and consider that any French authority with whom they deal should comply without question with their demands'.[7] Roosevelt was alerted to the 'strongly pro-de Gaulle' feeling in London, and was warned unofficially that 'any attempt to weaken or challenge his position will be unfavorably received by the British public'.[8]

While these debates ran back and forth across the Atlantic, the pro-Allied French were attempting to resolve their differences. The first move in that direction had come, oddly enough, from Churchill and Roosevelt, who in January 1943 had engineered a much-publicised handshake between Giraud and de Gaulle. Some weeks later both Generals were brought within the ambit of the French National Committee. There was no doubt that civilian members of the National Committee favoured de Gaulle's leadership, and the Americans strongly suspected that Britain held the same view. During one of his transatlantic visits, Churchill tried to persuade Hull that these suspicions were mistaken,[9] and a few days later pressed the same view on Roosevelt. Events, however, soon proved otherwise. The Prime Minister cabled home, suggesting that the French National Committee should be compelled by diplomatic and financial means to drop de Gaulle. This was too much for the War Cabinet to swallow, even from Churchill; and they returned a polite, but emphatic, denial of the Prime Minister's request.[10]

On 3 June 1943, the 'French Committee of National Liberation' was set up as successor to the old French National Committee. De Gaulle and Giraud were joint Presidents, and there were both civilian and military members. Four days later the new Committee sought Allied recognition as 'the body qualified to ensure the conduct of the French effort in the war within the framework of inter-allied cooperation as well as the defence of all French interests'.[11] The British were markedly embarrassed. 'Speaking frankly,' a junior Minister explained to an American official, 'the British were the victims of their own too successful build up of de Gaulle. They were thoroughly worried about his tendencies.'[12] Roosevelt was furious at the new French initiative. A fortnight after the Committee was set up, he told Churchill 'that there is no possibility of our working with de Gaulle'.[13] The Prime Minister was forced to remind the President that his own views were not endorsed by the War Cabinet. Pressures grew in Britain in favour of acceding to the French request, and a month later Churchill had to warn Roosevelt that Britain might soon recognise the Committee; if she did so, Russia would doubtless follow.[14] The two men were due to meet at Quebec in August, and a final decision was delayed until then. They had to acknowledge an impasse. Different formulae were devised by the two countries to define their relationship with the Committee. The British recognised it, in terms similar to those requested by the French; the American formula expressly averred that their attitude did 'not constitute recognition'. Astonishingly, Cordell Hull not merely had no part in this decision, but did not even know it had been taken until he telephoned the secretary to Roosevelt's Chief of Staff to enquire about the position.[15] The Secretary of State, not unreasonably, exploded – though perhaps not in the correct direction. 'We all had an awful time with Hull, who has at last gone off in a pretty sulky mood, especially with the Foreign Secretary who bore the brunt,'[16] reported Churchill to his Cabinet. The French, however, were apparently satisfied with the somewhat inconclusive result, and were persuaded not to emphasise the contrast between British and American statements.

Behind all this lay a great deal more than personal animosity. A strong current of American opinion regarded all European Empires as evil anachronisms. Neither Roosevelt nor Hull represented this opinion in its extreme form, but both leaned some way towards it. They were by no means anxious to restore the British Empire – still less the French Empire – to its pre-war glories. In the judgement of Harold Macmillan, British Minister resident in the Mediterranean area, Roosevelt was 'more than nettled' by the formation of the French Committee, which 'threatened to bring about the reunion of the French Empire which at heart he apparently wished to keep divided'.[17]

By contrast, there were few people in Britain who wished to see the British Empire dissolved – though a great many people thought that the dependent parts of the Empire should be encouraged towards self-government. Most Britons were disposed to think of the French Empire as in essentially the same position as their own. There was also a very influential body of British opinion, centring on the Foreign Office, which believed passionately in an Anglo-French alliance, and had done so ever since the *Entente Cordiale* of 1904. Eden epitomised the Foreign Office view, while Churchill perceived that, in the future, cooperation with the United States would be far more important. Perhaps neither man really appreciated at the time how radical was the difference between them.

Political questions cut across the dispute. In France itself, there was a strong resistance movement, in which (since Russia came into the war) the Communists played a large part. Although de Gaulle's own political opinions were much to the 'right', the Resistance was disposed to back him vigorously as he was the strongest available force of opposition to the Germans. In the prevailing atmosphere of pro-Russian, vaguely 'left-wing', feeling which prevailed around 1942–3, all this counted for virtue in the eyes of the British Foreign Office. By contrast, the American State Department noted with considerable disfavour the fact that de Gaulle was receiving support both from the well-organised French Communists and from the Foreign Office.[18]

A couple of months after the 'recognition' question had been patched up, further disquieting news came from the French. First, Giraud was removed from co-Presidency. Next, a number of French politicians were arrested by the Committee of National Liberation and charged with treason. In some cases there was strong *prima facie* evidence of complicity in treasonable activity, or even in atrocities; but the case which really highlighted the problem most sharply was that of Flandin, sometime Premier of the Third Republic, and briefly a Minister in the Vichy Government. No allegations of inhumanities were breathed against him; and his record with Vichy had certainly not been that of a man desiring to collaborate closely with the Germans. Churchill reacted violently to the news of Flandin's arrest.

. . . Having acquainted myself in detail with his acts over the last ten years I am of opinion that for the French Committee to proceed against him would be proof that they are small, ambitious intriguers, endeavouring to improve their position by maltreating unpopular public figures.[19]

The argument advanced, for the proceedings against Flandin were – in Churchill's view – 'little less than a declaration of civil war against the greater part of the people of France'.[20] Assurances were later given by de Gaulle that Flandin and the other Vichy Ministers would not be ill-treated, nor brought to trial until after the liberation of France.[21] Nevertheless, other Frenchmen were not covered by such assurances. Pierre Pucheu, who was also arrested by the Committee, was not merely brought to trial, but shot. By all accounts he richly deserved his fate; but the operative question was not the guilt of Pucheu, but the title under which the Committee had tried and executed him. If they could deal with one man in that way, they might presumably deal in a similar manner with others.

The wrangling continued. It was necessary to prepare a directive for General Eisenhower as to how he should treat French political authorities in the areas which would be liberated when the main European invasion began. A draft compiled by the American War Department caused Roosevelt 'some displeasure' because it was moving towards recognition of the French Committee.[22] Later, another draft was produced, which leaned the other way.[23] Churchill and Roosevelt both approved of this; but continuing difficulties at home made it impossible for the Prime Minister to sign it until these could be resolved. Meanwhile, the French Committee stole a march on the Anglo-Americans and assumed general authority over the armed forces – thus overriding Giraud.[24] In May, the Assembly – a sort of quasi-Parliament of the 'Free French' – took matters a stage further, and formally proclaimed the Committee as Provisional

Government of France. By this time the Allied invasion of
Normandy was only a month away, and some kind of understanding
about the status of the 'Free French' was apparently required. If the
invasion succeeded, an administration would have to be set up
behind Allied lines. Frenchmen of all opinions would resent
continuing military government by the Anglo-Americans.

At the end of May, an invitation was sent to de Gaulle to visit
Britain before 'D-day'. The Foreign Office had hoped that this might
be useful, not only in preparing for the General's eventual
Normandy visit, but also as a good occasion for reaching agreement
about the civil administration which would function after the
liberation. Such an agreement, however, presupposed American
concurrence, for the main control of the Allied expedition would be
in the hands of Eisenhower. Roosevelt was not prepared to authorise
an American representative to be present at the Anglo-French
discussions – an essential condition if their conclusions were to have
any real authority.[25] Thus when the invasion began on 6 June the
directive to Eisenhower which had been concocted in March was still
unsigned by Churchill, and no alternative instructions had been
agreed. It was evident that Churchill could go no further with his
Cabinet. Might Roosevelt be brought to make concessions? Henry
Stimson, Secretary of War, decided that 'an immediate reconciliation
between the British and American Governments' was necessary –
even if the price was provisional recognition of de Gaulle. Yet
Stimson could get nowhere with Hull, recording that the latter 'hates
de Gaulle with such fierce feeling that he rambles into almost
incoherence whenever we talk about him'.[26]

A considerable feeling was building up – even among leading
Democrats in Roosevelt's Cabinet, and sympathetic journalists – to
the effect that failure to recognise de Gaulle was 'on account of the
President's bullheaded obstinacy, based largely on a personal dislike'
of the General.[27] Meanwhile, de Gaulle was also in a very angry frame
of mind, claiming that he had been 'tricked into coming to London
and . . . presented with a *fait accompli*'.[28] He received a strong hint
from Eden that the difficulty lay with Churchill and the Americans
rather than with his own Department.[29]

So everything waited on Roosevelt. On 12 September came news
that de Gaulle had just formed 'what appears to be a pretty
representative Provisional Government.[30] Meanwhile, the Allies were
cutting into France. At first, the French people were by no means
unanimous in welcoming the Anglo-Americans as liberators, and
there were recorded cases of women snipers.[31] Later, however,
opinion swung strongly to the Allies, and it became more and more
clear that the majority of French people supported the General. It
also became increasingly desirable to transfer authority over the

liberated regions to a native French administration. At last, on 23 October, the three major Allies recognised the Provisional Government, and a 'Zone of Interior' was set up under its control.

France showed an immediate disposition to form close links with Russia. In November 1944, it was announced that de Gaulle wished to visit the Soviet Union. Churchill approved of the idea, expressing the hope that the French and Russian leaders would 'talk over the whole field together'.[32] Stalin warned Churchill that the French were likely to raise the question of establishing a Franco-Soviet Mutual Assistance Pact, similar to that already existing between Britain and Russia. The whole tone of the message suggested that Russia was anxious to avoid any commitments to France which would raise objections in Britain.[33] The British Government made no difficulties; but Eden – with War Cabinet approval – suggested an alternative kind of treaty: a tripartite pact between Britain, France and the Soviet Union.[34] Then both Churchill and Roosevelt began to express hesitations about such an arrangement. Stalin was indifferent; but the final word lay with France. De Gaulle decided against the British proposal, and concluded a simple bilateral treaty with the Soviet Union.

Relations between the major Allies over France contrast very sharply with their relations over eastern Europe. The sharpest differences lay within and between the Anglo-Saxons. What is most impressive is the extreme tact of the Russians in all these discussions. At no point did they give reasonable cause for offence to any of the parties concerned – British, American or French. They acted as though they had no special concern with either France or the French Empire, save only to ensure that no unnecessary impediment stood in the way of the Allied war effort. Beyond that, they were quite happy to leave all developments to the three western countries themselves. The effect of all this on the French is not difficult to understand. America was perceived as unsympathetic; Britain as a land of divided counsels. Russia, by contrast, was seen as a willing future associate, linked to France by a common fear of Germany. The many Communists in France would encourage that view of the situation; while people like de Gaulle, who were by no means Communist sympathisers but who smarted under the treatment meted out to them by Roosevelt, could perceive advantages in playing off Russia against the Anglo-Saxon Powers.

The story of relations between the major Allies and France invites comparison with their relations towards Italy in the same period. The Allied invasion of Sicily began in July 1943. Before the month was out, Mussolini had fallen, and in the course of September, the new government set up by King Victor Emmanuel III and Marshal Badoglio surrendered unconditionally to the Allies. There were numerous German troops in Italy, and they – predictably – refused to withdraw; so Italy declared war on Germany before she had concluded peace with the Allies.

As time went on, differences began to appear between the British and Americans, who were slowly working their way up the Italian peninsula. It was desirable to operate through some Italian civil administration if possible. The more representative such an administration could be, the better; and there was always the underlying suspicion that those few politicians who did happen to be to hand were claiming an influence far beyond their measure of popular support. Nobody had great confidence in the popularity of the King or Badoglio; but there seemed better prospects in November 1943, when a number of 'opposition' politicians, including Count Sforza and the scholar Bernadetto Croce, appeared on the scene. Such men would have given considerable 'credibility' to an Italian Government; but Badoglio discovered that they would not join his administration unless the King abdicated. Churchill concluded that, although 'King Victor Emmanuel is nothing to us', it was dangerous to make changes of such a drastic kind in the circumstances.[35] Abdication might have adverse effects on the Italian armed forces, which had hitherto been 'working well' with the Allies.[36]

Military progress continued to be slow, and in the early part of 1944, pressure for political action began to mount, both in Britain and in America. As early as January 1944, Cordell Hull had decided that 'reorganisation of the government of Italy should no longer be delayed'[37] – apparently implying that the King should abdicate at once. Churchill, however, remained adamant, and vigorously slapped down the British military men in Italy – who, in his view, gave too much attention to 'opposition' politicians; while Roosevelt, for the time being, checked the State Department.[38] The Italian 'opposition' soon developed an apparently powerful coalition of no fewer than six political parties, and Roosevelt began to weaken. Churchill, fortified by a decision of the British War Cabinet, maintained his stand.[39]

Help came to the beleaguered Churchill from an unexpected quarter. On 13 March, the Soviet Union restored diplomatic relations with Italy. This could be seen as an attempt to strengthen the position of the King and Badoglio – although the putative beneficiaries viewed this Greek gift 'with mixed feelings'.[40] Then, at the end of the month, the Italian Communist leader Togliatti returned to his country from Moscow. He soon swung round most of the 'opposition' to a more accommodating position, and in April a compromise solution was formally announced. The King should remain until the Allies reached Rome, when he would withdraw from public life and appoint his son Umberto as Lieutenant of the

Realm, who would exercise the Royal powers. Manifestly, the intervention had been inspired by some calculation of advantage by Russia, who thought benefit would derive from reducing political tension in Italy. As with Russian attempts to weld together the Western Allies in relation to France, these efforts were very likely connected with a desire to speed the 'Second Front' – though contemporaries were more impressed with the idea that Russia wanted the political situation stabilised until the northern parts of the country – where many Communists resided – could be reached by the Allied armies.[41] Whatever the reason for Togliatti's intervention may have been, it proved effective. Badoglio was able to form a government resting on several political parties – including Communists, Socialists and Christian Democrats.

The Allies eventually entered Rome on 4–5 June. Within hours, the King had transferred powers to his son. A day or so later, Badoglio was forced to resign, and a new government was formed under Bonomi, who had been Prime Minister in the days before Mussolini, but had withdrawn from public life for over twenty years. The transfer of power enraged Churchill: 'I am surprised and shocked about Badoglio being replaced by this wretched old Bonomi. We have lost the only competent Italian with whom we could deal.'[42]

Churchill did not accept the rebuff as final, and sought help from both Stalin and Roosevelt for the restoration of Badoglio. This action drew a gentle, but firm, reproof from Attlee, who contended that it was 'unfortunate' to approach other Allies until the matter had been discussed in the War Cabinet.[43] Nothing could be done, however, until the other major leaders replied. Stalin was non-committal; but Roosevelt firmly opposed interference with Bonomi's government.[44] So Bonomi remained in office.

Churchill continued to fulminate against Britons whom he blamed for allowing the change to take place: the High Commissioner, Sir Noel Charles ('a helpless kind of person'), and above all the Chief Allied Control Commissioner, General Mason-Macfarlane ('so far as I am concerned he will never have any post of the slightest military or political responsibility again').[45] This incident by no means terminated the Prime Minister's efforts to control the course of Italian politics; but the broad pattern in Italy had been largely decided. It bore many similarities to that which was developing behind the Allied lines in France. A Coalition Government, held rather at arm's length by the Anglo-Saxon Allies, was gradually taking over civil administration. The Communists occupied an important, but not a dominant, position within that Government. The Soviet Union was apparently behaving impeccably towards the Anglo-Americans; but it was not difficult to guess at ulterior designs.

The third large Latin country was also destined to play some part in relations between the Big Three wartime Allies. The Spanish Civil War of 1936–9 had exerted an immense effect on those Britons and Frenchmen who were deeply concerned over politics – though far less effect upon the man-in-the-street. In western Europe and to an extent in the United States, the 'left' and a section of the 'right' had given strong moral support to the Spanish Government, while a considerable element of the 'right' had afforded similar support to Franco. One side noted the assistance which Germany and Italy were affording to the insurgents; the other noted the assistance which Russia was giving to the Spanish Government. In retrospect, it is clear that both bodies of opinion in the democratic countries extolled the virtues of their favourites and vilified the other side with scant regard to the disgusting realities of the conflict; while neither cared to emphasise how complex and often conflicting were the interests which gave ostensible support to one side or the other.

When war came, the very important strategic location of Spain was evident, and for most of the period a major British political figure, Viscount Templewood – formerly Sir Samuel Hoare – served as Ambassador. The exhausted country was neither able nor willing to play a very large part in the conflict. At first neutral, she passed into a phase of pro-Axis 'non-belligerency'; but even in this period resisted the blandishments of Hitler to intervene strongly on the enemy side. Such intervention could well have proved of considerable importance in 1940, or at the time of the Western Desert campaign. The one respect in which Spain did provide active support for the Axis was by sending the 'Blue Division' volunteers to fight against Russia. As the tide of war turned towards the Allies, Franco returned to his original position of strict neutrality. Yet Spain's action against Russia, the memories of the Civil War, and real or supposed similarities between Franco's government and the political systems of the doomed central dictators, all ensured that the country would attract unfriendly Allied attention in the closing phase of war and the early days of peace. Russia had her legitimate grievance over the Blue Division, while many politicians in the Western Democracies – including very moderate men – could not forget that they had taken a strongly anti-Franco stand during the Civil War. Had the time now arrived for the Allies to take active measures to topple Franco?

In October 1944, Franco wrote to Templewood, indicating his own views about current developments. He saw the threat of international Communism: 'the European countries in a disintegrated continent will have to face the direst and most dangerous crisis of their history.'[46] The burden of the argument was that in future Britain should look sympathetically towards Spain, and even involve her actively in the task of peacemaking. All this precipitated one of the few sharp ideological disputes which took place during the existence of the British Coalition Government. Attlee argued that the 'disappearance' of Franco's régime 'would bring definite advantages to the Spanish people'. Furthermore, contended the Deputy Prime Minister, 'we should use whatever methods are available to assist in bringing about its downfall'.[47] Lord Selborne, the Conservative Minister of Economic Warfare, was equally emphatic for the opposite view. Franco's régime, he argued, showed less 'incompetence, corruption and oppression' than its predecessor, and its atrocities were 'fewer and less horrible'.[48] The dispute extended to the two men most intimately connected with British foreign policy. Eden, while not expressly committing himself to Attlee's view, certainly inclined towards it. In a telegram to Washington he argued that 'really friendly relations' with Spain were impossible while the existing régime persisted. There could be no question of Spain being represented at the Peace Conference, and it was unlikely that she would even be invited to participate in a future World Organisation.[49] Churchill reacted very sharply. The logical conclusion of Eden's ideas would be 'precipitating a renewal of the civil war',[50] which would lead to Communist control of Spain. Thereafter 'we must expect the infection to spread very fast through both Italy and France'. The Prime Minister contended that 'every country that is liberated or converted by our victories is seething with Communism' and 'only our influence with Russia prevents their actively stimulating this movement'. Eden back-tracked rapidly, assuring Churchill that the Foreign Office had no intention of fostering Communism in Spain;[51] but the general debate continued. It was eventually agreed that Churchill should write to Franco, firmly disavowing any idea of alliance against Russia; while nobody of importance pressed hard for any dramatic action against the Caudillo.

The United States came to a similar view towards the end of Roosevelt's life. Meanwhile, the General gradually removed the most objectionable features of his régime, perhaps in response to diplomatic pressure. The Democracies kept Spain almost in quarantine throughout the dictator's life, even when they later became engaged in a bitter Cold War with Russia. The Russians found Franco's continued existence a useful, though wasting, asset when they sought to criticise the Democracies for alleged toleration of fascist régimes.

6

Yalta

'The three heads of Governments consider that the eastern frontier of Poland should follow the Curzon Line, with digressions from it in some regions of five to eight kilometres in favour of Poland.' Yalta communiqué from Churchill, Roosevelt and Stalin, 11 February 1945.

'Germany, the United Kingdom, France and Italy, taking into consideration the settlement already agreed upon in principle concerning the cession of the Sudeten German districts ... declare themselves individually held responsible by this agreement for guaranteeing the steps necessary for its fulfilment.' Munich agreement by Chamberlain, Daladier, Hitler and Mussolini, 29 September 1938.

The 'Tolstoy' conference began only a few days after the final collapse of the Warsaw rising. Churchill and Eden gave no intimation before their departure that the Poles might have an important part to play in the Moscow conversations; but on 7 October 1944, an urgent message was sent to Mikolajczyk, urging him to fly to Moscow 'at once' to participate in the talks, bringing whatever colleagues he wished.[1] The Polish Prime Minister was far from eager to comply; but was brutally informed that refusal would 'relieve us from further responsibility' so far as the Polish Government was concerned.[2] So he flew to Moscow, accompanied by Romer, the Foreign Minister.

The particular concern of Britain, and probably of Russia too, was to establish a united Polish Government which would contain elements from the Government in London and also from the Lublin Committee. The existence of two Polish administrations presented obvious dangers to Allied unity. To the Russians, the accretion of well-known figures from London would add credibility to a government over which they might expect to exercise preponderant influence, while the London Poles could bring into the pool an army of nearly 100,000 seasoned men. For Britain the matter was not only important but urgent. The Lublin Committee, with Russian backing, was steadily establishing its authority: so delay would operate in Russia's favour. Eden therefore considered that Mikolajczyk should 'go straight to Lublin and set up a reconstituted Government there at once'.[3] – without even returning to London to consult his colleagues.

At the first meeting between Polish, British and Russian delegates, Stalin set down his terms. 'If the Poles wished to reach agreement with the Soviet Government, they must first accept the Curzon Line.'[4] Churchill set every pressure upon them to comply. Mikolajczyk, of course, had no sort of lawful authority to transfer any Polish territory to anybody; but in such circumstances constitutional niceties go by the board. Deepest problem of all was Lwow. The London Poles had reason for thinking that Roosevelt might eventually back them on their claim to that city. Churchill offered to intercede with Stalin on the Poles' behalf – but only on condition that they agreed to accept the general settlement proposed, even if he proved unsuccessful. Eden tried to discover whether the Russians were likely to yield on the matter, but indications were to the contrary.[5]

Yet more British pressure was set upon the Poles, and at last they were brought to accept the Curzon Line 'as the line of demarcation between Russia and Poland'.[6] Such *de facto* recognition was not enough for the Russians, who required *de jure* recognition as well. This concession the Poles were in no position to make, for they knew that their colleagues would repudiate them if they attempted it. Without agreement here Stalin was not prepared to proceed further with the attempt to form a united Polish Government – although he proclaimed himself willing that Mikolajczyk should head such a government if agreement could be secured. Gloomily, Churchill recorded that he had conveyed to Stalin 'all the dangers we see from the festering sore of Soviet-Polish affairs'.[7] Eden was in despair: 'And so at this time after endless hours of the stiffest negotiations I have ever known it looks as though Lwow will wreck all our efforts.'[8] Efforts, we may fairly ask, to do what, and for whom. Stalin, who always liked to pose as a 'moderate' when dealing with foreign statesmen, hinted privately to Churchill that he might be facing difficulties not wholly dissimilar to those of Mikolajczyk – claiming that 'he and Molotov were the only two of those he worked with who were favourable to dealing "softly" with Mikolajczyk'.[9] 'I am sure,' commented Churchill, 'there are strong pressures in the background, both party and military.' Stalin, of course, had every interest in persuading Churchill that this was so; but that fact does not necessarily make his statement false. The Americans received the impression that Stalin was unable to relinquish the Soviet claim to

Lwow, even if he wished to do so.[10] There is not much solid evidence about currents of opinion within the Soviet Union; but it does appear probable that there was a considerable head of steam behind Ukrainian nationalism at this time. The Ukrainians had singularly little reason to feel much gratitude towards any of the various people who had governed them at various stages in their history; and probably the best way of ensuring their future support for the Soviet Government was by treating their national aspirations – such as their claim to Lwow – with special favour.

Although Stalin would not allow a united Polish Government to be formed without capitulation by the London Poles on the question of the Curzon Line, a number of discussions took place at the Moscow meetings concerning the form which such a government might take if that question could be set out of the way. British delegates met the Lublin Poles in the presence of the Russians. Diplomatically, Eden told the Foreign Office that the principal figures, Bierut and Osobka-Morawski, 'did not make a good impression'.[11] Less diplomatically, Churchill amplified this view in a communication to the King. Contrasting the two Polish groups, he observed: 'Our lot from London are, as Your Majesty knows, a decent but feeble lot. The three delegates from Lublin seem to be the greatest villains imaginable.'[12] Matters hardly augured well for the prospects of a united government, or if one could be achieved, for the future of the country; but Mikolajczyk was nevertheless brought to make further contact with the Lublin Poles. The upshot of a series of discussions, involving British, Russians and the two Polish groups in various combinations, seemed to suggest that some kind of mutually acceptable formula – possibly on a basis of equal representation – might be achieved, provided that Mikolajczyk could sell the idea, along with acceptance of the Curzon Line, to his London colleagues. Eden cheered up a little at this turn of events, telegraphing the Foreign Office that Mikolajczyk 'will have a hard struggle but now seems confident that he will succeed. It is most important that he should succeed'.[13]

High tragedy, clumsily handled, may easily degenerate into farce. The Polish tragedy began to develop in that manner in the immediate aftermath of the 'Tolstoy' Conference. The task of persuading the Poles to accept what Eden and Churchill considered good for them proved more difficult than had been anticipated. Mikolajczyk found his colleagues in an enquiring mood. After a week or more of deliberations, they fired a series of questions at the British Government. Would Britain support Polish claims for compensation in the West, even if the United States disagreed?[14] The War Cabinet gave a conditional affirmative. The Polish frontier should be extended to the Oder 'unless Poland, of her own volition, should desire ... a more restricted territorial compensation in the west'. The Poles went on to ask about the composition of the united government which it was proposed they should enter. Churchill explained to the Cabinet that the Lublin Committee demanded 75 per cent of places, but in his view the London Poles should receive at least 50 per cent. The problem, the Prime Minister went on to tell his colleagues, could probably not be settled until the frontier question was out of the way. Even so, he added, 'The fact could not be concealed that agreement might be reached on the frontier, and yet everything might break on the question of joining forces with the Lublin Committee.' In other words, the London Poles might find themselves abandoning claim to Lwow, to the bitter dismay of their fellow-countrymen, and yet still not obtain a reasonable share in the new government. The next question was also difficult: 'Will H.M. Government guarantee the independence and integrity of the new Poland?' Here there was sharp division. Churchill favoured a guarantee. Viscount Cranborne – not a member of the War Cabinet, but a Minister invited to the meeting – dared to disagree. 'We had the lesson of 1939 before us and should not again give guarantees to Poland which we could not implement.' The War Cabinet, perhaps following the *argumentum ab hominem* rather than the force of reason, agreed with the Prime Minister. These views were then communicated to the Poles.

The Polish Government was also in close contact with the Americans. The State Department considered that both Polish and American opinion would be prepared to accept the territorial settlement if only Lwow could remain in Poland.[15] Harriman accordingly volunteered to make a further intercession with the Russians on the matter. Mikolajczyk's response to the suggestion was not encouraging. Even if Lwow remained in Poland, he explained, the only party in the Polish Government which would be prepared to reach agreement on the general terms envisaged by Russia was his own Peasant Party. Hence the Ambassador's suggestion was dropped.[16]

After long discussions amongst themselves, the Polish Government broke. Mikolajczyk resigned. He considered – so the British Cabinet minutes recorded – that it was 'still his duty to try for an accommodation with Russia', while 'most of his colleagues did not believe in Russian good faith or that, in these circumstances, negotiations with Russia would be of any value'.[17] Events would show whose judgement on the matter was correct. At first the British Government buoyed itself up with the hope that no other Polish Government could be formed, and Mikolajczyk would be recalled on his own terms; but – as usually happens when a man resigns in order to prove himself indispensable – exactly the opposite was shown.

After some delay, Mikolajczyk was succeeded by the veteran Socialist, Tomasz Arciszewski. This appointment was symbolic. Popular mythology in the West still suggests that the root of Polish intransigence lay in 'reactionaries'. A British Foreign Office minute of the time correctly recognised that it was the Polish Socialists who 'have all along been the main thorn in Mikolajczyk's flesh'.[18]

The change of Polish government set the British and Americans in an embarrassing position. They deplored it; and for a short time the British at any rate apparently anticipated the early return of Mikolajczyk. Soon, however, it became apparent that this would not happen.[19] They were under a deep moral obligation to the former Premier, which they could not decently abrogate; yet a Polish decision to cease backing the British protégé was hardly a good occasion for breaking relations with the London Poles. The view of both the American and British Governments was that relations with the London Poles would not henceforth be more than 'correct' – but 'we would not look favorably on full recognition of the Lublin Committee by the Soviets'.[20]

Matters were getting out of hand. Roosevelt, at last safely home for his fourth Presidential term, contacted Churchill in the middle of December with the suggestion that they should make a joint approach to Stalin, urging postponement of further action on Poland until the Big Three could get together.[21] This approach was endorsed by the Prime Minister. Yet, on the very day when Churchill heard and approved of Roosevelt's proposal, the Prime Minister took what looks like a wholly unnecessary and gratuitous action influenced by sheer spleen, on a matter which he and all others knew was considered vital by all London Poles. About the beginning of December, Churchill had agreed to back Roosevelt if the President interceded with Stalin over Lwow. Yet on the fifteenth of the month he made a public statement in the House of Commons indicating that the British Government would support the Russian claim to the Curzon Line – including Lwow and the oilfields of Galicia.[22] The Americans were compelled to meet this astonishingly imprudent announcement by a public statement by Edward R. Stettinius, who had just succeeded Hull as Secretary of State. This was to the effect that boundary changes should not be arranged during wartime, save by mutual consent of the countries concerned.[23] This may have helped the American Government with its internal critics, but it was too late to save Lwow.

The Russians, however, required a great deal more at Poland's expense than the Curzon Line – with or without Lwow. Even before the fall of Mikolajczyk, they had been edging towards formal recognition of the Lublin Committee.[24] On the last day of 1944, the Lublin Committee broadened its political base to an extent, and declared itself the 'Provisional Government of the Polish Republic'. Osobka-Morawski, technically a 'Socialist', became Prime Minister of an administration which was, in form, a multi-party coalition. As Eden explained, however, 'the Socialist and Peasant Parties in Lublin now appear to be little more than groups of left-wing dissidents'.[25] The Soviet Union promptly recognised the new 'Government'. A month later, the Czechoslovaks succumbed to pressure, and did the same. One story tells that the Czechs feared that Russia would otherwise set up a Committee in Slovakia, as rival to their own Government. Another suggests that they were bribed by a Russian offer to recognise their possession of Teschen – a town to which Poland also had a strong claim.[26]

The Polish situation was both dangerous and fatuous. There were two administrations, each headed by a Socialist, each consisting nominally of a broad coalition of parties, and each claiming to be the lawful government of Poland. Each of them knew that its chance of ever really governing Poland would depend on toleration of one or more of the Big Three. Each one in name possessed a substantial army, but would only be allowed to use that army with support of a major Ally. Neither 'Government' had been elected by the Polish people, nor depended on an elected Polish parliament for continuance in office. One was recognised by Russia, the other by Britain and America.

Just as there was great uncertainty about the future political orientation of Poland, so also was there great uncertainty about its future frontiers, both in the East and the West. In spite of his own public statement, Churchill continued to believe that the Russians might make a dramatic gesture over Lwow, relinquishing the town to Poland after all.[27] In the matter of the western frontier, the London Poles, at any rate, had perceived the dangers of making their demands too covetous. Now the situation was greatly complicated through the formation of the Lublin 'Government' and its recognition by Russia. The Lublin Poles predictably accepted the Russian view about the Curzon Line, which reduced the moral force of any representations which might later be made over Lwow. In the west they also followed Russian wishes, and demanded that their frontier should be the rivers Oder and Neisser. The great town of Stettin (Szczecin), which bestrides the Oder, should go entirely to Poland.

The River Oder has two tributaries called the Neisser. If the eastern Neisser was intended, then this would give Poland the Oppeln district – which Britain had long intended she should receive, along with East Prussia and Danzig – plus a good deal of territory about which Britain was more doubtful. The Lublin Poles, however, seemed to be demanding the western (Görlitzer) Neisser; and an article in *Pravda* confirmed and supported this claim. Eden now expressly admitted what had surely been plain all along: 'The Russians consider that they have an interest in pushing Poland as far to the west as possible, thus embroiling her permanently with Germany and making her dependent upon Soviet support and protection.'[28] In human terms, the effect of these changes would be enormous. The Poles, who had had more than enough of minority problems, would be bound to expel all, or most, of the Germans from any land which they occupied. Something like $2^1/_2$ million Germans had lived in pre-war Poland. The eastern Neisser frontier would bring in a further $2^1/_4$ millions, the western Neisser $3^1/_4$ millions more still. This grand total of eight millions, based on Eden's figures, may have been a considerable underestimate. The more territory the Poles were forced to cede to Russia in the east, the more urgently would they demand compensation in the west. It would be difficult for even the London Poles to act moderately in the matter, because of likely reactions within Poland itself. Yet there was some evidence that British public and parliamentary opinion was uneasy at even the Oder-Eastern Neisser frontier which the War Cabinet was prepared to support, should the Poles demand it. How would Britain react to new demands for territory, much of which had been practically 100 per cent German for centuries? There was no convincing argument based on recent history, or on security. The Polish claim was a simple demand for *Lebensraum*, which only arose because the Russians proposed to annex half the country, and most of the Polish inhabitants would wish to flee from Soviet rule. This was difficult to explain to Britons and Americans who still believed that the war had been entered in support of Poland and other small nations, or the principles of the Atlantic Charter.

On one matter, however, there was no dispute, at least within the British Government. 'It is essential for us,' wrote Eden to Churchill, 'that there should be an independent Poland. The danger is that Poland will now be insulated from the outside world and to all intents and purposes run by the Russians behind a Lublin screen.'[29] It is possible, however, that Roosevelt was not prepared to give this matter quite the same degree of primacy. Stettinius, who (far more than his predecessor) could be relied upon to echo the President's view, 'stressed that failure to find a solution would greatly disturb American public opinion, and might prejudice the whole question of American participation in the world organisation'.[30]

The 'world organisation' to which the Secretary of State was referring was what later became known as the United Nations – a new use of a term which had originally meant the countries at war with Germany. Roosevelt and Stettinius were both obsessed by the putative value of the 'world organisation' as a guarantee of future peace, and American diplomatic documents of the period give that matter an exceedingly high grade of priority – vastly higher than corresponding British documents allow. Roosevelt was apparently convinced that the success or failure of the 'world organisation' – and therefore, very probably, the future preservation of peace – would turn on whether Russia participated fully at the very start. This probably disposed him to regard such matters as the boundaries and political composition of Poland as, by comparison, of secondary importance.

In February 1945, the Big Three attempted to solve some of the principal problems at the 'Argonaut' Conferences. First Churchill and Roosevelt met at Malta, where they discussed mainly military matters. At this phase of the proceedings, Churchill was in a mood of deepest depression. In the presence of Eden, Cadogan, Hopkins and Stettinius, the Prime Minister 'became very emotional about the condition of the world. There were more units of pain at that moment than ever before in history. His outlook was very gloomy. He wept and his outlook . . . was extremely low, at the bottom of the barrel – no use going on – no hope for the world.'[31] But the Prime Minister's spirits were rapidly restored. British and American delegates soon proceeded to Yalta, in the Crimea, for the crucial rendezvous with Stalin. Even the most sympathetic observers could hardly fail to contrast the condition of the three leaders. Churchill's physician, observing the decrepit condition of Roosevelt, had 'no doubt which of the three will go first'.[32] In fact, a cardiac specialist had decided, nearly a year earlier, that the President might die at any time, though Roosevelt had not been told. Harry Hopkins, Roosevelt's closest adviser, had been in wretched health for years, and his condition at Yalta appeared, if anything, even worse than that of the President.[33] 'Pa' Watson, an important member of the American delegation, actually died on the return voyage. There is no reason for thinking that the precarious condition of those invalids seriously impeded their mental capacity; but they must have guessed that the end was not far off, and desired to round off their life's work. Some of the decisions taken at Yalta certainly look like the work of men in a hurry.

Cadogan considered that Stalin 'shows up very impressively against the background of the other two ageing statesmen'. Eden took a similar view. Stalin was 'the only one of the three who has a clear view of what he wants . . . P.M. is all emotion in these matters, F.D.R. is vague and jealous of others'.[34]

Records of the meeting leave no doubt that Poland preponderated over all other subjects of discussion put together. Roosevelt made a strong plea for the Poles to keep Lwow. Churchill's recent public statement on the matter set him in a weak position to second this, but he did the best he could – in vain; Stalin would not budge, and all prospects of the Poles retaining Lwow were abandoned. The Western Allies were not much more successful in restraining Polish claims in the west than they had been in advancing them in the east. Stalin made it clear that the Neisser tributary which he desired to form the frontier of Poland was the more westerly river of that name. Churchill warned that 'it would be a great pity to stuff the Polish goose so full of German food that it died of indigestion', and reminded Stalin that there was 'a large body of opinion in Great Britain which was frankly shocked at the idea of moving millions of people by force'. Stalin countered that one: 'No Germans were found in these areas as they had all run away.' This was a considerable exaggeration; but, insofar as it contained a grain of truth, it casts vivid light on the reputation which Soviet troops acquired when they advanced into Germany.

The British War Cabinet was even less pleased about Poland extending to the Western Neisser than was the Prime Minister. They sent him a rather forceful telegram, to the effect that any extension of Poland beyond the Oder and Upper Silesia should be a matter for the peace conference.[35] Roosevelt argued for delay on different grounds: no Polish Government acceptable to the three major Allies had yet come into existence; let no final decision be taken until the views of such a Government could be taken into consideration. Here matters were left, with the lands between the two Neissers still in doubt.

The question of an acceptable Polish Government seemed in sight of solution. The Big Three agreed that

> the Provisional Government which is now functioning in Poland should . . . be reorganised on a broader democratic basis with the inclusion of democratic leaders from Poland itself and from Poles abroad. The new Government should be . . . pledged to the holding of free and unfettered elections as soon as practicable on the basis of universal suffrage and secret ballot. In these elections all democratic and anti-Nazi Parties would have the right to take part and put forward candidates.[36]

Once this Government had been formed, all of the three Powers should recognise it. Churchill seems to have been genuinely pleased about the prospects. As he told the War Cabinet on his return,

> So far as Premier Stalin is concerned, he was quite sure that he meant well to the world and to Poland. He did not himself think that there would be any resentment on the part of Russia about the

arrangements that had been made for free and fair elections in that country.[37]

Yugoslavia proved no problem at all. Churchill was able to tell the other delegates that 'the King had been persuaded and indeed almost forced to sign a decree appointing Regents'.[38] This doubtless pleased Stalin, and Roosevelt made no difficulties. Evidently the Americans had not really objected to what Britain and Russia were trying to do, but were not prepared to have their assent taken for granted. Almost immediately after the conference, the War Cabinet was told that 'the Yugoslav Government would proceed to Belgrade immediately to settle the Regency question and to form a united Government' and that 'the Tito-Subasić agreement was to be put into force at once'.[39]

The discussions on Greece pleased the Prime Minister even more. He reported to his colleagues that

the Russian attitude could not have been more satisfactory. There was no suggestion on Premier Stalin's part of criticism of our policy . . . The emissary sent to the USSR by the Greek Communists had first been put under house arrest and then sent back.[40]

On their way home from Yalta, Churchill and Eden called at Athens. The experience there was tremendously gratifying. As the Prime Minister told the War Cabinet, 'the crowd which had welcomed them had been the biggest he had ever seen'. This incident was perhaps the final retort to those critics who had bitterly attacked the British Government for its action in Greece. Whoever else was displeased, the Greek people were satisfied.

Yalta decisions about specific countries were set in the wider context of a general 'Declaration on Liberated Europe'. The Great Powers agreed to utilise the period of instability which would inevitably follow expulsion of the enemy to concert their policies, and 'assist the peoples liberated . . . to solve by democratic means their political and economic problems'.

Other important matters received serious consideration. It was agreed – outside the main conference and in conditions of the utmost secrecy – that Russia should enter the war against Japan two or three months after the end of the German conflict, and receive substantial territorial and other concessions for her trouble.[41] Stettinius was able to give assurances to Molotov on another matter of Russian interest. The United States, he declared, was willing at any time to discuss the grant of large credits to assist the Soviet Union after the war.[42]

The question of a permanent 'World Organisation' came up in the discussions. Preliminary arrangements had been made long before. The statesmen assembled at Yalta now agreed that the 'United

Nations', in the old sense of the term, should be invited to the initial conference, which would be held in the United States late in April.

In this atmosphere of apparent general agreement, the Big Three departed from Yalta. Roosevelt, despite his rapidly-declining health, was in a mood of euphoria, and declared that the conference

> spells – and it ought to spell – the end of the system of unilateral action, exclusive alliances, and spheres of influence, and balances of power and all the other expedients which have been tried for centuries and have always failed.[43]

Many criticisms would doubtless be levelled against Churchill and Roosevelt when they reached their own countries, though they had every reason for believing that this criticism could be beaten down fairly easily. Yet few even of the most bitter critics could have guessed how fragile and ephemeral the Yalta agreement would prove.

7

Disillusion

[Churchill] 'Premier Stalin was a person of great power, in whom he had every confidence. He did not think that he would embark on any adventures . . .' War Cabinet Minutes 19 February 1945 (Confidential annex). W.M.22(45). CAB 65/51.

'Herr Hitler then said . . . he did not wish to include Czechs in the Reich. . . . [Chamberlain] said that the impression left on him was that Herr Hitler meant what he said.' Cabinet Minutes 17 September 1938. Cabinet 39(38). CAB 23/95.

Just as the Polish settlement had formed by far the most difficult area of the Yalta discussions, so also would that part of the agreement prove by far the most controversial throughout the democratic world. Doubts and apprehensions were expressed almost at once. On 17 February, Arciszewski sent a message to Roosevelt, declaring that the decisions 'were received by all Poles as a new partition of Poland leaving her under Soviet protectorate'.[1] A week later the London Polish Government attacked the arrangement root and branch.[2] More independent observers shared this feeling of disquiet. Peter Fraser, Prime Minister of New Zealand, telegraphed Churchill to express the view that a settlement which made Poland's future dependent exclusively upon Russian support was 'clearly unwise'.[3] To this Churchill replied, indicating his 'good hopes that Russia, or at any rate Stalin, desired to work in harmony with the Western Democracies'.[4] A Confidential Annex to the Cabinet Minutes of 19 February records the same view: 'he was quite sure that (Stalin) meant well to the world and to Poland'.[5] Right at the end of the month he spoke in the same spirit when defending the Yalta decisions before Parliament.

Public reactions in Britain were uncertain and hesitant. When the agreements were voted on in the House of Commons, the Government won what looks like a most satisfying victory. A critical

amendment on the Polish policy, whose principal but not exclusive
support came from back-bench Conservatives, was defeated by a
vote of 398 to 27, including tellers.[6]

Yet in reality there was abundant evidence of disquiet. Nobody was
more conscious of this than the Prime Minister. In private he
admitted that 'it would . . . be a mistake to suppose there is not a
good deal of uneasiness in the House which will not find expression
in the Lobby on a vote of confidence'.[7] This 'uneasiness', the Prime
Minister confessed to Roosevelt, existed 'in both Parties'.[8] The
principal Labour spokesman was Arthur Greenwood, the party's
Deputy Leader and a former member of the War Cabinet. The Prime
Minister considered Greenwood's speech 'extremely hostile to the
Crimea policy about Poland'.[9] The principal Liberal spokesman was
Sir William Beveridge, who showed doubts both about Poland and
about proposals for the future of Germany. Lord Dunglass (the
future Lord Home) elaborated the many ways in which the Crimea
decisions violated the Atlantic Charter. Yet none of these critics
actually voted against the Government. Nor did H. G. Strauss, a
junior Minister who felt so strongly on the matter that he resigned
his office in protest; two other junior Ministers abstained.[10] The
Government had made the Yalta division 'vote of confidence', and it
is not difficult to believe that this fact deterred many potential rebels.
Others, no doubt, felt that the best thing they could do for the Poles
was to suppress their private apprehensions and rally behind the
Government.

Reactions in the United States were similar to those in Britain.
With less than truth, Roosevelt assured Congress on 1 March that
'the Crimean Conference concerned itself only with the European
war and with the political problems of Europe'.[11] He went on to tell
them that 'never before have the major Allies been more closely
united – not only in their war aims but in their peace aims'. In the
United States, as in Britain, foreign policy was in this period more or
less bipartisan – members of both Parties actually participating in the
administration – and this effectively held back the most dangerous
political criticism. The bulk of the American press was 'strongly
enthusiastic' over Yalta;[12] 51 per cent of the people questioned in a
survey regarded the Conference as 'successful' from the American
point of view, against only 11 per cent who thought it
'unsuccessful'.[13] A considerable overall majority even considered the
agreement over Poland to be 'about the best that could be worked
out under the circumstances'. Yet – as in Britain – the warning voices
were heard. Representative Smith of Wisconsin told the House that

Britain and the United States have acquiesced fully in the demands
of Stalin for his self-selected sphere of influence not only in Poland

and the Baltic area, but in the south of Europe also. That . . . constitutes a retreat from the high moral ground we have been resting upon in this war; it can but lead to another war, more deadly, more devastating, more cruel and costly than this one.[14]

It was events in Poland which disillusioned even the political leaders. Even while the debate in the British House of Commons was proceeding, Churchill began to feel new worries about the implementation of the agreements. At the time of Yalta, Stalin had complained that Poles had been killing members of the Red Army. Arciszewski's Government had many counter-charges to make. 'The London Poles,' Churchill wrote to Clark-Kerr, 'have been spreading it about among Members of Parliament that there have been wholesale deportations and liquidations in Poland. We have no means of denying or disproving this.'[15] At one point, indeed, Molotov actually invited the Anglo-Americans to send observers to Poland; but this offer was evidently designed as no more than a subterfuge to secure tacit recognition of the Lublin 'Government'. When the democracies eagerly accepted Molotov's offer, but made it clear that this acceptance did not imply recognition of Lublin, the offer was speedily withdrawn.[16]

As soon as the diplomats set to work to establish a Polish government which all the Big Three could recognise, they ran into grave difficulties. On 27 February, the British and American Ambassadors complained to Molotov that Bierut's government 'had a completely false understanding of the agreement reached at the Crimea'.[17] Manifestly, Bierut was only acting under Russian orders, and the 'false understanding' represented in truth a fundamental difference of intentions.

Everything really turned on Roosevelt. Britain could do little by herself; Molotov and Bierut were acting under orders from above; the American diplomats and State Department officials could not intercede with Stalin. Churchill tried to galvanise the President into action. On 8 March he sent him a copy of Arciszewski's representations, with comments. Molotov, observed the Prime Minister,

clearly wants to make a farce of consultations with the 'non-Lublin' Poles, which means that the government in Poland would be merely the present one dressed up to look more respectable to the ignorant, and also wants to prevent us from seeing the liquidations and deportations that are going on and all the rest of the game of setting up a totalitarian regime before elections are held and even before a new Government is set up.[18]

Five days later Churchill expanded on this theme.

> A month has passed since Yalta and no progress of any kind has
> been made. Soon I shall be questioned in Parliament on this point
> and I shall be forced to tell them the truth. Time is, of course, on
> the side of Lublin, who are no doubt at work to establish their
> authority in such a way as to make it impregnable.[19]

'If we do not get things right now,' the Prime Minister had written
not long before, 'it will soon be seen by the world that you and I by
setting our signatures to the Crimea settlement have underwritten a
fraudulent prospectus.'[20]

Thus within a fortnight of Churchill's spirited defence in the
House of Commons of the Yalta decisions, the Prime Minister had
almost completely changed his mind about Russia, and even his close
relations with Roosevelt were being shaken. 'I do not wish to reveal a
divergence between the British and United States Governments,' he
told the President, 'but it would certainly be necessary for me to
make it clear that we are in presence of a great failure and an utter
breakdown of what was settled at Yalta, but that we British have not
the necessary strength to carry the matter further and that the limits
of our capacity to act have been reached.'[21]

Eden, who in the past had often shown much more sympathy with
Russia than his chief, perceived the danger inherent in the protracted
negotiations, and pressed for action. 'Of course Molotov does not
want a breakdown,' wrote the Foreign Secretary, 'he wants to drag
the business out so as to consolidate their power. We cannot be
parties to this and must force the issue.'[22]

The Foreign Secretary called for a joint message from Churchill
and Roosevelt to Stalin. 'Is there any other way in which the Russians
can be forced to choose between mending their ways and the loss of
Anglo-American friendship?' he asked rhetorically. 'This is the only
method by which we can hope to obtain anything approaching a fair
deal for the Poles.' Yet – as Churchill replied – 'we cannot press the
case against Russia beyond where we can carry the United States'.[23]

Without requiring any prodding from Britain, some important
Americans were beginning to feel considerable concern about the
drift of events, as early as mid-March. Stettinius noted that the
'Declaration on Liberated Europe' was coming under strain in
Romania,[24] while he was acutely conscious of the problems which
would be presented if agreement had not been reached over the
Polish Government by the time of the first plenary meeting of the
United Nations, due in mid-April: 'people felt it was a test of Russian
good faith', the Secretary of State noted in his 'Record'.

On 27 March, Churchill considered the question of relations

between Russia and the West in a long and pungent telegram to Roosevelt,[25] which had already been discussed by the War Cabinet. 'I am extremely concerned at the deterioration of the Russian attitude since Yalta', he told the President. Molotov, the Prime Minister explained, 'persists in his view that the Yalta communiqué meant merely the addition of a few other Poles to the existing administration of Russian puppets and that these puppets should be consulted first ... It is as plain as a pikestaff that his tactics are to drag the business out while the Lublin Committee consolidate their power.' He warned Roosevelt that 'you and we shall be excluded from any jot of influence' not merely in Poland, but throughout eastern Europe.

The President was cautious in his reply to Churchill. 'The agreement on Poland at Yalta,' he wrote, 'was a compromise between the Soviet position that the Lublin Committee should merely be "enlarged" and our contention that we should start with a clean slate and assist in the formation of an entirely new Polish Government.'[26] Unfortunately the President was right. Molotov was putting a doubtful, but a quite arguable, construction on a highly ambiguous document. The leaders of the Western Democracies had been so overwhelmingly concerned not to leave Yalta without the form of an agreement that they had done something far worse: they had reached what looked like an agreement, but was really nothing of the kind. Indeed, this confusion over the meaning of the Polish agreement was only part of a much wider disagreement over interpretations between Russia on the one hand and Britain and America on the other. As Harriman pointed out, 'the words "independent and friendly neighbors" and in fact "democracy" meant different things to the Soviets and to us'.[27] The intentions of Churchill and Roosevelt had been clear enough: to establish conditions in Poland in which the people of that country could freely choose their own government in the future. The intention of Stalin was equally clear: to strengthen the Lublin 'Government' and eventually saddle Poland with a Communist-dominated dictatorship. These two objectives were utterly irreconcilable. In any case, there was no impartial arbitrator to whom anyone could appeal: Stalin had his army in Poland, and the Western Democracies did not.

Roosevelt nevertheless agreed that the time had come for the Anglo-Americans to take the whole matter up with Stalin in a joint message. Roosevelt, Churchill and Eden all seem to have agreed that the real test of Soviet sincerity was whether Mikolajczyk was offered a place in the Polish Cabinet; and that in addition to him 'genuinely representative party leaders' from among the Poles living in Poland must be incorporated into any remodelled Government, before they would recognise it.[28] They very soon learned, however, that Molotov at any rate entertained 'strongest opposition' to Mikolajczyk, and also appeared unwilling to include other representative Poles.[29]

Soon the American Government received other information which made them less sanguine about good future relations with Russia. On 4–6 April, Harriman sent a series of telegrams to Stettinius, indicating that the Soviet attitude to the matter of relief supplies for Europe was cynical in the extreme.[30] Roosevelt nevertheless remained willing to do all that was possible to bring the Russians to a reasonable frame of mind over Poland. The President's last message to Churchill was sent on 12 April. That afternoon, he suddenly collapsed, and died a few hours later.

The Vice President, Harry S. Truman, automatically succeeded Roosevelt. Truman was not well known outside his own country. His main interest had been in domestic rather than international affairs. Yet, under the system of government which Truman inherited, conduct of foreign affairs was very much a matter of Presidential prerogative. Cordell Hull had been repeatedly by-passed or ignored. Stettinius, who – unlike Hull – had no political power-base, was a creature of the President. A plan had been evolved towards the end of Roosevelt's life, under which Charles Bohlen acted as a sort of liaison officer between President and State Department, charged to keep each of them informed of what was happening in the other's province. Truman knew little of current foreign policy developments, and Stettinius was compelled to inform him that Harry Hopkins was 'the one person who really thoroughly understood the various ramifications and the relations between Roosevelt and Churchill and between Roosevelt and Stalin'.[31] Several weeks were bound to pass before Truman could assume fully the reins of American foreign policy. Neither Churchill nor Stalin knew the new President; and the opportunity which Roosevelt's funeral afforded for the Prime Minister to travel to the United States and meet him was missed – to Churchill's later regret.

Negotiations with Russia over Poland did not abate. Messages continued to pass between the 'Big Three' under the new Presidency, as before. Truman was as anxious as his predecessor to avoid announcing a breakdown in negotiations – which would have the direst effects not only in Poland but elsewhere.[32] Meanwhile, Russia continued to build up the Lublin 'Government' in a manner which would ensure that no infusion of new blood could substantially alter its character. A treaty was concluded between Russia and her satellite Poles on similar lines to the Russo-Czech treaty which had caused such anxiety long before.

Russia began to show increasingly blatant contempt for opinion in the Western countries. Arciszewski's Government received an invitation for their delegate in Poland, Janowski, to attend a conference with a representative of the Soviet Command. A promise of safe conduct was given. Janowski returned to Poland, and assembled leading members of the democratic Parties within his country to meet the Russians. The upshot, as a senior Foreign Office official explained to Churchill, was that 'practically all the leaders of the democratic Parties [were] arrested'.[33] British remonstrations with Russia at the diplomatic level produced a positively insulting reply.[34]

At last the American patience began to run out. On 23 April, Truman had his first proper meeting with Molotov. The President gave the Commissar for Foreign Affairs to understand that 'the United States Government could not be a party to any method of consultation with Polish leaders which would not result in the establishment of a new Polish Government of National Unity genuinely representative of the Polish people'.[35] Molotov fenced a little; whereupon Truman retorted that 'an agreement had been reached on Poland and that there was only one thing to do and that was for Marshal Stalin to carry out that agreement in accordance with his word'.[36] The two men repeated themselves several times to the same general effect. Finally, Truman made it plain that he was not interested in exchanging dialectics with the Commissar for Foreign Affairs, but only in ensuring that the American view was conveyed to Stalin. According to Truman's account, the discussion concluded on an acid note: ' "I have never been talked to like that in my life," Molotov said. I told him, "Carry out your agreements and you won't get talked to like that" '.

Truman met the Secretaries of State, of War and Navy, plus several other leading policy makers. 'Our agreement with the Soviet Union so far had been a one-way street and that could not continue; it was now or never', observed the President.[37]

Truman's truculence towards Molotov bore on another matter where he found himself thinking on lines similar to Churchill. The first meeting of the United Nations in its new form was due to be held a very few days later in San Francisco. The Russians were demanding that their own satellite Polish 'Government' should be present as one of the founder-members, and a few days before Roosevelt's death had hinted strongly that they would not themselves participate unless their protégé was invited. Such an invitation would of course more or less imply recognition, and nobody in the West was disposed to give way to such blackmail. The suggestion was made that the whole Conference should be called off; but Churchill and Eden concurred 'that it would be a great blow to our cause and prestige and also to the cause of a free Poland if the mere sulkiness of the Russians prevented the world conference from being held'.[38] As the Prime Minister commented in private, 'although I have never been at all keen on this Conference I should then in that event become very keen on it'. Truman's mind in that matter too was similar to Churchill's. At the meeting with his own leading colleagues which followed the stormy meeting with Molotov, he told them that 'he intended to go on with the plans for San Francisco, and if the Russians did not join us they could go to hell'.[39] In the end the Russians climbed down, and attended the Conference. The new organisation, however, was crippled from the start by the 'Great Power veto', which meant that any of the major Powers could block action which ran counter to its own interest.

Meanwhile, the Polish Government in London was in an extraordinary limbo. At Yalta the Western Allies had agreed to cease recognising it as soon as an acceptable new administration had been formed. Yet that new administration had certainly not come into being, and there was some chance that it never would. The Western Allies were powerless to influence the London Poles by either threats or promises. General Anders, known for his strong anti-Russian views, was appointed deputy Commander-in-Chief of the Polish forces under the absent General Bor-Komorowski. Soon doubts arose as to whether Arciszewski's Government really possessed full support among the exiled Poles themselves.[40] In Mikolajczyk's time, it was generally possible to restrain the public controversy between rival groups of Poles; now this was impossible. Fulminations between Arciszewski's Government and Lublin were unmeasured; while neither body had much reason for loving Mikolajczyk. Yet, while any possibility of agreement remained, neither the British nor the American Government was disposed to state its own opinions fully in public. To do so would be to admit that Churchill and Roosevelt had both been duped at Yalta, and for long before; while it would also destroy whatever chance remained of a general agreement with Russia.

Although it was events in Poland which proved crucial in changing British and American attitudes to Russia, there were other places where abundant signs existed to show that inter-Allied cooperation was disintegrating. Brigadier Fitzroy Maclean had played a large part once in persuading the British Government to establish close links with Tito. The same Brigadier Maclean reported in February 1945 that Yugoslavia was developing 'an authoritarian system of government, based on a single party system, and a single party line, with all real power concentrated in the hands of one man'.[41] He went on to record the view that 'Yugoslavia, under the able leadership of Marshal Tito, appears to have been singled out to play an important part as a bastion of Soviet power' in a Soviet bloc which 'already includes Poland, Hungary, Czechoslovakia, Bulgaria, Romania and Albania'.

Czechoslovakia was another country whose future orientation was for a long time indeterminate, and where a power struggle between

Russia and the West was likely. When the Red Army moved into Czechoslovakia, the first province it reached was Ruthenia – where an agitation was immediately worked up for incorporation in the Soviet Ukraine. Beneš prevailed on the Russians to halt the agitation; but there was a strong suspicion that it would soon be renewed.[42] By March 1945, enough of Czechoslovakia had been cleared of German troops for Beneš and his Government to return to their country. The original idea had been that members of the Diplomatic Corps should accompany the Ministers; but at the last minute the Russians refused permission to the diplomats, while allowing the politicians to proceed.[43] Soon after their arrival, a new Czechoslovak government was set up. Its composition scarcely augured well for the future. Fierlinger, the new Prime Minister, was technically a Social Democrat, but was observed to have 'become very pro-Communist as well as pro-Russian'.[44] Two of the five Deputy Prime Ministers were Communists. The crucial Ministry of the Interior was held by a Communist. Apart from Fierlinger, there were only two social Democrats in the Government, and one of those was virtually a Communist. The old Agrarian Party had been completely excluded. There were no representatives from Ruthenia: which was taken as a sign that the province had 'gone east'. Hugh Dalton recorded a conversation with a Czech diplomat on 5 April:

> He thinks the Communists are increasingly in control. 'National Committees' are being formed everywhere in liberated Slovakia. . . . Anyone who criticises them is accused of not being 'democratic'. He thinks that the Communists will soon get rid of Beneš. They will show no more gratitude to him than he has shown to his old supporters.[45]

While all this was happening, Western diplomats and other observers were still excluded from Czechoslovakia, as they had been excluded from Poland; a matter which gave considerable concern to the Foreign Office.[46]

In the last few weeks of war, the advancing armies of the Western Democracies seemed to have the Czech situation partly in their own hands. On 18 April, the British Foreign Office contacted their American counterparts, 'pointing out how important and valuable it would be from the political standpoint if the American forces could press forward into Czechoslovakia and liberate Prague, supposing that military considerations allowed'.[47] The Americans did not answer immediately, and the Prime Minister himself was urged to intervene. A good deal of correspondence passed between senior British and American political and military men. Eden pressed that liberation of western Czechoslovakia by the Americans 'might make the whole difference to the post-war situation in Czechoslavakia and might well influence that in nearby countries'.[48] Stettinius argued the same way; but in vain. On 24 April, Churchill discovered that Eisenhower 'never had any plan or idea of going into Czechoslovakia'.[49] The Western Allies would later have bitter cause to regret this omission. The Czech capital was still in German hands at the moment of surrender, on 7 May 1945.

8

Stocktaking

On 30 April 1945, Adolf Hitler committed suicide. On 7 May the German Reich, surrendered unconditionally to the Allies. At that moment, there were already several places in Europe where the victors were engaged in deep and dangerous disputes. Most of those disputes were concerned with the system of government which should prevail in liberated or conquered territories. One was concerned with a military question: which Ally should occupy a piece of territory. When the disputed area is viewed on the map, it scarcely appears to be of primary importance; but to both Churchill and Truman, the issue appeared for a time more urgent than any other, and to carry with it the serious danger of actual warfare between erstwhile Allies.

Venezia Giulia was the area at the head of the Adriatic, which included the towns of Trieste, Pola and Fiume (Rijeka). It had belonged to the Austro-Hungarian Empire until 1918, and was later acquired by Italy. The urban population was predominantly Italian, the rural population Slav. Tito and the Italians both lay claim to it. In theory, the Big Three all accepted the view that the fate of Venezie Giulia would need to be decided at the eventual Peace Conference; but experience tells that possession is nine points of the law. There were further complications. The Supreme Allied Commander in the Mediterranean area, Field Marshal Alexander, was British, but many of the troops he commanded were Americans, and important decisions required consultations between the two governments. Alexander's original proposal, bruited in February 1945, was that a military boundary be defined in Venezia Giulia, designed to ensure that the Western Allies had control of essential supply lines into Italy and central Europe. Areas west of the line would be administered by Allied Military Government. Tito would be asked to withdraw Yugoslav troops from that area; but if he insisted that they should remain, they should come under Alexander's command.[1] It was emphasised that any arrangement reached would in no way prejudice the ultimate destiny of the province.

The American State Department view was different. They considered that the whole of Venezia Giulia should be placed under military control of the Supreme Allied Commander, and political control of the Allied Military Government.[2] The American object was to ensure that the fate of Venezia Giulia really was left open until the Peace Conference; for they suspected – not without reason – that the alternative would mean a further definition of 'spheres of influence'. A protracted and leisurely debate ensued between the British and Americans. Meanwhile, Tito gathered military strength in the vicinity, and his bargaining position therefore improved.

Just as Churchill's views about Russian intentions towards Poland underwent a dramatic change in the first fortnight of March 1945, so also did his appreciation of the significance of Venezia Giulia. 'My feeling is that henceforward our inclination should be to back Italy against Tito,' he wrote to Eden on 11 March.[3] 'The fact that we are generally favourable to Italian claims at the head of the Adriatic will give us an influence over Italian internal politics as against Communists and wild men which may assist the re-integration of the Italian state.' Later the Prime Minister developed the idea further. 'The only way to split the Communist Party in Italy,' he told Eden, 'is upon Tito's claims. It is in our interests to prevent the Russian submergence of central and western Europe as far as possible. The Italians would certainly form on this point.'[4] The Prime Minister concluded that 'we should therefore be drawn into joint action with the United States and smooth out our affairs with Italy and win ardent support from the majority of Italians. This is a fairly good line-up.'

The British began to press for an early decision. On 7 April, Harold Macmillan, Resident Minister, 'expressed considerable concern over the lack of progress . . . and was apprehensive that we would find ourselves again faced with a *fait accompli*'.[5]

Towards the end of April, after well over two months of Anglo-American wrangling, the dispute over Venezia Giulia began to pass from a matter of diplomatic speculation to an acute military problem. The area was still more or less in German hands, but no fewer than three armies were converging upon it. Western Allies and Titoites were both poised to enter in force; while the Germans had apparently permitted 'considerable anti-partisan Yugoslav forces whose total strength is believed to be over 20,000 men'[6] to move northwards towards Venezia Giulia. These units were thought to be Croatian Ustashi – 'without exception completely compromised by open collaboration with the Germans' – rather than Četniks who 'when last heard of were bottled up in southern Bosnia'.[7] No doubt the British would not regret seeing Ustashi exclude Tito from

Venezia Giulia – for the former would readily relinquish their prize and consent to be disarmed and interned – while the latter would certainly not yield a square inch if they could help it. It was unthinkable, however, that any kind of encouragement should be given to the Ustashi.

Churchill tried to force the pace. There was no longer any remote possibility that Tito would agree to the American suggestion, while it was becoming increasingly unlikely that he would willingly assent to a division of Venezia Giulia. 'The great thing is to be there before Tito's partisans are in occupation,' the Prime Minister telegraphed Truman on 27 April. 'Therefore it does not seem to me there is a minute to wait.'[8] Two days later, a common policy was at long last agreed. The Supreme Commander was to 'establish and maintain Allied Military Government' in what was virtually the whole province.[9] Diplomatic victory, no doubt, for the State Department; but how should these brave words be set into effect?

Nobody was more worried over that question than Henry Stimson, Secretary of War. 'The problem of just how much force will be used against the Yugoslavs and against the Russians if they cooperate with the Yugoslavs may quickly become pressing,' he urged with commendable understatement, 'and it is requested that the State Department furnish clear cut guidance at once.[10] Stimson, a Republican who had been Secretary of State in the days before Roosevelt, was probably the most experienced man in the Truman administration and the President had to give some kind of answer. If the Titoites 'failed to cooperate', he decided, then Alexander should 'communicate with the Combined Chiefs of Staff'.[11]

By 2 May, the situation was even more alarming. Tito indicated 'that he intended to establish a wartime line of operations from the mouth of the Izono . . . to Tarvs'.[12] Alexander could use Trieste and Pola; but there was evidently no intention of allowing him to take over the towns. At this point, the State Department suddenly began to wonder about a new danger. If for any reason the Allies backed down before Tito, there was a substantial risk of civil and even military disturbances in Italy.[13] They were all too conscious of the political risks at home from infuriated voters of Italian extraction.

As the European war ground to a halt, relations between Titoites and forces of the Western Allies were extraordinary. Parts of the towns Trieste, Monfalcone and Gorizia were occupied by troops commanded by Alexander, other parts of those towns by troops commanded by Tito.[14] In Trieste, sentries from the two sources paraded side by side, and sometimes personnel were billeted in the same house.[15] Yet – as Churchill wrote a week after 'V.E. Day' – 'at any time we may be in armed collision with them'.[16] Nor did the

Yugoslavs confine their attention to Venezia Giulia. The American State Department was convinced that they were 'even trying to establish civil control in the eastern part of Udine . . . beyond Venezia Giulia'.[17] Soon came news that Titoite forces were also moving into Carinthia – that part of Austria immediately to the north of Venezia Giulia, where lived substantial numbers of Slovenes. Tito backed this military action by a speech laying claim to Carinthia. The British Ambassador was instructed to remind Tito that the Big Three had agreed that the area should be occupied by British troops; but even this information did not suffice to persuade the Yugoslavs to withdraw.[18] The Americans feared that Tito 'may have similar designs on parts of Hungary and Greece if his methods in Venezia Giulia succeed.[19]

On 10 May, Truman took a momentous decision. He told the Acting Secretary of State 'that he . . . had finally come to the conclusion that the only solution was to "throw them out". He realised that this was a reversal of his former position but that developments were such that it left no alternative.'[20] The State Department received the news with relief. This was exactly the sort of language Churchill had long been trying to persuade Truman to employ, and his enthusiastic approbation followed as a matter of course.

The situation was not only complex and dangerous, but also obscure, both as to current facts and to likely developments. Harold Macmillan reported on 14 May that between 30,000 and 40,000 'so-called regular' Yugoslav troops 'and about 10,000 to 20,000 partisans'[21] were operating in a small part of western Venezia Giulia. Just across the Austrian frontier – other information told – something like 300,000 surrendered enemies and refugees had come under care of the Anglo-Americans; while 600,000 German and Croat troops were converging there, anxious to surrender.[22] No commander could be very certain who was where at what moment; what intentions they might have; or how various bodies of soldiers might act when they met.

Although the Western Allies had agreed on the principle of 'throwing out' Tito, it was by no means clear exactly which areas he should be required to evacuate, how much force should he employed to evict him, or what should be done in the not impossible event of Stalin rendering military assistance to the Yugoslavs. On 14 May, the British and American Ambassadors were instructed to order Tito out of a defined area which included Trieste, Monfalcone, Gorizia and Pola.[23] This order was not couched in the form of an ultimatum, and a good deal of diplomatic fencing took place. We may conjecture that Tito sought assistance from Stalin but received a disappointing reply. In any event, on 25 May the State Department learnt that forces from the Western Allies had entered the whole area which was under dispute.[24] From this point forward the Yugoslav claims were pursued at the diplomatic rather than the military level. The fate of Venezia Giulia was by no means settled; but the immediate danger of erstwhile allies shooting each other had been removed.

In the dispute over Venezia Guilia, principal initiative had come from the United States, even though the commander and most of the troops immediately involved were British. This was no more than tacit acknowledgement of the new world situation: a situation which, for different reasons, the British and American leaders both disliked. There had been a great shift in relative importance of the Anglo-Saxon countries. Though Britain was still accorded formal rank as co-equal to Russia and the United States, this was more a courtesy than an acknowledgement of reality. Churchill had begun to sense this at the beginning of 1945. When Peter Fraser of New Zealand cabled him in February in criticism of the Yalta agreement, the Prime Minister drafted a reply containing a paragraph which the Dominions Secretary persuaded him to excise. That passage is illuminating:

> ... You do not seem to realise that Great Britian and the British Commonwealth are very much weaker militarily than Soviet Russia and in the regions affected we have no means, short of another general war, of enforcing our point of view. They are also far weaker than the United States, both financially and militarily. We are not, therefore, in a position to give clear, cool, far-seeing, altruistic directions to the world. We have to do the best we can. We cannot go further in helping Poland than the United States is willing or can be persuaded to go.[25]

On 3 April, Churchill developed a similar theme at a joint meeting of the War Cabinet and certain leading Commonwealth statesmen. He warned them of the 'predominant power and influence' which Russia currently exercised throughout Europe; but he went on to add: 'The resources in men and materials commanded by the United States were vastly superior to our own ... In natural resources we could not hope to equal either of these Powers.'[26] The Prime Minister argued that 'the unity of the British Commonwealth of Nations' and (incredibly!) 'our superior statecraft and experience' might compensate for these disadvantages. Yet the whole tone of Churchill's messages to Truman – particularly on European questions – indicates that he now perceived that Britain could do little without backing from America. During the war, diplomatic initiative had frequently originated from Britain; in the immediate aftermath, the Prime Minister's messages to the President are those of an adviser, or even a suppliant.

Yet British advice still had great weight. The reason is partly grounded in American political practice. While policy initiatives in Britain largely originated from the Foreign Office, American initiatives came from the President much more frequently than from the State Department. Roosevelt had been visibly losing drive for several weeks before his death, and Truman, when he succeeded, took several weeks to take full measure of the world situation. So the American initiative was missing.

In this period, Churchill's mind was changing radically on the question of Russia. So also were other minds. In the middle of May, Attlee complained that the Russians were ' "behaving in a perfectly bloody way", telling us nothing but setting up puppet Governments all over Europe as far west as they could'.[27] Several of the Prime Minister's later messages to Roosevelt had evinced growing alarm. His communications to Truman, and particularly those written after the collapse of Germany, make this point again and again, with increasing emphasis. Russia, he pointed out, now stood right in the middle of Europe; within a short time, on current plans, British and American armies on the continent would melt away, while Russia might keep 200 or 300 divisions on active service.[28] The only chance of saving Europe from 'another bloodbath'[29] was by handling the situation 'firmly'. Specifically, Anglo-American troops should remain in Europe, and there should be an early meeting of the 'Big Three'.

On 12 May, five days after the German surrender, Churchill used the term 'iron curtain' to describe the barrier existing between territories controlled by Russia, and the rest of Europe. The Prime Minister won no immediate response from Truman on the proposal which followed a couple of days later, that the Americans should issue a 'standfast' order to their forces in Europe.[30] The President, even if he was convinced by the Prime Minister's arguments, was scarcely a free agent in the matter. The military claims of the Far East were hard to resist; while it was exceedingly doubtful whether Truman, any more than his predecessor, would be able to obtain authority from Congress to remain in Europe for long. The general situation nevertheless worried the American leaders profoundly. Three weeks after the European victory, Truman was reported by one of his senior colleagues to be 'greatly disturbed by the spreading feeling that a war between us and Russia is inevitable'.[31]

Everything seemed to suggest that a Big Three meeting was vital, not to say urgent. The President agreed;[32] so did Stalin; and by the end of May it was generally agreed that a conference should be held at Potsdam, in the environs of Berlin, during the latter part of July.

Suddenly political troubles in Britain threatened to throw those arrangements into the melting pot. Parliament had prolonged its own life several times by special legislation, and the House of Commons elected in 1935 was still sitting almost ten years later. In the immediate aftermath of V.E. Day, Labour Party leaders were disposed to agree that the Coalition ought to remain together for some months – but they were conscious that Churchill was under Conservative pressure to call a much earlier election.[33] The Prime Minister suggested to Attlee that the Coalition should continue until the defeat of Japan.[34] Current military thinking did not suggest that this would take place for many months, and the Labour Ministers decided to withdraw from the Government[35] and – with one exception – the Liberals did the same.[36] A General Election was promptly set in motion. Churchill formed a 'Caretaker Government', predominantly of Conservatives, which was to hold office until the election results were in. Polling would be on 5 July, but it would not be possible to announce the results until service votes could be collected and counted – which would be three weeks later. Thus the Potsdam Conference would begin in the period between polling and the count of votes, and a new Government might take office either during or immediately after the Conference. Churchill accordingly offered Attlee the opportunity 'to share in the Government's anxieties, though not in their responsibilities'[37] by receiving papers on foreign affairs and strategy, and later followed this by a further invitation for the Labour leader to be present at Potsdam. Both proposals were accepted.[38]

A somewhat fatuous little crisis suddenly threw this eminently sensible arrangement into serious doubt, and the Prime Minister – getting matters out of proportion – vainly suggested postponing the date of Potsdam for a month or more, to clarify the British political situation. Another problem with constitutional overtones arose in the United States, and was to exert a more serious effect on world affairs. As in Britain, the wartime government had included members of what might normally be considered the 'opposition' party; indeed, one of the most remarkable features of the American Government was that many of its leading personalities were not political figures in the ordinary sense at all.[39] When Truman succeeded Roosevelt, all of the old Cabinet agreed to remain for the time being. The position of Stettinius, however, was soon perceived to present dangers for the future. If Truman should himself die in office, then – as the Constitution currently stood – his successor would be the Secretary of State: a man who, in this instance, had never held elective office of any sort. Truman also had political debts to discharge within the Democratic Party, and at the end of June, Stettinius was persuaded to withdraw to the position of American representative at the United Nations. The new Secretary of State was

James Byrnes – a much stronger political figure, who, as we have noted, was a serious contestant for the Vice Presidential nomination a few months earlier. There was no doubt about either the ability or the ambition of 'Jimmy' Byrnes. When Truman succeeded to the Presidency, 'there was a general feeling that Jimmy was willing to take over and tell Truman how to run his job'.[40] It was not difficult to predict that friction would eventually arise between Byrnes and Truman, for personal reasons. There was another important characteristic possessed by the new Secretary of State which was likely to prove of importance in the conduct of his office: his strong predisposition to compromise.[41]

In preparation for Potsdam, a good deal of work was done behind the scenes. Truman made it his business to establish special contacts with both of his major allies. Averell Harriman contended – and Truman agreed – 'that Stalin was not getting accurate reports from Molotov or any of his people and as a result had grown deeply and unjustifiably suspicious as to our motives, which he probably thought were designed to deprive him of the fruits of victory.[42] This linked with American suspicions that Soviet failure to carry out the Yalta agreements had been due in large part to opposition inside the Soviet Government which Stalin encountered on his return. If this was anything like the truth, then it was important to secure direct access to Stalin and bypass Molotov. One is strangely reminded of the widespread British official feeling in 1938 that it was important to secure direct access to Hitler and bypass Foreign Minister Ribbentrop.

On many occasions in the past, Roosevelt had used his close personal friend Harry Hopkins for special diplomatic contacts. Hopkins was widely disliked by political opponents of the late President – and, indeed, by political supporters who were suspicious or jealous of his influence. Yet he knew Churchill and Stalin well, and was apparently well liked by both of them, and his altruism could not be gainsaid. Hopkins's health was poor, but he was without difficulty persuaded to engage in this, his last great public mission. In the latter part of May, Hopkins was despatched as Truman's special emissary to Moscow, where he engaged in long discussions with Stalin and the other Soviet leaders. Churchill heartily approved of this approach.

The most important feature of Hopkins's visit was the discussions over Poland. Hopkins sought to explain to the Russians how people of the United States regarded the matter as a touchstone of Russia's attitude towards the liberty of other countries. 'Our whole relationship,' he told Stalin, 'was threatened by the *impasse* over Poland.'[43] The Russians, Hopkins went on to suggest, should not give much weight to certain virulently anti-Soviet elements in the

American press; but they must appreciate the deep feelings stirred by doubts over the preservation of civil liberties. He could instance the shock felt by even well-disposed Americans at the news of the recent Polish arrests. Stalin assured Hopkins most emphatically of Russia's intention to restore liberty to Poland.

Hopkins's arguments seemed to produce practical results as well as promises. At the beginning of June, Stalin agreed to invite 'non-Lublin' Poles to Moscow for conversations. These would include some of the 'London Poles' who had broken with Arciszewski – though not Mikolajczyk. Some Poles who had remained in the country during the occupation – including the peasant leader Witos – would also be called.⁴⁴ The British and American Governments both felt particular obligations to Mikolajczyk, and the Russians were eventually persuaded to invite him too. A conference was held in Moscow at which the three acceptable Polish groups (not, of course, Arciszewski's Government) were all represented. On 28 June, the formation of a new 'Government of National Unity' was announced. It would be headed by the 'Lublinite' Prime Minister, Osobka-Morowski. More than three-quarters of the members of this Government had been in some way connected with the 'Lublin' group, but Mikolajczyk became Deputy Prime Minister and Minister of Agriculture, while important non-Lublin figures like Witos, Stanczyk and Grabski also entered the Government. The 'Government of National Unity' promptly announced that it accepted the Yalta decisions, and would organise free elections under a secret ballot. Meanwhile, the sixteen Poles who had been kidnapped earlier were brought to trial in Moscow. As usually happens in spectacular trials held in totalitarian countries, the majority of the accused pleaded guilty. The sentences awarded were – by Soviet standards – light; no one was condemned to death, and the longest term of imprisonment imposed was ten years. These events satisfied the rather easy consciences of the British and American Governments. In the early morning of 6 July, both countries withdrew recognition from Arciszewski's Government, and transferred it to the 'Government of National Unity', which was now established at Warsaw.

Just before the Potsdam Conference opened, Mikolajczyk gave his own appraisal of the situation into which he had been pushed. He told a British diplomat 'that Poland was in a state of chaos so complete that he was inclined to believe that there had been a brain at work behind it'.⁴⁵ The reason, he suspected, was 'the intention of the Lublin people . . . to sovietise the country'. Political arrests, he declared, were still being made; most of the Polish press was not free; and the Communists in the Government were trying to delay elections. Meanwhile, the Russians

were taking away not only every machine upon which they could
lay their hands, but also every beast that stood upon four legs . . .
The peasants in the high roads over which the Russians were
withdrawing were betaking themselves with their animals to the
woods and leaving their villages to be picked clean.

Mikolajczyk believed that a number of these deplorable features of
the new Poland would soon improve; but his description of the
situation as he found it could hardly give much ground for a very
sanguine view. Internal conditions in Poland, however, were no
longer matters of deep concern for the leading Allied statesmen;
their diplomatic agreement, such as it was, had already been more or
less concluded well before Potsdam.

For weal or woe, the President's contacts with Russia appeared to
have delivered results. At the same time he made a similar approach
to Britain. Here again the President needed to evaluate the true
situation, though for very different reasons. The weighty and
alarming messages with which Churchill had bombarded Truman
could not be lightly brushed aside in any assessment of either Russian
or British policy.

The President's emissary for the British mission was less qualified
for his task than Hopkins, and Truman's private notes suggest that
the President never felt the same measure of confidence.[46] The man
selected was Jospeh E. Davies, a former American Ambassador to
Russia and a noted sympathiser with the Soviet regime, who appears
to have entertained the view that he could convert Churchill to his
own opinions about the Soviet Union. Like Hopkins, Davies was in
poor health. The ex-Ambassador protested that his sole desire was to
be of service, and Truman was a little distressed to discover that he
had been 'pestering the Department of State . . . to see that Hopkins
received no bigger headlines than he did.[47]

Discussions between Churchill and Davies covered a wide range of
international problems, and by any test were no more than a very
qualified success. Davies suggested that the Potsdam Conference
might commence as a discussion *à deux* between Truman and Stalin;
whereat Churchill bristled, and indicated that he would not
participate at all in such conditions. More serious was the dispute
between Churchill and Davies over Russia.[48] The Prime Minister was
'vehement and even violent' about Russian behaviour in the
occupied areas. 'What was more horrible to him than communism
was the imposition of the secret police and Gestapo methods . . . He
elaborated . . . at length and with great emphasis and emotion,
[upon] the grave dangers which would arise with the withdrawal of
American troops from Europe.' The continent 'would be prostrate
and at the mercy of the Red Army and of communism'. All this

shattered the President's representative:

> I told him frankly I had been shocked beyond words to find so violent and bitter an attitude and to find what appeared to me so violent a change in his attitude towards the Soviets. Its significance was appalling. It staggered me with the fear that there could be no peace. I had heard of such attitudes in Britain but I had discounted these reports.

So ran the account which Davies sent to Truman; but the story as recorded in Davies's own notes suggests that the exchanges were even more polemical. He accused Churchill of having 'confessed that Hilter was right' about Russia, 'and now that we had jointly defeated Hitler, the Russians could not be trusted in the execution of the "Grand Design" of preserving the Peace we had won'.[49] 'He pulled no punches,' added the ex-Ambassador, 'neither did I.' The scene may be imagined.

But were the Prime Minister's views nevertheless correct? Nobody, not even Davies, could gainsay that they provided a possible and legitimate interpretation of available facts. Right or wrong, their existence only underscored the need for an early and frank talk between the Big Three.

Events in those parts of eastern Europe where Russia was the dominant military power were not at this point following a consistent pattern. In Finland, there was nothing to suggest that Russia intended to interfere with the ordinary process of democratic government, although the country would doubtless be required to cede some territory and to pay some kind of reparations. In Hungary, the picture seemed even more encouraging, for there were signs that a strong and genuine democracy was taking root for the first time in the country's history. Yet in Romania the ruling coalition, headed by Dr. Peter Groza, was to all appearances a mere puppet of the Russians, devoid of popular support. In particular, it did not include the Peasant Party, which seemed to command much wider allegiance than any other political group. Iuliu Maniu, the Peasant Party leader, was described as 'the only Romanian elder politician whose personal honesty has never been questioned'.[50]

In Bulgaria, there was a general reign of terror. 'Between 1500 and 2000 politicians, professors and journalists,' reported *The Times*, 'have been sentenced to death and executed'.[51] In addition to these official executions, early reports told of 15,000 to 20,000 murders: a figure which later information suggested was a gross understatement of the true number.[52] In all probability some of these people were suffering rough justice for collaboration with the Germans; but it looked as if the majority were being punished primarily for opposition to the new régime. Yet there were paradoxes, even in Bulgaria. Some important opponents of the Communists remained at large, and one popular Agrarian figure with firm democratic principles, Nikola Petkov, actually remained within the government.

The fate of ex-Allied countries in central and eastern Europe also gave cause for alarm. Diplomatic reports from Czechoslovakia suggested that the country was far from happy in its 'liberated' condition. The population

> give the general impression of being cowed . . . The Germans have now been replaced by the Russians and in the eyes of a few the change is for the worse . . . Under the Russian occupation only the Communists feel they are supported and non-Communists are correspondingly dejected and apprehensive.[53]

Deportation of Sudetendeutsch and of the Hungarian population of southern Slovakia was bound to occur; but the Czechoslovak Government was accused in some quarters of conducting the process with 'great inhumanity'.[54]

Territorial questions were also involved in Czechoslovakia. The Czechs, with apparent Russian connivance, occupied Teschen when the Germans left. More important was the fate of Ruthenia. At the end of July, it was announced that this province would be transferred to the Soviet Union. It is surely remarkable that the transfer of the Sudetenland to Germany in 1938 caused the most immense international furore, while the transfer of Ruthenai to Russia seven years later attracted relatively little interest. As in the earlier transaction, there were ethnic arguments for the change – in this case, the population was largely Ukrainian. But it was evident that these were no more than a pretext, and nobody seriously tried to discover what the local population thought on the matter. The Czech Government was probably relieved to lose Ruthenia, which was the most backward and impoverished area of the country. The Russians rejoiced for a different reason. When they took Lwow from Poland, they acquired a common frontier with Czechoslovakia. Their main reason for desiring Ruthenia was perceived by an American diplomat at the time: 'its strategic position and desire of Moscow leaders to have common frontier with Hungary'.[55] These new routes into two more European countries would be used repeatedly, and to great effect, by the Russians.

In Yugoslavia, there were other causes for concern besides the frontier problems. When the dust began to settle on the agreement, it was evident that this was not working as the Western Allies had hoped. The new 'United Government' had twenty-eight members. Only six had belonged to Subasić's government in London, and three of those six had been incorporated at an earlier stage to please Tito. The twenty-two Belgrade members could all be regarded as Tito supporters of one kind or another, and the great majority were Communist sympathisers.[56] Thus, at most, three of the twenty-eight members of the government could be regarded as anti-Communist.

For all these considerable matters of concern, a situation rather similar to that in the run-up to Yalta appeared to be developing. Immense differences remained between the major Allies; but the 'first step which counted' towards their resolution was the decision to hold the Conference at all. Once the Big Three had agreed on that, they had effectively decided that all points at issue were negotiable. The most immediately dangerous problems – Poland and Venezia Giulia – appeared to have been 'de-fused'. Other issues, important as they were, were not 'vital' in the sense that the Allies were likely to start shooting each other in order to enforce their particular wishes.

9

Potsdam

'Marshal Stalin said that in all the countries liberated, the Russian policy was to seek a strong, independent, sovereign state. He was against Sovietisation of any of these countries.' Private talk between the Prime Minister (Churchill) and Stalin, 18 July 1945. PREM 3/430/6 fo. 45 s.

'Herr Hitler then said that what he was concerned with was the German race. He did not wish to include Czechs in the Reich. When he had included the Sudeten Germans he would be satisfied.' Private talk between the Prime Minister (Chamberlain) and Hitler, 15 September 1938. Cabinet Minutes 17 September 1938. CAB 23/95.

When it became clear that the war in Europe would probably end in the complete defeat of Germany, questions relating to the country's future came under serious examination by Allied statesmen and diplomats. Throughout 1944, a body known as the European Advisory Commission had been working on a variety of matters relating to the immediate aftermath of war, including the future military occupation of Germany. Many of the Commission's recommendations were accepted readily by the Big Three. Germany should be completely occupied, and divided into military zones, each administered by a specific Power. Geography prescribed that Russia should occupy the east, which was generally considered to be the epicentre of German militarism. There was a great deal of argument between British and Americans about allocation of the other two zones, but it was eventually decided that the United States should receive the south west, and Britain the north west.

One aspect of the occupation arrangements greatly perturbed Churchill. As far back as February 1944, Roosevelt had warned him that he would be unable to leave American troops in France for a pro-tracted period after the war.[1] Later the President returned to the point, explaining that he 'must bring the American troops home as rapidly as transportation problems will permit'. If this happened, urged the Prime Minister, 'how will it be possible to hold down western Germany. . . ? We certainly could not undertake the task without your aid and that of the French.'[2] The President protested that he had no legal authority to equip a post-war foreign army – 'and the prospect of getting such authority from Congress is more than doubtful'.[3] The dangers which would follow from American withdrawal were truly appalling; but for the time being nothing could be done about it.

It was more or less taken for granted that Germany's territorial gains since 1937 would be returned after the war. She would also lose East Prussia, and probably a good deal more land in the east. There were discussions about possible territorial losses in the west, and about whether the country should be preserved as a unity or broken up. The question of possible 'reparations' in money, kind or labour was also being discussed. Some of these matters could perhaps wait for a while; but it was predictable that the immediate aftermath of war would present urgent problems of starvation and very likely disease, while millions of 'displaced persons' of German and other nationalities were likely to be migrating in every direction across Germany and contiguous parts of Europe. To a considerable extent, the way in which these problems would be handled might be related to the views which the Allies entertained about the eventual fate of the country. Discussions raged in Britain and America – and, no doubt, in Russia too – about the exact fate of Germany; but no clear consensus emerged which makes it possible to speak confidently of a 'British' or 'American' or 'Russian' point of view.

Most far-reaching of all proposals for Germany's future was that of Henry Morganthau, United States Secretary to the Treasury, who proposed to turn Germany from a mainly industrial country into an agricultural and pastoral country. The matter had been discussed between British and American representatives at the Quebec Conference of September 1944; but again no clear 'national' points of view emerged.[4] As time went on, however, the leading men in both countries tended to view the whole idea with increasing disfavour.

Like so much else which was thrown up by the war, the Morganthau Plan was almost entirely counter-productive in its effect. The object of the Plan had been to ensure that Germany could never fight a future war; but knowledge of the Plan soon leaked to the enemy, and the practical effect was to make her fight a good deal harder in the current war. Byrnes records how a German-speaking sergeant retailed to him every night the Berlin broadcasts.

These invariably included an appeal to the people of Germany not to consider the proposals of the Allies to surrender. Surrender, they warned, meant enforcement of the 'Morganthau Plan' . . .[5]

There can be little doubt that another effect was to check any disposition to allow the Anglo-Americans a fairly easy ride into Germany, in order to forestall the Russians.

At Yalta, the future of Germany was seen to present serious difficulties; but many of these could be conveniently shelved for a long time. There was no call for immediate decision over either eastern or western frontiers, and nobody was very firmly committed over the country's political future, save in the sense that anything which savoured of militarism or Nazism must be eradicated. The prevailing view of the Big Three leaned towards 'dismemberment' into two or more successor states – a policy in which one may see the hand of Morganthau – and the Foreign Ministers were instructed to consider 'the best method of studying the question of dismemberment'.[6] This form of words hardly suggested any large measure of real consensus. Even this tentative proposal generated a vigorous reaction in the British War Cabinet. Clement Attlee, leader of the Labour Party and Deputy Prime Minister, cabled Churchill to express his colleagues' concern that no decision should be taken until the matter had been discussed in Cabinet.[7] The protocol which eventually emerged from Yalta was even more tentative than the original proposal.[8] As the War Cabinet minutes sagely record, 'while the dismemberment principle had been agreed, ample elbow-room had been retained'.[9] In fact, the committee to discuss German dismemberment never met.

Yalta discussions on Germany's immediate future were more productive. Roosevelt told delegates that American public opinion would not allow his country's troops to remain for more than two years. Events would later disprove this prophecy, but it was important for immediate plans. It provided Churchill with a powerful argument for an idea which only the British regarded with any enthusiasm: that France should receive a zone of Germany to administer. The European Advisory Commission proposals included no such provision, and Stalin argued rather gently against the innovation. Churchill appeared to prevail against him; but the victory was one of appearance rather than reality: for Roosevelt and Stalin had already decided privately to allocate a zone to France – 'out of kindness', as the President put it.[10] Arrangements were also made for division of Austria and the cities Berlin and Vienna, each into four zones. It was further agreed that Germany must pay reparations. The nature and quantity of these should be fixed by a Reparations Commission sitting in Moscow. Other questions relating to Germany were less urgent, and no one seems to have felt that they would prove intractable in future.

When the various Allied troops were advancing into Germany in the spring of 1945, it was generally agreed that their progress should be regulated by the need to secure 'maximum surrender' from the enemy, and thus would inevitably mean that troops would sometimes move into areas destined for eventual occupation by somebody else. At the conclusion of hostilities, there were several aberrations from the pattern which the Big Three had agreed should eventually obtain. The Anglo-Americans had advanced well to the east of their proposed zonal boundaries in Germany, but the Russians held Berlin. Eisenhower had had the chance of taking the capital, but held back – largely through the political directive he had received to destroy the German army.[11]

Austria presented special problems, which perhaps derived in part from the general uncertainty about whether the country should be regarded as a defeated enemy – part of Hitler's Reich, and indeed his country of birth – or as the first victim of aggressive German expansion. In the general scramble of the last few weeks of war, the great bulk of the country was occupied by Russians. A week or so before the German surrender, Russia set up a 'Provisional Government' under a Social Democrat, Karl Renner, in which Social Democrats, Christian Socialists and Communists were represented in approximately equal numbers. On 14 May, a 'Democratic Republic' was proclaimed. This action caused considerable irritation in the West, for the Anglo-Americans had not been consulted.

Yet the very confusion over the former Reich really contained seeds of a tolerable solution; for both Anglo-Americans and Russians had in places advanced ahead of their agreed positions, and could, without loss of face, retreat thereto. The British in particular were very anxious to avoid the appearance of a deal with Russia to withdraw to the agreed zones; but the Powers certainly acted as if such a deal had been struck, and their occupation armies gradually assumed control of the areas allocated at Yalta. The most important surviving enemy weapon was the German fleet, and some anxious discussion took place within and between the Powers as to its fate. The Allies seemed to be moving towards the view that most of the submarines should be sunk, while vessels which could be readily converted to peacetime use should be divided between the Big Three.

In the immediate prelude to the Potsdam Conference, a vital decision about Germany's future was taken almost casually. Morganthau wished to attend as a delegate, but the President thought otherwise. The Secretary of the Treasury proffered his resignation, which was promptly accepted, probably with relief. Nobody else was prepared to espouse the 'Morganthau Plan' or anything like it; and the idea of forcibly dividing Germany into successor states as originally conceived also passed gradually out of sight – although division of Germany would later take place along lines which nobody envisaged in 1945.

.When the delegates assembled at Potsdam, other equally far-reaching decisions were taken, apparently without their full implications being appreciated at the time. In wartime discussions over Germany, it had been generally accepted that the country would be treated as an economic unity for the immediate post-war period – the predominantly agricultural east balancing the predominantly industrial west. Much turned, however, on what was meant by 'Germany'. The Western Allies appear tacitly to have assumed that 'Germany', for current purposes, meant Germany as it existed before Hitler began his road to conquest. No doubt much of eastern Germany would eventually go to Poland, and some to Russia – but surely not before the Peace Treaties?

The definition, and the future, of Germany tied up with the question of Poland's western frontiers. This matter had been shelved at Yalta, for Roosevelt was able to argue that the views of the Poles themselves were not ascertainable yet, for no generally-acknowledged Polish Government was in existence. By the time of Potsdam, however, all the Big Three were recognising the new Warsaw regime. President Bierut was invited to Potsdam, and there spoke the lines which he had been taught by his Russian mentors. He wanted Poland to extend to the Western Neisser. As the Red Army was in occupation of the whole area in dispute, nobody could reasonably doubt that this would be the eventual settlement. Decencies, however, should be observed, and everybody still acknowledged that the final decision must await the Peace Conference.

All this had great bearing on the immediate as well as the long-term future of Germany. The delegates at Potsdam discovered that a vital fact was in dispute. What had happened to the eight million Germans who had inhabited the various places Russia proposed to give to Poland? Stalin had said at Yalta that all had fled; but Churchill's information was that 'great numbers, running into millions, were still there'.[12] If Stalin's statement was correct, then only Poles could cultivate the land. The western countries were not free to send observers to see for themselves, and were compelled to take Stalin's word for it. It was therefore apparent that the Poles either had already moved in, or were in the process of moving in, to the area, with full Russian connivance; and that they had no intention of treating it as German territory on either a long-term or a short-term basis. The fact that the change was in theory provisional until the peace settlement gave no comfort to anybody.

'My appeal came to nothing. The world has yet to measure the "serious consequences" which I forecast.'[13] Thus wrote Churchill long after Potsdam. It would be comforting, perhaps, to believe that the Prime Minister was overwhelmingly concerned over the ethnic and human problems posed by the new Polish frontier. Alas, evidence suggests that what exercised him most were problems of a very different kind. If the area east of the Oder was still part of Germany, then the vast quantities of food which it produced would be available to feed the swollen population of the industrial western zones. If it was part of Poland, then no such obligation existed, and the western countries must make different provisions, at great expense, to compensate for those supplies.

Britain and America did not even use the one weapon which Providence had set in their hands in relation to Germany's immediate economic future. The principle was laid down at Potsdam that reparations could be taken by each Ally from its own zone, provided that these 'should leave enough resources to enable the German people to subsist without external assistance'. The Allies would satisfy their reparation claims by removing material from their own zones, and by seizing external German assets. As Russia had suffered more damage than the Western Allies, the Big Three agreed that she should also be entitled to a stated proportion of capital equipment and other products from the western zones. It is surely curious that this Russian demand was not bargained against the Western requirement for food.

Agreement was reached at Potsdam on other matters relating to Germany's future. It was confirmed that she should be treated as a single economic unity for the occupation period – barring, of course, the provinces which had become, for practical purposes, Polish or Russian. As a small concession to Morganthau's ideas, 'at the earliest practicable date the German economy shall be decentralised' – and in future the Germans should not be allowed to produce any kind of armaments, aircraft, or seagoing vessels. The German Navy should be divided between the Big Three, and special arrangements made for the disposal of U-boats. Transfers of the German population from Poland, Czechoslovakia and Hungary, the Big Three agreed, 'will have to be undertaken', but 'should be effected in an orderly and humane manner'. In the matter of civil liberty, Germany would benefit from defeat. Democratic political parties and Trade Unions should have the right to organise throughout the country, while freedom of speech, press and religion should be permitted – subject only to the need for maintaining military security.

The Powers did not propose to set up immediately an overall political authority for Germany, and no real decision was reached about the one already established by the Russians in Austria. German local government would be built up, and gradually form a decentralised structure for the country as a whole. Certain departments of state for the whole country should be set up, under German civil servants. They would be directed by the Control Council – an inter-Allied body operated by the four occupying Commanders-in-Chief. Wider questions about the country's political future, and about possible truncations in the West, could be set aside indefinitely; and for the time being the Powers might cooperate in an empirical manner and gradually allow a de-nazified Germany to come into existence. Meanwhile, those accused of war crimes should be brought to trial. Only ex-enemies, of course, would come into this category; nobody thought of seeking out and bringing to trial those responsible for the atrocities at Katyn or Dresden.

Some discussions took place about areas of Europe which presumably belonged to the 'spheres of influence' of western Allies. Spain was difficult. The Russians submitted a memorandum which recommended that the United Nations should break relations with Franco, and 'render support to the democratic forces in Spain and ... enable the Spanish people to establish such a régime as will respond to their will'.[14] This evidently implied renewal of the civil war, and probably the eventual establishment of a Communist régime. Neither Churchill nor Truman had any cause for loving Franco, but they had no wish to exorcise Beelzebub by conjuring Satan; so the matter was dropped. Russia was evidently prepared to take the rough with the smooth so far as spheres of influence went; she expected others to recognise her areas of dominance, but was prepared – if all else failed – to grant grudging reciprocity in theirs.

A not dissimilar view was taken about Greece. The Western Allies feared Yugoslav and Bulgarian aggression against Greece; Stalin complained at Potsdam about Greek aggression against Bulgaria and Albania. Churchill volunteered that 'Greece was to have a plebiscite and free elections', and offered the Russians an opportunity to send observers.[15] Stalin was not interested – pointedly observing that 'he was not meddling in Greek affairs'. Yet he went on to complain about American proposals for changes of government in Romania, where – so he assured the Prime Minister – 'everything was peaceful'. Whatever Roosevelt might have thought about the 'Tolstoy' agreement and spheres of influence, for all practical purposes the Americans tacitly accepted its implications.

One change during the Potsdam period seems to have come as a surprise to most participants at the Conference, and would prove of some importance in their future relations: the new Labour government in Britain. On 18 July, Stalin had assured Churchill that the Prime Minister would have a majority of about eighty seats.[16] The Labour leaders themselves had not expected to win.[17] Yet results confounded such judgements: Labour won an overall majority of 146. Stalin; like most prophets whose forecasts are belied by events, gave his own interpretation: 'the British people had decided that the war was over, that Japan was far away and that the Americans could finish it off. They were turning their minds to peace problems.'[18] The new Prime Minister, Clement Attlee, strenuously denied this assessment; but perhaps it was not far wrong.

Most observers had assumed that the Foreign Secretary of a Labour administration would be Hugh Dalton. There were problems of personalities connected with other offices, and in fact the post was given to the great Trade Unionist, Ernest Bevin – Dalton receiving the Exchequer. Both men were initially disappointed;[19] but in later times the wisdom of Bevin's appointment would be seen. As a Trade Union leader in 1920, he had played a large part in blocking supplies to the enemies of Russian bolshevism; but his subsequent experience involved abundant encounters with Trade Union Communists, whose minds he came to know a great deal better than aristocratic Foreign Office men could even hope to do. Those who feared, or hoped for, a swing of British foreign policy towards Russia would be equally amazed. Truman soon observed with some astonishment that British foreign policy did not change with changes of government – and regretted that the same was not true in his own country.[20] A joke would eventually become current that 'Bevin treats the Soviet Union like a breakaway from the Transport and General Workers' Union'. There were occasional similarities between the two.

10

Tube Alloys

'. . . the intense atom glows
A moment, then is quenched in a most cold repose.'
Shelley, *Adonais*, 179–80.

In nearly all Europe west of the USSR, the challenge which
Communism posed in 1945 came either from the Red Army, from
small and ruthless groups of armed partisans, or from even smaller
groups of men who had established themselves in the governments
of their countries. Only in Yugoslavia and Albania was there the
slightest indication that Communism might be winning support
from a majority of the people.

In China, the situation was radically different. Great areas of the
country were occupied by the Japanese. By no means all of the
remainder was held by Chiang Kai-Shek's Kuomintang, for
Communists controlled 'large portions of north China and
disconnected areas to the east and south'.[1] These districts were
largely behind the Japanese lines, and therefore immune from
Kuomintang intervention. As early as the beginning of 1943, both
Communists and Kuomintang were using their best efforts not
against the Japanese but in preparation for conflict against each
other. 'It is no longer wondered whether civil war can be avoided,'
wrote an American official, 'but rather whether it can be delayed at
least until after victory over Japan.'[2]

Even at this early date, American diplomatic literature was full of
gloom and despair at the failures of Chiang's government. 'Had the
Kuomintang had the foresight to adopt simple effective measures for
agrarian reform, equitable taxation and for promotion of home
industries,' wrote another American diplomat in 1943, 'it could have
cut the ground from under . . . the communists . . . This could still
be done, but it is feared that the present Kuomintang leadership, sterile
insofar as social reform is concerned, is incapable of altering its
conservative course.'[3] When a great famine struck the Honan

province, the American *Chargé d'Affaires* reported that 'there is no mention of any movement whatever of actual food or relief commodities into the region'.[4] The American Ambassador confirmed these general opinions, and added a significant rider: 'The end of the war in Europe will find a militarily strong Soviet Russia which may be expected to take an active interest in the Far Eastern situation.'[5]

By 1945, the situation had not improved. Henry Stimson, Secretary of War, could certainly not be regarded as a 'left winger'; but he described the Kuomintang as 'a mere surface veneer (more or less rotten) over a mass of the Chinese people'.[6] Another influential American wrote to Truman that the Kuomintang was 'now widely regarded by the Chinese masses as the party of the big bankers, merchants, landlords and owners of industry. Its prestige rests largely on the personal reputation of Chiang Kai-Shek.'[7] American uneasiness over the Kuomintang was closely paralleled by Russian doubts about the Chinese Communists – whom Stalin described privately at Potsdam as 'a bunch of fascists'.[8]

Chiang's followers were an acute embarrassment – military, moral and political – to the American Government. To make matters even more difficult, the Chinese Communists exhibited a façade of great moderation. In 1945, President Truman was told that they were operating a policy of 'redistribution of land to eliminate absentee ownership; drastic lowering of farm rents; better wages, treatment, living conditions and education for workers and peasants and their families'. The report added that 'the small farmers of China, who comprise 70 per cent of the total population, and the coolies of the cities, who comprise approximately 20 per cent, are generally eager for the protection, security and improved working conditions offered by the Communist program. Many of the intellectuals, even in Chungking, are also sympathetic to the communists.'[9] Such information should be treated with caution, for the informant was anxious to make a point, and there were doubtless vast local variations; yet if the general picture even remotely resembled the truth, it serves to explain a most remarkable difference between Communism in China and Communism in Europe. The immediate Chinese programme seemed to pivot on rural land reform, with an ingredient of mild social and economic reform – almost in the spirit of the 'New Deal'. A very moderate-looking Communist Party faced a very unattractive Kuomintang; and there was nothing else.

Attitudes of the Great Powers to this situation were uncertain. The American view was clearest. Admiral Hurley, United States Ambassador to China, reported to Truman that he had been charged by Roosevelt to bring Churchill and Stalin to an agreement on the policy that the United States has been pursuing in China, namely

1. To take all necessary action to bring about unification under the National Government of all anti-Japanese armed forces in China;

2. To endorse the aspirations of the Chinese people for the establishment of a free united democratic Chinese Government;

3. To continue to insist that China furnish her own leadership, make her own decisions and be responsible for her own policies and thus work out her own destiny in her own way.[10]

Hurley obtained formal concurrence from Churchill and Stalin; but the Americans continued to feel considerable doubts about the sincerity of both major Allies, whom they deeply suspected of desiring to keep China divided.

To an extent, Generalissimo Chiang Kai-Shek seemed to be responding to the American initiative by the summer of 1945; but the Communists in their turn were stepping up demands. There seemed little hope of peace in China, save from 'the concerted use of influence by the Great Powers'.[11] It was still, apparently, Stalin's view that 'the only chance ... for a stable government in China was the Kuomintang around the Generalissimo'.[12] Unfortunately, the only direction in which the Great Powers were exerting 'concerted influence' in China was one which was most unlikely to encourage internal peace. At Yalta, a personal agreement was concluded between Roosevelt, Stalin and Churchill. Stettinius knew little about the agreement; while Eden, who did know, disapproved.[13] Stalin told Churchill and Roosevelt 'in the most rigid secrecy of the willingness of the Soviet Government to enter the war against Japan two or three months after the surrender of Germany'.[14] For this favour, Stalin demanded consideration. The Kurile Islands should pass from Japan to Russia, while southern Sakhalin and adjacent islands, which the Japanese had taken from Russia in 1904, should be returned. The port of Dairen – once Chinese, but currently held by Japan – should be 'internationalised', 'with safeguards for the pre-eminent interests of the USSR'. Russia should recover her lease of Port Arthur – also originally Chinese, but now in Japanese occupation. The '*status quo* in Outer Mongolia' should be preserved: that is, a province which was technically Chinese should be recognised as nominally independent – but in practice would become a dependency of the Soviet Union. The Chinese Eastern Railway and the South Manchurian Railway should be operated by a Soviet–Chinese company 'in the understanding that the pre-eminent interests of the USSR would be safeguarded'.[15] Thus, most of the territories and privileges affected by the agreement were currently held by Japan; but the natural reversionary upon Japan's defeat would in most cases be China, who at one time had owned them. The effect of the secret clauses of the Yalta agreement was therefore to benefit the Soviet Union and to disadvantage China. Such an arrangement would be sure to reduce Chiang's moral authority considerably. Nevertheless, Roosevelt undertook to secure his acquiesence. In fact, the President had been dead for a couple of months before the Chinese were approached. T. V. Soong, the Chinese Foreign Minister, was particularly appalled at the proposals concerning Outer Mongolia – explaining to Stalin that although China was manifestly incapable of currently exercising sovereignty in the area, yet formal abandonment of the Chinese claim would mean an irretrievable loss of 'face'.[16] Chiang's reactions were similar: the news came to him as 'a great shock'.[17]

Yet even before the Chinese were informed, there were signs of unexpected American hesitation over the secret Yalta agreement. A few days after V.E. Day, Halifax sent a telegram to Churchill, seeking advice about Britain's attitude to the proposed Soviet intervention against Japan. The Ambassador reported that policy-forming elements in the United States

> appear to be in a state of indecision. On the one hand the view is expressed that it would be just as well on political grounds if the job could be finished without Soviet intervention. This opinion is said to be particularly favoured by the Navy Department. On the other extreme there are those who would welcome early Soviet belligerency as a means of saving lives and of obviating a protracted American campaign on the Asiatic mainland.[18]

Churchill's answer was emphatic: 'We desire the entry of the Soviets into the war against Japan at the earliest moment.'[19]

While this debate was proceeding, the large cat which had been stuffed into the bag at Yalta suddenly escaped. On 27 June, the Canadian Prime Minister sent a message to Churchill. By a rather roundabout route, Mackenzie King had learnt 'certain conditions to be accepted prior to Soviet entry into the Pacific War'.[20] These corresponded generally, though not quite accurately, with the secret agreement at Yalta. In Cadogan's view the information was communicated 'by someone on the Chinese side, in the belief that China is being subjected to Russo-American pressure of which we know nothing, in the hope of getting us to redress the balance'.[21] This revelation that Canada had her own sources of information made it necessary for Churchill to tell all the Dominions what had been agreed at Yalta. Further news soon followed from Mackenzie King. Russia had stepped up her demands, and the Chinese were under great pressure to complete an agreement before Potsdam.[22] The Chinese Foreign Minister received hints that 'he would incur the enduring ill-will of Stalin if he did not clinch in Moscow'.[23] The British and Americans, however, advised him not to make the concessions demanded by Russia.[24]

Why were the Western democracies now opposed to these Chinese concessions? During the Potsdam meeting, Churchill gave Eden the sensational information that 'it is quite clear that the United States do not at the present time desire Russian participation in the war against Japan'.[25] This statement, as we shall later see, was an over-simplification at the best. Insofar as it contained a grain of truth, it posed a much more fundamental question. Why had the Americans changed their minds so dramatically in the short period since Yalta?

The answer may be given in two words: atomic bomb. Long before America came into the war, the principle that enormous quantities of energy could be liberated by processes of atomic fission was understood in both America and Britain, and the potential military applications of this knowledge were appreciated.[26] It was also appreciated at an early stage that atomic energy might have exceedingly important applications for peaceful uses as well. Churchill and Roosevelt agreed that research should be conducted on the safer side of the Atlantic, and in August 1943 concluded a written agreement not to use the atomic bomb without each other's consent, nor to communicate information about it to others. Canada was brought into the arrangements to an extent; she would supply raw materials, and provide facilities for part of the project.

It was not possible to keep these developments wholly secret between the three countries. There was some leakage to the Russians, who sought information through members of the Communist Party employed in laboratories and plants in America. Fragments of information reached Governments of the Netherlands, Belgium and Brazil, in connection with supplies of raw materials. The French had done some of the early research, before the collapse in 1940.[27]

During the period of Roosevelt's Presidency, Henry Stimson was the only American in a leading official position who knew much about the work, although Stettinius had some information. When Truman became President in April 1945, he knew that a great military secret was being prepared, but had not the least idea what it was. Stimson told him something of the plans next day; but the new President also soon discovered that certain apparently competent experts were firmly convinced that the new bomb would never work.[28]

On 7 June 1945, leading members of the British Government learned that the 'Americans will be ready in a month's time to undertake the first large-scale tests of Tube Alloys' – code name for the project – 'and hope to use it against the enemy within a month thereafter'.[29] They were warned that it was 'a weapon which already far outstrips in destructive power all known weapons, while the process of development has by no means come to a halt'. The necessary British assent for use of the weapon was granted early in July.[30]

Uncertainties over the political consequences of the bomb had already exerted an important effect on arrangements between the Big Three. Truman had taken care that the Potsdam meeting should not be held before mid-July 'on purpose to give us more time'.[31] At the beginning of the Potsdam meeting, Churchill learned that the Americans had successfully exploded the first, experimental, atomic bomb. This radically altered the whole prospect of the Far Eastern war. Instead of fighting a protracted and bloody campaign extending over many months, the Americans could hope to bring Japan down in defeat within a short time by one or two dramatic incidents. The reason for inviting Russia to participate had been to reduce the expenditure of Anglo-American blood. Did the atomic bomb remove the need for Russian help? Churchill, as we have seen, told Eden at the time that it caused the Americans to cool off from the idea, and declares in his book on the Second World War that 'the President and I no longer felt that we needed Stalin's aid to conquer Japan'.[32] Astonishingly, Truman writes the opposite in his own book on the period – claiming that he, Churchill and the Chiefs of Staff concurred at Potsdam in the view that 'Russian entry into the war against Japan should be encouraged'.[33] Stimson's recorded statements uphold Truman's view.[34] Perhaps the Americans were still not unanimous; or perhaps the effect of the new developments on American thinking was to reduce enthusiasm for Russian participation, but not turn them against it altogether.

Whether or not the Japanese knew anything of the fearful new weapon which was being prepared for them, they could fairly guess that the Big Three were about to conclude an agreement at Potsdam to finish off Japan between them; even if this agreement for some reason miscarried, defeat was still inevitable. The most important card which the Japanese held was the power to kill many Allied soldiers, and impose heavy economic burdens on their enemies in the process. The Americans and British now perceived that they possessed a card to trump that one.

Just before the Russian delegation left for Potsdam, a message from the Emperor was delivered through the Japanese Ambassador. It 'stated that "unconditional surrender" could not be accepted by Japan but, if it was not insisted upon, Japan might be prepared to compromise with regard to other terms'.[35] Stalin told Churchill of this approach. The Prime Minister also discovered that 'Russia intended to attack Japan soon after August 8 (the Marshal thought it might be a fortnight later).'[36]

By a curious coincidence, Churchill learnt from Stalin of the Japanese approach on the same day as he heard from Truman of the first atomic explosion. He advised each of his informants to tell the other the important tidings. Stalin was not apprised of the atomic explosion until 24 July, when the President

> casually mentioned ... that we had a new weapon of special destructive force. The Russian Premier showed no unusual interest. All he said was that he was glad to hear it and hoped we would 'make good use of it against the Japanese'.[37]

Whatever else was implied by the invention of the atomic bomb and the diplomatic situation developing between the Allied Powers, Britain, America and China now had more reason than ever to conclude the Far Eastern war with all possible speed – even at the cost of various other desirable objectives. Even before the experimental explosion, documents had been passing and discussions were being held, at high levels in the United States. On the day of the explosion, Stimson sent Truman a memorandum urging 'that we formulate a warning to Japan to be delivered during the course of this Conference, and rather sooner than later'.[38] The War Department had already prepared a draft, which had apparently been approved by the two Service departments. On 24 July, a draft declaration from the United States, Britain and China was circulated, and Stalin was informed. On 26 July, the document was issued. It called upon Japan 'to proclaim now the unconditional surrender of all the Japanese armed forces'. The disastrous phrase, 'unconditional surrender', had been repeated so often that its use here was inescapable; but the body of the document made it absolutely plain that the surrender demanded was by no means unconditional. The enemy was promised sovereignty over the truly Japanese islands; was assured that Japanese forces, after being disarmed, would be allowed to return home; that the country would be allowed to retain peaceful industries and eventually return to world trading relations. There was a further promise that Anglo-American forces would withdraw once the essential Allied objectives had been secured.

Just as Britain, America and China had every reason to make the terms as attractive as possible to the Japanese, so also had Russia every reason to hope that the offer would fail, and the war continue until she had time to participate and thus lay claim to spoils of victory. In the event, the Japanese rejected the terms, and war continued.

On 6 August, the first atomic bomb was dropped on Hiroshima.

The devastating and probably decisive effect of the weapon was apparent immediately to all. It was imperative for Russia to intervene at once, before Japan surrendered. On 8 August, the Soviet Union declared war on Japan, with effect from midnight. Now haste became imperative for the Western Allies. Once the Russians invaded in force, it would be impossible to shift them from any territory, whether *de jure* Japanese or Chinese, which they happened to occupy. The other Allies could not wait for dilatory, face-saving procedures to run their course in Japan. On 9 August, the second atomic bomb – once planned for Kokura – was dropped on Nagasaki. It was constructed on a different technical principle from the Hiroshima bomb, and was far more effective. Next day, the Japanese decided to accept most of the Allied terms, reserving only that the Emperor should retain his prerogative. There was some more delay while the Allies argued about this point, and about the technicalities of the surrender; but on 14 August the Japanese condition was accepted, and the surrender announced.

There has been, and will probably long continue to be, much discussion as to whether the atomic bombs were exploded primarily to defeat Japan or primarily to exclude Russia, as far as possible, from the Far Eastern settlement. The answer would seem to be that either of these considerations would by itself have provided adequate justification in the minds of the political and military leadership. Yet ordinary experience suggests that men engaged in one great conflict do not readily turn their minds to another possible one in the future; and this makes it likely that the consideration uppermost in their minds was to expedite defeat of Japan. This, after all, had been the sole reason for wanting Russia to enter the Far Eastern war in the first place. A war fought from island to island against desperate Japanese defence would not only have been exceedingly costly in men and materials, but would soon have caused many people in the democracies to ask whether the game was worth the candle.

Statesmen began to grasp at a very early stage the enormous consequences which would derive from the new weapon. More than a month before the first, experimental, bomb was exploded, the Americans had tried to work out ways of controlling its use after Japan was defeated. The conclusions were scarcely encouraging. Stimson reported to Truman that 'the only suggestion which our Committee had been able to give' was an international agreement to publicise all work done on the matter, and full inspection of all countries 'to see whether this promise was being carried out'.[39] The Secretary of War, however, was doubtful whether Russia would assent to inspection, and was convinced that no disclosure should be made until effective plans for inspection and control had been devised.

The British, not knowing as much as the Americans, could not react so quickly; but on the day after the Nagasaki bomb was dropped, a high-powered advisory committee was set up by leading members of the Cabinet 'to submit proposals as soon as possible about the international handling of the new discovery'.[40] Attlee soon drew sweeping conclusions on the matter.[41] There was no effective protection against atomic bombardment, save the threat of retaliation. International agreements to abstain from using such an overwhelmingly effective weapon would probably not be honoured. Strategic bases and strategic frontiers were henceforth useless. Nothing could halt the march of future discovery. Even the hope that expense might limit the bomb to a few super-powers was futile:

> The Americans placed speed above every other consideration and backed heavily all the horses in the race. As a result they have spent something like £500,000,000. But it is estimated that any country developing the process now could produce bombs with plant which might cost as little as £25,000,000.

This brought the bomb within the capacity not merely of Russia but of countries like France, Belgium, Holland, Switzerland and Sweden. Nor could one hope to restrict production because there were so few known sources of the raw materials. Further sources would doubtless be found; and one of the likely places 'from the general nature of the country' was Russia.[42] Nuclear power would certainly be used for industrial purposes, and the scientific principles involved would be similar to those used in the Nagasaki bomb. Thus it was not possible to keep peaceful and warlike developments of nuclear energy in more or less watertight compartments.

Just what immediate conclusions Russia drew is more speculative. One consideration which must have been recognised was that the military situation had been altered beyond recognition, to the immediate disadvantage of the Soviet Union. When Roosevelt talked at Yalta about withdrawing American troops from Europe in a couple of years, it looked as if nobody would be in a position to face two or three hundred Soviet divisions with a remotely comparable force anywhere on the Eurasian continent. This new bomb was worth all the Soviet divisions put together. No doubt Russia was already preparing her reply. In September, Molotov – very much in his cups – proposed a toast, 'Here's to the atom bomb' – adding, 'We've got it'.[43] This was not true when uttered, but nobody doubted that it would be true within a few years.

So, far from feeling safe in the new situation, the Americans saw cause for deep alarm. George Kennan, Chargé in Moscow, contended that 'the men who are now in power in Russia . . . would

[not] hesitate for a moment to apply this power against us if by doing so they thought that they might materially improve their own power position in the world'.[44] Yet – for the time being – the Americans were the only people who possessed the bomb. Meanwhile, there was considerable speculation in the West as to whether the American monopoly exerted much influence on current Soviet policy.[45] Yet whether or not Russia was inhibited in her immediate policy by the American monopoly, she would most certainly not risk challenging America in any 'vital interest' while that monopoly remained.

The sorcerer's apprentices continued to argue desperately about the new power which they had acquired, and various questions posed by the atomic bomb continued to be debated in all countries – but most intensely in Britain and the United States. Memoranda passed and discussions took place between leading members of the Governments concerned. There was little suggestion that atomic research should cease, but there was a great deal of debate in both countries – much of it at cross purposes – as to whether Russia should be informed of current atomic knowledge, and what sort of international controls could be devised to prevent the proliferation of nuclear weapons, the multiplication of nuclear powers, and the development of new and more terrible nuclear techniques. In these early discussions, the disputants did not divide into 'natural' pro-Russians favouring disclosure and 'natural' anti-Russians opposing it. At this stage, the most influential advocate of sharing the atomic secret was Henry Stimson. The Secretary of War told the American Cabinet on 21 September 1945 that scientists working in his department were unanimous in the view that there was no way of keeping technology of the bomb secret for long; therefore, it should be formally shared with Russia, to avert ill-feeling. The Under-Secretary of State, Dean Acheson, agreed with him.[46] Other members of the Cabinet took very much the opposite view. The Democrat James Forrestal, Secretary of the Navy, adopted 'the most extreme attitude of all' against disclosure, while some Ministers gave compelling evidence for what was perhaps the clinching argument: that disclosure would be deeply resented by public opinion.[47]

The most authoritative statement of Russian opinion at this early stage came from Stalin, at a press interview given in September 1945. While he considered that the current American monopoly posed some threat, he was convinced that that monopoly would not last long, and his general approach was by no means alarmist.[48] Eventually, the whole discussion more or less ran into the sands. It became increasingly clear that unilateral disclosure by the American Government was politically impossible; while no international agreement could be meaningful unless accompanied by full rights of inspection within all countries – a condition to which the Russians would never agree. It might be possible for Western countries to reach agreements about exchange of information – perhaps even about control – but that was the most that could be hoped for.

It is impossible to this day to assess the international consequences of the atomic bomb in the 1940s, beyond saying that it brought the Japanese war to an abrupt end. Arguably, the existence and latent threat of that bomb saved both western Europe and the eastern fringes of Asia from Russian control; arguably, it destroyed the last hope of real collaboration between Russia and the West, and condemned them to a permanent condition of mutual fear and Cold War; arguably, it saved the world from a Third World War by imposing a 'balance of terror' which no Power dared to upset; arguably, it did none of these things, and the broad course of events outside eastern Asia was not radically affected by the invention. Certainly the Soviet Union exploded her own first atomic device in 1949, and Britain followed suit not long afterwards. Since then, nobody has been quite sure who was ahead of whom in atomic technology, and all Powers have shown very marked reticence in using their own possession of advanced nuclear devices as a diplomatic weapon.

11

Calm between Storms

'There has been no decrease in the determination of the Soviet Union to produce world revolution. Diplomatic relations with friendly states are not regarded by the Soviet Government as normal friendly relations but "armistice" relations and it is the conviction of the leaders of the Soviet Union that this "armistice" cannot possibly be ended by a definitive peace but only by a renewal of battle.' William C. Bullitt (United States Ambassador to the Soviet Union) to Cordell Hull, 19 July 1935. Quoted in J. W. Pratt, *The American Secretaries of State* . . . xii, p. 600.

Progress of events in the first half of August 1945 was so rapid that the actual framework which would determine future development of the Pacific area was largely improvised. On 13 August 1945, the day before the Japanese surrender, Byrnes proposed to Truman that 'the occupation authority of Japan should be organized on the principle of centralized administration, avoiding the division of the country into zones of independent responsibility administered separately'.[1] There should be no repetition of the disastrous German experience – where action by the Control Commission could be vetoed by any of the occupying powers, and the separate zones were already developing into miniature states. Japan should indeed be jointly occupied, but under a single Commander-in-Chief, who must be appointed at once. When the second suggestion was put to the Russians they at first demurred, proposing joint command by an American and a Russian; but they swiftly withdrew this demand[2] and the American General Douglas MacArthur was promptly appointed Commander-in-Chief.

The American public received a colourful and garbled account of some of these transactions through the *New York Herald Tribune*[3] and British officials were also considerably confused. The Attlee government was far from clear whether Churchill had made secret verbal agreements in the early part of the Potsdam Conference about occupation and administration of Japan, and even whether he had entered secret undertakings at Yalta about Korea. On both matters it was necessary to check with the former Prime Minister, who was able to assure the government that no such agreements had been made.[4]

There were complex discussions between the Allies over the nature of the control to be exercised in metropolitan Japan. The eventual upshot was a more or less amicable agreement reached later in September to the effect that a multiplicity of states should participate in a Far Eastern Advisory Commission; but control should rest firmly with MacArthur. These debates coincided with a somewhat unseemly scramble between the Allies as to who should receive surrender where from the defeated Japanese. Eventually agreement was reached, prescribing certain areas for each of the recognised belligerents. There was some anxious discussion about Hong Kong, but eventually a 'face-saving' compromise was achieved between the British and Chinese. More serious was the position in areas under control of Chinese Communists, who were organised virtually as an independent state. They claimed that they were entitled to receive surrender in the areas in which they were operating, since they had borne the brunt of the fighting. The Americans had the gravest misgivings on the point, for they were well aware that this would mean ceding arms and strategically important territory to the insurgent forces, whose main weakness had hitherto been a shortage of weapons. In the end, the Americans did what they could to help Chiang's troops to occupy the places concerned;[5] but it was impossible to stop much material passing to the Communists.

The fate of Korea would eventually prove of exceptional importance – though the most dramatic events lie outside the present field of study. The country became a Japanese dependency in 1895, and was formally annexed fifteen years later. A Declaration had been issued from the Cairo Conference of 1943, to which China, Britain and the United States were signatories, promising independence after an Allied victory. Russia, not being at war with Japan, was not included. Independence, however, would present considerable practical difficulties. The administration, the police force and the land-owning classes were largely Japanese. The most numerous body of Koreans who might be in a condition to run their country were some 300,000 exiles residing in Siberia.[6] The country's post-war future was in fact decided more or less by accident. Although the Allies decided at Potsdam that there should be some division between areas of occupation in Korea, there was no decision as to where this division should lie. When Japan did collapse, the State Department wished United States forces to occupy the whole country: an operation militarily feasible, though only at considerable risks to the landings in Japan itself. A proposal was eventually drawn up by the 'State-War-Navy' Coordinating Committee to the effect that the parallel 38°N be taken as the line between where the Soviets and the Americans should accept surrender, though this was not meant to delimit the eventual areas of occupation. The principle was endorsed by the President and issued as 'General Order No. 1' by MacArthur on 2 September – by which time Russian troops had already been present in the peninsula for three weeks.[7] The largely industrial north and the agricultural south were economically complementary, and it appears generally to have been assumed by all concerned that after a brief period of military occupation which was necessary to expel the Japanese and allow political institutions to establish themselves in Korea, both American and Russian forces would be withdrawn, and the country left to its own devices.

Problems of eastern Asia could wait for some time for solution. By general consent, the fate of European countries was far more urgent. The Potsdam agreement included provision for the Foreign Ministers of the Big Three to constitute themselves a 'Conference' which would discuss preliminary arrangements of peace treaties, and various other matters. The first meeting of the Conference assembled in London on 11 September 1945. As far back as June, Stettinius had been of the opinion that 'a formal peace conference would be slow and unwieldy and ratification of the resulting document might be long delayed';[8] whereas many problems could 'be dealt with on an *ad hoc* basis' in this manner.

The position of France and China in these discussions would later prove important. The published wording of the Potsdam agreement did not authorise countries outside the Big Three to be present at the Foreign Ministers' Conferences, unless they were signatories to the surrender terms of a particular enemy country which was under discussion, or were specially invited by the Big Three to participate when matters touching their own interests came under discussion. There was apparently a verbal agreement at Potsdam, however, to the effect that France and China could participate in discussions, but could not vote, on other matters pertaining to the Peace Treaties. When the London meetings commenced, it was unanimously agreed that these verbal arrangements should apply.[9]

Eleven days after the Conference began, Molotov suddenly announced that Russia would not attend further meetings unless France and China were excluded from discussions, save where they were authorised to be present under the written Potsdam agreement. This announcement was greeted with consternation. Truman intervened with Stalin, but to no effect. The British and American Governments both decided that it was better to allow the talks to collapse than proceed in such conditions. The most positive achievement of the Conference had been a substantial measure of agreement over the future treaty with Finland. Beyond that, relatively little was accomplished, and a lot of bad feeling generated. As Foreign Secretary Bevin reported to the British Cabinet, disagreement on procedure was 'only the outward manifestation of the fundamental disagreement on principle' between Russia and the others.'[10]

The Big Three had agreed at Potsdam that preparation of an Italian peace treaty was 'the first among the immediate tasks to be undertaken by the new Committee of Foreign Ministers'. Italy was in Anglo-American military occupation, and nobody doubted that her immediate political future would be as a parliamentary democracy on the Western pattern. The main interest – now that Venezia Giulia had been set in cold storage – centred on her overseas possessions. Two parts of the former Italian empire had already been settled. There could be no question of Albania returning to Italy, and Ethiopia had been restored long ago to the tender, or otherwise, mercies of its Emperor. There remained various territories in Africa, and numerous islands in the Mediterranean, which were subjects of much doubt. In Britain, there was considerable disagreement between Bevin and Attlee;[11] but eventually the British decided to defer their various proposals in favour of the American view. Parts of Eritrea should go to Ethiopia; the other African territories should be set under United Nations trusteeship, with an Administrator assisted by an international Advisory Committee. Eventually the territories should become independent. What really set the cat among the pigeons was the Russian suggestion that they should themselves acquire trusteeship of Tripolitania – a proposal which would have set them in a position to wreak unlimited mischief on British and French interests in the Mediterranean, the Arab lands, and throughout Africa. It is difficult to believe that the Russians ever really saw Tripolitania as more than a bargaining counter for tangible advantages elsewhere. Bevin, however, was thoroughly alarmed, expressing privately the view that 'what the Russians really wanted was uranium'.[12] This view was reinforced when Molotov blandly suggested, 'if you won't give us one of the Italian colonies, we should be quite content to have the Belgian Congo'. Perhaps this was a joke; but the Belgian Congo was scarcely Bevin's to give, and he could hardly forget that it was the world's principal source of uranium.

Important though the Italian question was, it was apparently not the main cause of breakdown of the Foreign Ministers' Conference. Bevin made two serious attempts to discover from Molotov the gravamen of the trouble. A good many issues were discussed between the two men;[13] but they agreed that the main difficulty concerned Romania and Bulgaria. The British and Americans had both refused to recognise the new governments in those countries until they were satisfied about internal conditions.

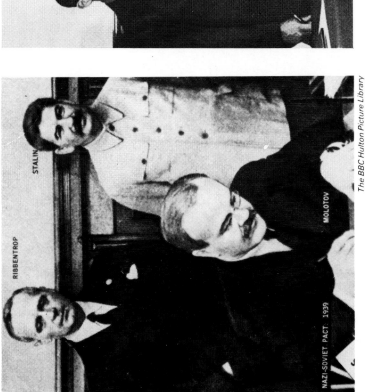

The BBC Hulton Picture Library

The Mansell Collection

RIBBENTROP

STALIN

NAZI-SOVIET PACT 1939

MOLOTOV

1 Different friends.
Molotov signs, and Stalin witnesses, (a) the Soviet-German Pact of August 1939 along with Ribbentrop; and (b) the Anglo-Soviet Mutual Assistance Pact of July 1941, along with Sir Stafford Cripps.

Blut, das sie nicht mehr abwaschen können:

DOKUMENTE

aus dem Walde von Katyn zeigen die Mordfratze der Sowjets

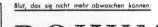

Die hier veröffentlichten erschütternden Bilder über den Massenmord von 11000 polnischen Offizieren durch die jüdische GPU, sind für alle Völker der Erde ein gellendes Alarmsignal: Vereinigt euch zum Kampf gegen die Weltpest!

Aufnahmen: Kremitz (Union)

Nun wissen sie, was Bolschewismus ist! Mit tiefstem Entsetzen finden Mitglieder einer polnischen Abordnung, denen Zutritt zu der Massenmordstätte gewährt wurde, die deutschen Nachrichten nicht nur bestätigt, sondern von der grausamen Wirklichkeit weit übertroffen

Offiziere aller Dienstgrade im Massengrab
Die Überreste des polnischen Brigadegenerals Bronislaw Bohatorewicz. An seiner Uniform und an gut erhaltenen Briefen, Ausweispapieren und Orden konnte er, wie zahlreiche seiner Kameraden, einwandfrei identifiziert werden

„Saubere" Arbeit der Sowjethenker: Genickschuß! Dieses grausige fotografische Dokument zeigt den Tod von bolschewistischer Mörderhand. Der Genickschuß, den fast alle bisher ausgegrabenen Leichen zeigen, ist die bevorzugte Justizform Moskaus

Sie hatten nicht einmal
Krieg mit den Sowjets!
Als die Bolschewisten im Herbst 1939 in Ostpolen einrückten, wurden 300000 polnische Soldaten darunter etwa 11000 Offiziere von ihnen interniert. Ein großer Teil davon verschwand spurlos. Jetzt enthüllen die Massengräber von Katyn, von denen wir hier eines zeigen, die gräßliche Wirklichkeit: Die polnischen Offiziere wurden allesamt von den Sowjets ermordet. Dieses Blut, das sie nicht mehr abwaschen können. Die Welt kann auf diese Schandtat nur eine Antwort geben: Kampf dem Bolschewismus bis zur völligen Ausrottung!

2 Katyn Massacre.
A German paper of 1943 gives pictures of the mass-grave of Poles who were probably massacred by the Russians in 1940.

3a Poles in exile.   *BBC Hulton Picture Library*

General W. Sikorski, Polish Prime Minister; Count E. Raczynski, Ambassador to London and A. Zaleski, Foreign Minister, in London, November 1939.

3b Czech crisis.   *BBC Hulton Picture Library*

Klement Gottwald, Communist Prime Minister of Czechoslovakia (back to camera, right) discussing composition of the new Government with President Benes, Mr A. Zapotocky and Mr V. Nosek (facing camera, left centre), 27 February 1948.

4b The Rival Buses.

4a Soviet wartime poster.
Translation: 'A year ago the struggle began for your liberation . . .
Your thanks is your work'.

ВАША БЛАГОДАРНОСТЬ—
ЭТО ВАШ ТРУД

Год тому назад началась борьба за
ваше освобождение!

5b The Loan Horse.
Ambassador Lord Halifax, and economist Lord Keynes, return from Washington with the American Loan. 'and don't look too carefully in his mouth'.

Punch, 12 December 1945

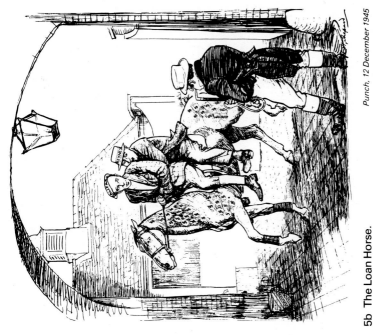

Punch, 7 February 1945

5a Trouble with some of the pieces.
Roosevelt, Stalin and Churchill at Yalta.

6a Special relationship.   *BBC Hulton Picture Library*
George C. Marshall (left), U.S. Secretary of State, and Ernest Bevin, U.K. Foreign Secretary at U.N.O. meeting in Paris, September 1948.

6b American diplomacy.   *BBC Hulton Picture Library*
Dean Acheson (facing camera) talks with Lewis Douglas, U.S. Ambassador in London, May 1950.

BBC Hulton Picture Library

Ivan Subasić

BBC Hulton Picture Library

Stanslaw Mikolajczyk

BBC Hulton Picture Library

Cordell Hull

BBC Hulton Picture Library

General Charles de Gaulle

Marshal Pietro Badaglio

7 Men of the time.

8 Turning point.
Pictures from the Berlin Air-Lift, 1948.

There had been some remarkable developments in both places immediately before the Conference. In Bulgaria, arrangements had been made for elections, which were due to be held on 26 August. The British and American Governments, however, soon reached the conclusion that these 'elections' would be a farce, for the electors would have no chance of choosing between conflicting points of view. A clear indication of the way the wind was blowing was provided when the Bulgarian émigré Communist Georgi Dimitrov was released from his various offices in the Soviet Union and authorised to return to Bulgaria, there to stand as a candidate for the ruling 'Fatherland Front'. The British and American representatives in Sofia were instructed to protest at the character of the elections. The ambit of State Department instructions to the American, Maynard Barnes, was not very clear, and he requested the Russian Chairman of the Control Commission to postpone the elections. Byrnes, the Secretary of State, sent an angry telegram to Barnes, claiming that the latter had exceeded his instructions – but not ordering him to withdraw his demand.[14] The British interpretation was that Byrnes would wait events and then repudiate Barnes, 'should the situation deteriorate'.[15] In other words, the Secretary of State would be in the clear, whatever happened. In the event, a message from Barnes to the effect that representations had succeeded crossed with Byrnes's remonstrances.[16] The election was delayed until mid-November, and, for a time, the Opposition was allowed the widest freedom of criticism.[17]

In Romania, a crisis occurred about the same time as these Bulgarian events, but with even less certain results. With encouragement from British and American representatives, King Michael formally requested Groza to broaden his government. When that demand failed, the King appealed to all the Big Three to assist in the formation of a more representative administration. The Americans made it clear that they were not prepared to recognise the ruling coalition as it stood.[18] Yet the State Department soon revealed a pusillanimity similar to that which it had shown in Bulgaria. The strongest constitutional weapon the King possessed was power to refuse assent to decrees promulgated by the Groza government. When he sought advice from the Americans as to whether he should use that power, the State Department told its representative at Bucharest to give the King no advice at all on the matter.[19] Groza was similarly unsure of the degree of support likely from his principal backers, and departed for Moscow early in September. He returned with some assurance of Russian support – though perhaps not quite as much as he had hoped.[20]

After the Foreign Ministers' Conference, Byrnes resolved to send a personal envoy, Mark Ethridge, to discover the true position in the

eastern Balkans. Ethridge's report confirmed the impressions of the
men on the spot. In Bulgaria, the Fatherland Front régime was
originally representative – though this 'has long ago ceased to be the
case'.[21] The elections which had been postponed from August to
November would not be 'a fair expression of the popular will'. In
spite of this, Barnes was not authorised to take action similar to that
which he had employed so effectively in August. Byrnes would do no
more than send a letter for transmission to the Prime Minister,
Kimon Georgiev, denying the representative character of the
elections. Georgiev, a strong anti-Communist, was already deeply
alarmed at tendencies within his country, and doubtless knew quite
as much about the situation as his informant. Unlike Byrnes,
however, he was not in a position to take action which would rectify
the situation. In the circumstances, the elections proceeded, and the
Fatherland Front achieved a huge majority.

Ethridge's report from Romania was equally emphatic and
depressing.

> The position of the Western Democracies is disintegrating fast, the
> Russian position becoming stronger all the time, and unless we
> can take firm and effective action in Romania it will soon be too
> late . . . The two political groups which have the support of the vast
> majority of the Romanian people are not only out of the
> government but their leaders are being harassed by the
> government, their political clubs largely taken over, their
> newspapers entirely suppressed and all public meetings of the
> opposition barred.[22]

The Western Democracies, the report added, would lose much moral
authority if they recognised a government constituted in such
circumstances.

In Hungary, progress towards democracy on the Western pattern
appeared a good deal more certain than in the eastern Balkans. In
September 1945, the American mission reported that non-
Communist political leaders were 'losing the sense of physical and
spiritual isolation which has frozen their will to resist the communist
drive'.[23] Early in October, municipal elections were held in Budapest,
in circumstances which seemed particularly favourable to Russian
wishes. The Communists and Social Democrats formed a common
list, and their only serious opponents in this highly urban
environment were the Smallholders Party. That essentially rural
party won a substantial majority. In the view of one qualified
American observer, 'many socialists voted for Smallholders as
protest against their party combining with communists'.[24] General
elections were due in Hungary a month later. Marshal Voroshilov,

the Soviet commander, suggested to the Smallholders leader that a common electoral list should be drawn up by all parties to the Coalition – which would have meant in effect that the voters would have no chance of choosing between rival candidates.[25] This advice was rejected. The component parties would make their individual appeals to the electorate – but it was agreed that the coalition would be reconstituted in the light of the result.[26] Polling took place in conditions to which no possible exception could be taken. The result was a great overall win for the Smallholders party, who polled 61 per cent of the votes, and won a slightly larger proportion of the seats. The Communists ran third, a little way behind the Social Democrats.[27]

Reconstitution of the Coalition was not easy, because – as in most European countries about this period – the Communists demanded the Ministry of the Interior, which would give them control of the police. Another spell of intense negotiations followed, with the eventual upshot that the Interior did indeed go to a Communist – but the official directly concerned with police was a Smallholder. Any dispute between him and his immediate chief would be referred to the Prime Minister, who was also a Smallholder. The net effect was that neither Communists nor opponents of Communism were able to 'purge' the police in their own favour.[28] The real irony of the situation was that the new Minister of the Interior, on whose appointment the Communists insisted so strongly, was Imre Nagy, who – eleven years later – would play the leading heroic and tragic role in the Hungarian rising.

In Austria, which was occupied by the four major Allies, political tendencies were not very different from those in Hungary. The occupying Power recognised the provisional government towards the end of October, and elections were held the following month in free conditions. The Catholic-Democratic People's Party won eighty-five seats, the Social Democrats seventy-six, the Communists only four. Nor was there much evidence of Russia 'tightening the screw' in other countries under her own occupation during the closing months of 1945. Czechoslovakia had been under mainly Russian occupation at the end of the war, but a small area was held by the Americans. Before the year was over, both Allies agreed to withdraw their troops. In Poland, the Anglo-Americans seemed to believe that they had at least saved the Peasant Party by injecting Mikolajczyk into the government; and so long as he considered it useful to remain, it seemed fair to assume that the Communists were not having everything their own way. In fact the clearest example of Communists grasping for absolute power came from Yugoslavia – the one significant country whose indigenous Communists had 'made their own revolution'. Final collapse of the Tito-Subasić

agreement was signalled early in October, when Subasić himself and
the remaining anti-Communist ministers finally withdrew from the
government.

In Greece, where the British were in occupation, the trend was very
different. At the beginning of 1945, the threat to liberty came
exclusively from the Communist-dominated EAM. As the year
advanced, 'right-wing' forces began to behave as badly as those on
the 'left'. Meanwhile, the authority of regular political government
began to collapse. The 'Varkiza agreement', which was concluded in
February, had promised the establishment of a parliamentary
democracy; but this soon became a mockery, as a series of weak
governments followed each other in quick succession, amid a welter
of intrigues and recriminations. Fortunately, it was possible to
dissuade the King from returning to Greece, for violence would
assuredly have flared up more strongly had he appeared on the
scene. There was an uneasy realisation that British troops must
remain in Greece for a considerable time. The alternative was civil
war, in which – whoever won – democracy would surely perish.

Thus the broad pattern of events in eastern Europe shortly after
Potsdam was strikingly different from the immediate aftermath of
Yalta, and also from what was to happen from 1946 onwards. The
Russians seemed to be feeling the ground, rather than acting with
ruthless determination. In Bulgaria and Romania, they drew back
when the Americans challenged them, and only tightened their grip
when it became apparent that the United States was not really
determined to resist the Soviet hegemony. In Finland, Hungary,
Austria and Czechoslovakia, Russia did not seriously interfere with
progress towards parliamentary democracy. In Greece and
Yugoslavia, developments were in less felicitous directions; but in
those places too the Russians appeared to be leaving matters to
internal forces, or to other Allies, rather than attempting to compel
the pace. Why, we may fairly ask, were the Russians acting in this
unwontedly moderate manner, which contrasts sharply with the
general course of their behaviour during the closing years of war and
the first few years of peace?

A simple answer might be that the Russians were moved by fear of
the atomic bomb; but they must have guessed that the number
currently in existence was small, and in any event attitudes in the
United States were not approaching the point where conflict with
former Allies came within the range of general contemplation. A
much likelier reason for the Soviet Union to desire friendly relations
with the United States at that stage was economic. During the war,
America had distributed vast quantities of material through 'Lend-
Lease' to her various Allies. By far the largest recipients were the
United Kingdom, which had obtained over $13 thousand million of

assistance, and the Soviet Union which had received $9 thousand
million. In the British case, over $4 thousand million had been sent
to the United States in 'reverse Lend-Lease' while the Soviet Union
had sent practically nothing; so the net receipts were equal in the
case of America's two principal Allies.[29] As far back as October 1943,
Russia had evinced interest in acquiring capital goods from America
after the war, with some kind of financial aid to support her in so
doing.[30] Lend-Lease supplies were cut off when war ended, as
everyone had anticipated – though resentment was caused by the
peremptory way in which this was done.

Early in January 1945, Molotov presented Harriman with an *aide-
memoire* requesting a thirty-year credit of $6 thousand million at $2^1/_2$
per cent interest.[31] In the next day or two, the Americans were given
to understand 'that the Soviet Government placed high importance
on a large post-war credit as a basis for the development of "Soviet-
American relations" '.[32] Morganthau was willing to recommend an
even larger sum for a longer period at a lower interest rate 'for the
purchase of reconstruction goods in the United States'.[33] The
American Treasury view was that the advantage to Russia of taking
the loan was by no means enormous: '$2 thousand million in credits
would speed up reconstruction only by some three or four months'.
Thus the Soviet Union was 'in a position to take a highly independent
position in negotiations regarding foreign credits'.[34] Yet the
importance of American loans to the Soviet economy would depend
in part on the degree of wartime destruction, which the Americans
could not possibly know. They may well have underestimated the
urgency of Russia's needs, and therefore the international
advantages which could be obtained by a disposition to
accommodate them on suitable terms. A 'package deal' involving a
generous American loan to Russia on the one side, and Russian
military and political withdrawal from much of Europe on the other,
might have been within Soviet contemplation. A loan, however,
would require Congressional approval. No American Government
can ever take such approval for granted to the extent that a British
Government backed by a 'safe' majority may take parliamentary
approval for granted; and in the current atmosphere of increasing
suspicion among the American people, Congressional approval was
– as Eden wrote to Churchill – 'at the moment out of the question'.[35]
The Russians did not immediately abandon the idea, and it remained
sufficiently important in Stalin's mind for the Marshal to raise it
when a delegation of Congressmen visited the Soviet Union in
September.

If there is doubt to what extent financial questions affected
America's relations with Russia in the immediate aftermath of war,
there is no doubt that such questions radically affected her relations

with Britain. These relations fell far short of the idyllic. After the ill-fated Foreign Ministers' Conference, Bevin reported to the Cabinet: 'We were faced with increasing hosility and distrust between the United States and Soviet delegations, each of whom sought to strengthen its own position without regard to our point of view.'[36] Nor were the diplomatic questions to which the Foreign Secretary was alluding the most serious points of difference. The main problems were financial, and here a great deal of largely gratuitous misunderstanding arose. Well before the end of the war, American official opinion was moving to the view that the policies of trade restriction which had been so generally pursued during the inter-war period had led to a general reduction of trade, to the disadvantage of all. The United States was well conscious that she was in the strongest economic position in the world. This gave her an opportunity to curtail these restrictions, which was – in the words of the London Ambassador – 'unparalleled but fleeting'.[37] This view appears to have been generally accepted by those guiding American policy. Britain's part was perceived to be of crucial importance. Her immediate financial condition was precarious; but she nevertheless preserved a position of great influence upon other countries. There was considerable danger that the British would 'work out their financial problems within the sterling area by the devices of blocked balances, exchange control, exchange pooling, bilateral clearing arrangements and forced exports in liquidation of sterling balances'.[38] In order to avert such policies, the American Government contemplated making Britain a loan, which would be tied to policies of trade liberalisation. This feature was a far more important consideration, from the American point of view, than any interest which such a loan would secure. Far from wishing to damage or exploit Britain, the United States considered it imperative from the aspect of her world economic strategy that Britain should prosper. People in Britain who had long fulminated from the political platform against the iniquities of bankers in general and American bankers in particular, forgot that it is not in a banker's interest to ruin his best potential client.

In the late summer of 1945, conversations began between financial representatives of the two countries. The most prominent members of the British team were Lord Keynes, who stood at the height of his world fame as an economist, and the Ambassador to Washington, Earl Halifax. The abrupt end of most forms of Lend-Lease made a loan urgent for Britain. Yet the talks did not lead to an early agreement. Within the British Cabinet itself there was a sharp division between the majority, who were anxious to clinch with the Americans, and two 'left-wingers', Emanuel Shinwell and Aneurin Bevan, who would not accept the idea of a loan with 'strings'.[39] By the end of November – in the words of the Chancellor of the Exchequer – the British negotiators in Washington were 'completely spun out'.[40] The talks seemed about to collapse. In desperation, the Government despatched Sir Edward Bridges, Permanent Secretary to the Treasury, to Washington. 'It became clear,' wrote Dalton just afterwards, 'that he had taken command.' Where the celebrities had failed for three months, it took the civil servant less than a week to secure agreement, which became known to the British Government on 6 December.

It was one thing for the negotiators to agree on a basis of recommendations, but a very different thing to persuade the respective governments and legislatures to accept the substance of these recommendations. While the Washington discussions were still in their final and critical phase, the existence of the Cabinet split and the identity of the two main opponents of the loan were communicated to the press – in circumstances which suggest a political leak rather than journalistic acumen. When the proposals came before the House of Commons, a somewhat astonishing situation developed. The official Opposition leadership recommended abstention on the ostensible grounds that they had not been parties to the negotiations, nor kept currently informed: hence they could not properly judge the merits of the arrangement. This – as the American Ambassador observed – was 'political and weak'.[41] The real reason was obviously to avert a split in the Conservative Party. As it was, both main parties were deeply divided. Including tellers, a hundred MPs voted against the agreements: seventy-three Conservatives and associates, twenty-four Labour and three Independents. Eight Conservatives rebelled in the other direction and supported the Government. Only the Liberals – a highly fissile group in this period – showed unanimity in favour of the agreements, to the amazement and delight of their parliamentary leader, Clement Davies.[42] The profound intra-party disagreements revealed in the division lobbies were quite exceptional in British political experience, and the grounds for dissent from the agreements astonishingly diverse; for Protectionist Conservatives well to the 'right' of the party joined hands with Labour rebels, of whom some were near-Communist. Even the House of Lords could not be taken for granted. The loan agreements as such constituted a 'money' matter, outside the power of the upper House to block; but the general trading agreements which had been concluded at Bretton Woods long before were tied indissolubly to the loan question, and these could be delayed for a very long time if the Lords proved recalcitrant. At one time, it appeared that Lord Beaverbrook would head a formidable opposition; but this fizzled out, and the eventual hostile vote was derisory.

The battle, as we shall see later, was still far from over, and several months would elapse before Congress gave its rather grudging approval. What admitted no doubt, however, was that Congress was in no mood to make the vast loan to Russia of which people had been talking glibly earlier in the year. Whatever positive incentives the Russians once had to accommodate American opinion had now disappeared.

In this far from felicitous atmosphere, the Foreign Ministers of the Big Three met at Moscow in the second part of December 1945. American diplomatic documents do not seem to treat this meeting as a resumption of the Council of Foreign Ministers. The French and Chinese were not invited; and the Americans did not send a bipartisan delegation. Agreement of a sort emerged; though hardly the kind of agreement which either the Americans or Russians had originally desired. The agreement turned on political division rather than economic cooperation.

Byrnes made huge concessions to the Russians over Balkan questions. As a particularly well-informed American diplomat wrote, he 'signed, against the advice of almost all the members of the American delegation, an agreement that we would not put up for membership in the Bulgarian Government two men who had every right to be there'.[43] So also with Romania; the Secretary of State did not baulk when the Russians made it clear that Maniu and like-minded men would be excluded.[44] In other words, Byrnes conceded without difficulty that the governments of both countries should exclude the men who were likeliest to form nuclei of opposition to an eventual Communist take-over. The road now seemed open for American recognition of the two governments, without taking too seriously the Yalta 'Declaration on Liberated Europe'.

There seems some connection – though it is not easy to prove this – between the American concessions in the Balkans and the Russian behaviour over Japan. We have already noted how determined the Americans were that MacArthur should be allowed a free hand, unencumbered by a Control Commission. Since the time of Potsdam, considerable correspondence had been passing between Stalin and Truman on the matter. Talks now took place at Moscow between Byrnes and Stalin, outside the main discussions, and seemed to produce agreement in favour of retaining the *status quo*, with America firmly in command. There was the form of an agreement over Korea: three-Power trusteeship, leading to the establishment of a credible independent government. Byrnes was also able to report 'complete agreement' over the mechanics of devising peace treaties with Italy and the 'minor enemies'.[45] Was there perhaps a tacit deal to the effect that America would wink at Russian domination in the eastern Balkans and in north Korea – in return for Russian toleration of American control in Japan? This is impossible to prove; but after the Foreign Ministers' meeting, both countries behaved as if that was the case.

There were moves towards some agreement on the question of nuclear energy. On Byrnes's suggestion, it was agreed that the Big Three, along with France, China and Canada, should sponsor a commission of the United Nations to study problems of control, and submit recommendations. This was very far indeed from a full solution – but it seemed a useful first step.

Both the character of the American delegation and the nature of the decisions which emerged from the Moscow conference brought the 'bipartisan' character of American foreign policy under severe strain. The position of Senator Vandenberg, a very influential Republican and Chairman of the Senate Foreign Affairs Committee, is crucial here. After a long career as an isolationist, Vandenberg announced his conversion to collective security earlier in 1945, and from then on was in close and generally friendly contact with the administration. Vandenberg had already evinced some doubts about the proposed British loan – though not outright opposition.[46] What particularly disturbed the Senator about the Moscow conference were the atomic energy proposals – which he apparently misunderstood.[47] When Truman was able to assure him that 'as long as he was President, no production secrets would be given away prior to arrangements for a system of inspection',[48] Vandenberg was more or less mollified. No less significant were the doubts of Admiral Leahy, the President's Chief of Staff. The attitudes of such men could be vital when the administration required Congressional support on matters touching on foreign policy. For Congress was becoming restive. The House of Representatives passed a resolution to the effect that American funds should not be used in support of United Nations relief operations 'in any country which impeded American newsmen in reporting UNRRA operations'.[49] This would, in current conditions, have excluded UNRRA support from countries under Soviet military control. The amendment was later dropped; but it was surely significant that nearly all the Republicans and a substantial contingent of southern Democrats had given it support.

Doubts were also sown in the President's mind about the general value of the Moscow decisions. Unfortunately, irreconcilable accounts have been preserved of meetings between Truman and Byrnes shortly after the return from Moscow.[50] It is not easy to evaluate the various factors – human and political – which determined relations between the two men, or to be sure how far Truman's confidence in his Secretary of State was undermined. Byrnes was certainly behaving in a very high-handed manner; and Truman had good grounds for thinking that he had not been kept as closely in touch with negotiations as his responsibilities demanded;[51] for the President's position as Chief Executive makes him ultimately accountable for diplomatic decisions. America's closest Ally also had grounds of complaint against the Secretary of State. Bevin's report to the British Cabinet suggests that there were important features of the situation on which Britain was kept in the dark.[52] Perhaps there were overriding reasons for some of this secrecy; but the whole atmosphere was not one to inspire confidence.

Thus did matters stand at the turn of 1945–6. People still spoke of the 'Allies', though the term 'Iron Curtain' was coming into currency on both sides of the Atlantic. The general picture suggested that Russia on one side and the Western Allies on the other were gradually disentangling their conflicting interests, in an atmosphere, no doubt, of hard bargaining but scarcely of conflict. The 'spheres of influence' principle first applied at the 'Tolstoy' conference in 1944 and initially opposed by the Americans was being tacitly accepted by all concerned. The Allies would not share power or 'influence' but could apparently agree more or less amicably to divide it. This 'Iron Curtain' situation was in one sense the very antithesis of a 'Cold War'; for an Iron Curtain implies mutual withdrawal to impregnable positions; while any kind of war – cold or otherwise – implies that at least one party is attempting to push back the frontiers of the other. Many people, both in Britain and in the United States, were uneasy about the intentions of their countries' governments; but in neither place had the somewhat rickety structure of a 'bipartisan foreign policy' broken down.

12

1946

'The fundamental tenet of the communist philosophy embraced by Soviet leaders is that the peaceful coexistence of communist and capitalist nations is impossible.' Report by Clark M. Clifford, Special Counsel to President Truman, 24 September 1946. HST/MISC. 14.

In the course of 1946, many of the issues at stake between the Big Three were apparently resolved: most of them very much in Russia's favour. The countries of eastern Europe provide a series of striking object-lessons which show the incredibly versatile behaviour of the Communists, and the great skill with which they adapted themselves to the special circumstances of the individual countries in order to tighten their grip, without dangerously antagonising the Governments of Britain and America. These methods were applied whether the countries concerned had been allies or enemies.

It had been agreed at the December Conference in Moscow that the Romanian Government should be broadened, by incorporating members of the Opposition. The two Opposition politicians who really mattered were the Peasant Party leader, Iuliu Maniu, and the Liberal Party Leader, Dinu Bratianu. Both men were passed over, and two nonentities brought in as 'representatives' of those parties. This slight genuflexion in favour of representative institutions enabled the American and British Governments to recognise the new Romanian administration early in February. Thereafter, the newcomers were excluded from influence by first giving them no Ministerial portfolios, and later not inviting them to Cabinet meetings. Notes of protest from Britain and America fell thick and fast during all these proceedings; but no more effective action was possible.

In July, two new electoral laws were approved by the Romanian Cabinet, in the teeth of opposition by the Peasant and Liberal parties. One – to abolish the Senate – was plainly unconstitutional; the other 'was drafted to facilitate all possible electoral frauds'[1] The

Opposition leaders tried vainly to persuade the King to refuse assent to these laws – thus forcing a major crisis and compelling the Russians to show their hand. In November an election was held in conditions of general intimidation and electoral malpractices – with inevitable results. It was swiftly followed by a mass trial of ninety-one defendants, much on the model which Vyshinsky had established a decade earlier in the Soviet Union.

In Bulgaria, the Opposition members whom the Foreign Ministers had decided to inject into the Government were a good deal more wary than their Romanian counterparts, for they insisted on receiving either the Ministry of the Interior or the Ministry of Justice. The last thing the Communists would do was to yield control of the police or the courts, and this condition was refused. The British and American Governments therefore decided not to recognise Bulgaria. This did not radically affect the course of events within the country. There followed a series of political crises, as a result of which more and more of the anti-Communist members of the Fatherland Front were dropped from the government. A referendum on the monarchy was held in September, with the predictable conclusion that nine-year old King Simeon departed to join his grandfather Victor Emmanuel III of Italy (who had recently abdicated), in exile. In October a General Election took place. There appears to have been a good deal of intimidation during the campaign period, but the actual polling was held in conditions 'certainly no worse than is usual on Balkan election days'.[2] The Opposition, who mustered about 100 seats, did not represent a wholly negligible factor in Bulgarian politics. In November, however, the last significant anti-Communist – Prime Minister Kimon Georgiev – was driven to resign from the government, and was succeeded by the erstwhile Soviet citizen Dimitrov.

Hungary presented different problems both for the Soviet Union and for the West. It will be recalled that a truly free election in 1945 had delivered a huge majority to the Smallholders, who thereafter formed the main partners in the inevitable coalition. The Russians, whether by accident or design, undermined the authority of the Smallholders by wrecking the country's economy. As victors in a defeated country, they followed the ancient practices of looting, requisitioning and taking reparations – the borderlines between the three always being doubtful. The country was also forced to support 600,00 occupying troops – a contingent for which no imaginable military justification could be conceived. To set this figure in perspective, we may observe that the British Government took it as self-evident that Greece (whose population is similar to that of Hungary) could not possibly support an army one-sixth as large, composed of its own citizens.[3]

These and other economic burdens imposed by Russia were – as the American Minister in Hungary wrote in April – 'largely responsible for rapid deterioration of Hungarian economy and for runaway inflation now ravaging the country'.[4] The measure of inflation in Hungary in 1946 exceeded even the worst period of the Weimar Republic. In one week in February, the pengö was seen to drop from 800,000 to 1.8 millions to the dollar: and when finally replaced by a new currency in August, rated well over four million millions to the dollar. In such circumstances, the rural population abandoned money for barter; while the townspeople more or less starved.

Thus was the morale of the Smallholders Party sapped. As the Hungarian Prime Minister explained to an American representative, his party must somehow preserve the coalition; for the only other courses possible were either a Smallholders Government which would catch the blame for all the country's troubles, or a 'leftist' coalition which would act like the Bela Kun regime of 1919.[5] In such circumstances, the Communists and their associates could ask more or less their own price for remaining in the coalition. They first required that elements whom they described as 'reactionary' should be eliminated from the Smallholders Party itself. Thereafter, with assistance from the Soviet-dominated Control Commission, they compelled the Government to dissolve a wide range of bodies to which they had objection – even organisations as apparently innocuous as the Boy Scouts and the Catholic youth organisation. Meanwhile, Communists and their associates had thoroughly entrenched themselves in administrative positions of the state.[6]

As Poland was an Allied country, and the Anglo-Americans were deeply committed to Mikolajczyk, more caution was required. The Communists preferred for the time being to attack weaker foes. A referendum was held on 30 June, on various questions of government policy: abolition of the senate; nationalisation of industry; division of large estates; and the new western frontiers. On some of these matters, public approval would probably have been granted freely; but to forestall difficulties over the others, more than twelve hundred members of the Peasant Party were arrested shortly before the poll, and the eventual results were, apparently, falsified.[7]

The overriding concern of the government majority in Poland was so to manipulate matters that they would win clear control in the election which was due in the early part of 1947. The Peasant Party was offered 25 per cent of seats in the Cabinet if Mikolajczyk himself were excluded – but refused the temptation. The Socialist Party was more vulnerable, because it had no member who enjoyed special protection from the Western Democracies. A combination of bribes and threats prevented the party from holding its Conference in July;

while the Government proceeded to give its fullest support to a small dissident group within the party who were prepared to take the line required of them.[8] By the end of 1946, terrorism was general. It was said that 150,000 people were under arrest for political reasons; while 10,000 members of the Peasant Party had recently been arrested, in evident anticipation of the forthcoming elections.[9] Mikolajczyk seriously considered withdrawing his own party entirely from those elections, or making a formal appeal to the Yalta Powers to intervene in support of their promises. British and American authorities were appalled at the consequences which would ensue in that event, and worked desperately to prevent any such action.[10]

Czechoslovakia affords a striking and unique example of a country which, throughout the past crucial decade, had sought to retain genuine parliamentary democracy, yet to adopt a foreign policy thoroughly consonant with the wishes of the Soviet Union. Like so many other countries, it experienced its first post-war elections in the spring of 1946. Only citizens of Slav race were permitted to vote. As well over a quarter of the pre-1938 population had been non-Slav, a great many people were excluded. This strange electorate left the Communists as the largest single party, with about 38 per cent of the total vote and a similar proportion of seats. No government could possibly be formed without some kind of coalition. It took considerable time to produce a new Cabinet; but eventually the Communist Klement Gottwald presided over a government in which all of the substantial parties were represented in approximate proportion to their electoral strength, while the portfolios of Foreign Affairs and National Defence were held by the important non-party figures Jan Masaryk and General Svoboda respectively. The key post of the Interior – most important of all for totalitarian parties who are preparing to take over control of a country – was firmly in Communist hands.

In those countries of continental Europe which had been liberated by the Anglo-Americans, the issue between Communists and their enemies was not yet clearly decided at the beginning of 1946 – nor, indeed, at the end of the year. In Greece, the overriding concern of the occupying British forces was to fend off all insurgent bands, whether of right or of left, and to protect the land from possible invasion by its three northern neighbours, in the hope that a plebiscite on the monarchy could be held in conditions of freedom. Once the country could be established as a functioning parliamentary democracy, secure from external attack and internal violence, British troops could be withdrawn. Matters, however, were not working out that way at all. An all-party British parliamentary delegation was present in Greece during the plebiscite period, and reported in December 1946. The delegation concluded that 'while intimidation and malpractices existed on both sides and was on the whole more pronounced in the case of the right, there is no reason to doubt that the King would in any event have secured a majority'.[11] In more general terms, 'the delegation's conclusion is that right and left wings share responsibility to the disorders and they are not prepared to say which group is the more culpable'.[12] The presence of British troops was 'appreciated by all but the extreme left'[13] – but the delegation was very far from sanguine about the country's prospects of internal peace.

More critical still was the situation in western Europe, and above all in France. Late in 1945, a coalition government, bearing all the superficial marks of real strength, was set up under General de Gaulle. Within weeks it collapsed, and the General withdrew temporarily from politics, amid widespread mutual recriminations. In the early part of 1946, the Russians supplied France with large quantities of wheat, for palpably political motives. Similar considerations prompted the Americans to do the same.[14] During 1946, the country experienced two General Elections and two constitutional referenda; and not one of them gave a really convincing verdict. The referendum in May resulted in rejection of a constitution which had been supported by the Communists and (with less enthusiasm) by the Socialists. In the following month a General Election was held in which the Catholic MRP was returned as the largest single party, and the Communists secured marginally more than a quarter of the places in the Chamber. A second referendum in October at last gave the country a Constitution; but another General Election the following month produced a substantial increase in the Communist poll, and set them by a narrow margin as the largest single party in the Chamber.

Here was a situation which, on the face of it, might easily lead either to Communist control or to civil war. Yet a curiously undramatic conclusion emerged. The Communists demanded that their leader, Maurice Thorez, should be appointed Prime Minister; but he was voted down by the Assembly. Then the MRP proposed their own Georges Bidault, and he was likewise rejected. Finally, the President turned to the veteran socialist, Léon Blum. After vainly trying to form a coalition, Blum eventually produced a purely Socialist government. This received almost unanimous support from the Deputies, though only about one-sixth of the seats were held by that party. On this strange political note, the year 1946 came to an end.

Nowhere else in western Europe did the Communist tide run as high as in France. In Italy, Belgium and the Netherlands, elections were held in the course of 1946. In all of those countries the Communists secured substantial representation, but they did not come in sight of power. Even in Spain there was no attempt to spark off an armed revolt against Franco.

On the other side of the world, in eastern Asia, a kind of uneasy truce prevailed. The process of disarming the Japanese and evicting them from occupied territories was a slow one: late in November 1945 there were still 700,000 Japanese soldiers in Manchuria alone.[15] Nor was it by any means clear how the major Allies would line up in eastern Asia. Truman was still convinced 'that both England [sic] and Russia wanted a weak and divided China ... We were the only big nation that wanted a united democratic China.'[16] Nobody in Britain or America seemed very sure how close relations were between Russia and the Chinese Communists, and American efforts were still bent towards securing some kind of reconciliation between the Kuomintang and the Communists. There were intermittent outbreaks of fighting between the two forces in China; but it was far short of all-out war.

Control of Japan rested firmly in the hands of General MacArthur. As in the European countries, elections were held; but the Communists here secured only a derisory share of the seats. The likely development of Korea was less certain, with the north currently under Russian occupation, the south under American. At the Foreign Ministers' Conference at the end of 1945, it had been agreed to set up a democratic government for the whole country, and the decision taken to establish a commission, with representatives from the two Commands, charged to consult with Korean organisations and thereafter to submit proposals for consideration by the Big Three and China. In March 1946, the Joint Commission met. The Americans contended that all Korean groups should be free to express their views to the Commission. The Russians, however, argued that only those Koreans who had accepted the Moscow proposals should be invited. As nearly all the political parties in Korea had criticised the proposals sharply because they were seen to delay independence, this suggestion would mean that only Communists and their associates could participate. This was obviously unacceptable to the Americans, and the Joint Commission broke down on 8 May.

The American Government – conscious of the strength of Korean nationalist opinion, and under strong domestic pressure to retrench on military spending – was all too anxious to pull out of Korea. By the end of the summer, they had decided to withdraw 10 per cent of their troops each month, with the intention that these should be replaced by Koreans, who would gradually develop experience.[17] The situation in the North was utterly different. Just after collapse of the Commission, Truman sent a personal representative to the Russian zone. The report showed that the Russians were in the process of establishing a Communist state, under firm surveillance of the Red Army, and in conditions closely resembling those operating in eastern Europe.[18]

In some matters, cooperation between Communist and non-Communist countries continued. The Council of Foreign Ministers held long and complex meetings, as a result of which a Peace Conference was eventually convened to deal with Italy and the 'minor enemies'. The Peace Conference concluded its meetings in the autumn, with recommendations for peace treaties which were to be signed formally in the new year. Heavy economic penalties were exacted from Germany's eastern associates, but Soviet troops were soon to be withdrawn. Territorial arrangements in the Balkans followed broadly the pattern prevailing immediately before the German invasion of Russia, save that the whole of Transylvania reverted to Romania.

Italy presented more serious problems. Most of Venezia Giulia passed to Yugoslavia, but Monfalcone and Gorizia remained with Italy, and Trieste was established as a 'free territory'. France secured minor gains in the north-west of Italy. The Dalmatian islands passed to Yugoslavia, the Dodecanese to Greece. Italy was required to renounce all her colonies; but the victors could reach no agreement about their ultimate destiny, and were forced to advertise that disagreement to the world by announcing that the matter would be reviewed within a year.

The future of Germany remained unresolved. Meanwhile the Western Powers found maintenance of their Zones an increasingly burdensome operation. Any attempt to alleviate these burdens would, to a large extent, predetermine the character of the future Germany. The Morganthau Plan was undeniably dead; but any other sort of Germany could pose the gravest difficulites and dangers for all the Allies. If Germany was to be a unitary state, then any kind of balance between the Allies would be upset. The Western countries were appalled at consequences which would flow if a united Germany became Communist; no doubt the Russians were equally alarmed at the prospect that it might form close links with the West. A loose federation would probably be the best solution if it could be made permanent; but this presupposed genuine goodwill between ex-Allies, which palpably did not exist. The one solution which neither Eastern nor Western Allies favoured or perhaps even considered possible was that Germany should be permanently divided into two states, one associated with the West and one with Russia; yet, in the course of 1946, matters began to drift in that direction.

The Russians clearly had no intention of cooperating closely with the other occupying Powers. The French, for the time being, were satisfied with existing arrangements, for their own zone was economically profitable; furthermore it included the Saar, which many Frenchmen desired to incorporate into France. The precarious political balance in France itself made any strongly pro-Western or pro-Russian policy impossible, and there were perceived advantages in trying to play one side against the other. The British and American zones, however, were economic liabilities.

In May, Bevin circulated a Memorandum to the Cabinet, in which the possibility of zonal fusion was considered. Arguments were adduced for both sides; but the general tenor was against fusion – for such a policy 'would in effect amount to bringing western Germany into a Western anti-Soviet bloc [and] would mean an irreparable break with the Russians'.[19] A further consideration was that Berlin would be isolated within the Russian zone. In Bevin's view, the Western Powers would soon be dislodged from the capital.

In the early part of 1946, the Americans were also undecided whether to try to unite their own German zone with that of any other cooperative Ally. In the middle of the year, however, they came strongly to the view that economic fusion of the British and American zones was both possible and desirable. Byrnes approached Bevin privately on the matter in July,[20] but no immediate British decision was taken. Indeed, it was not until December that the British Cabinet accepted the idea of fusion of the two zones.[21] Even so it was to be for economic purposes only, and there was an open offer to the French and the Russians to bring their own zones into the union whenever they wished.

Broadly speaking, the Eastern and Western Allies were disentangling their interests during 1946, and retreating into separate compartments. The diplomatic trend, in other words, was towards a kind of 'iron curtain' situation. The differences between them, however, were increasingly made matters of intense public controversy – and in that sense there was a clear beginning to the 'Cold War'. The process of exhibiting and parading differences became increasingly deliberate and pointed on both sides. The United Nations provided a particularly spectacular forum for dialectics and histrionics.

The original issue concerned Iran. Curiously, it appears that none of the Big Three had intended the controversy to be raised in the manner in which it was. During the war, northern Iran had been occupied by Russians, the south by British. There was good reason for this: as matters stood at the time, either Germans or Japanese or both of them might have driven through to the Gulf. In 1943, Britain and the United States signed agreements guaranteeing the future independence of Iran; but Stalin demurred when Roosevelt suggested that Russia should do the same – indicating 'that Russia needed a warm-water port and would like to have one on the Persian Gulf'.[22] When the war ended, the Russians showed no disposition to leave the country, and the Iranian Government resolved to lodge a complaint before the Security Council of the United Nations, which was currently meeting in London. Neither the British nor the Americans wished that the new organisation should be confronted at such an early stage in its career with a dispute in which major Allies were likely to take different views; but neither had any very good technical grounds for objecting. After all, the principal purpose of the United Nations was to solve international disputes.

Within forty-eight hours of the Iranian complaint, the Soviet Union had moved to the counter-attack – not against Iran, however, but against Britain. Formal complaint was lodged because British forces remained in Greece; while the Ukraine delegate at the same time protested against the presence of British trops in what was then still the Dutch East Indies. The Soviet and Ukraine delegates were on much weaker technical ground than the Iranians, for the British troops were present with the willing – indeed, eager – permission of the recognised political authorities in the territories concerned, while in Iran, the lawful government was the complainant.

The real point of the Soviet and Ukrainian attacks was an appeal to world public opinion, rather than an appeal to the assembled diplomats. Neither the Greek nor the Iranian government was particularly attractive, while British action in the East Indies could readily be represented as an imperialistic venture – which would be highly unpopular in much of the world, not least in the United States. At a meeting of the American Cabinet in November 1945. Byrnes had declared that 'the British were as bad as the Russians in wanting to hold their troops in Iran';[23] so on that issue too, the Americans could hardly be expected to rush to Britain's assistance. At this stage of proceedings, Russia's main international antagonist appeared to the world to be Britain, rather than the United States. That condition of affairs would not last long; but in a wider sense these encounters very much set the tone for future sessions of the United Nations. Although its agencies continued to perform many useful functions, sessions of the General Assembly and of the Security Council were very soon seen by journalists and the public mainly as great sounding-boards for complaints and counter-complaints by erstwhile Allies against each other.

Next blast came from Stalin. On 9 February he delivered a speech which – as regaled to most British readers[24] – appeared to be no more than a Marxist analysis of the genesis of the Second World War – contentious, no doubt, but scarcely a matter for international concern. Americans noted the sting in the tail. Stalin went on to declare that the forces of imperialism and capitalism – which, in his view, had caused the recent war – were still operating; and the Soviet Union must therefore arm to resist them. The Soviet people, he declared, must build up their strategic industries in preparation for 'any eventuality'. Where in the world, we may ask, could those forces exist which Stalin feared, save in other Allied countries?

When the British House of Commons came to debate foreign affairs, in the latter part of February, the discussion was described by one newspaper as 'being on Anglo-Russian relations rather than on foreign relations in general'. The undercurrent, cabled the American Ambassador, 'was one of heightened apprehension as to Soviet motive and intentions, coupled with the hope of ascertaining them specifically and dim realisation that solution was not in Britain's hands'.[25] Early in March, Churchill delivered a speech at Fulton, Missouri, which reverberated round the world. As with so many speeches which produced great excitement among contemporaries, we may read it today and wonder what all the fuss was about. This particular oration contained many unexceptionable features. The ex-Prime Minister called for strengthening of the United Nations, and of the 'fraternal association' between Britain and America. He pressed for a proper understanding with the Soviet Union. In a more controversial, but scarcely original, vein, he confuted the idea of disseminating atomic secrets until the organisation of the United Nations had emerged from its infancy. The particular feature of the Fulton speech which attracted most criticism was Churchill's concern to check further advances by the Communists, who – in the view of the ex-Prime Minister – sought the 'fruits of war', but not war itself. Many people read into this a strong hint that a military alliance should be developed between Britain and the United States.

Churchill's massive prestige, and the fact that Truman was present on the platform when the speech was delivered, raised the question of whether he was speaking the views of the British or American Governments, or both. Today it is clear that the British Government at any rate had no foreknowledge of the speech;[26] but it is also clear that the Russians did not believe this, and continued to feel resentment and suspicion long afterwards. When a new British Ambassador, Sir Maurice Peterson, was accredited to Moscow late in May, Stalin raised the matter of the Fulton speech. Peterson explained that Churchill did not speak as a member of the British Government, nor with its encouragement. Stalin, reported the Ambassador, 'continued to dispute this. When I insisted that Mr. Churchill had spoken as a private individual he said, "There are no such private individuals in this country".'[27] That was true, and Stalin knew full well why it was true; but it does exemplify the way in which even the best-informed people in totalitarian countries may honestly misjudge the way matters work in democracies.

The Fulton speech also produced a great deal of comment in the United States. Much of this was strongly favourable; other parts bitterly hostile. Most important of all the American critics at this stage was Henry A. Wallace, Secretary of Commerce in Truman's administration, who called the speech 'shocking'. Wallace's activities will shortly demand much attention; but it is important to bear in mind the fact that a substantial number of Americans considered it had been no more than a regrettable accident which gave the first office to Truman.

Even measures designed to improve international relations came to produce the opposite effect as 1946 wore on. The original object of a great American loan to Britain had been to deflect her from restrictionist trade policies – for the very reason that the United States desired to liberalise trade throughout the world. So far from desiring to use such a policy against the Soviet Union, the United States had once viewed with considerable favour the issue of a similar loan to her. Yet the drift of events had already driven this from the realms of practicality, before the end of 1945. The acrimonious negotiations over the British loan, and the considerable lack of enthusiasm with which it was eventually greeted in the United Kingdom, can hardly have given Americans a favourable view of that prospect either. At the beginning of 1946, it was far from a foregone conclusion that Congress would ratify the loan; and the Government of the United States saw that the final decision would be likely to turn on the attitude of men like the Republican Senator Vandenberg, the banker Bernard Baruch, and also Irish-Americans who supported the Democratic Party, but had strong anti-British proclivities.

When Churchill was in the United States, he was in close contact with some of these people. Whatever attitude his party might have taken in the House of Commons, there can be no doubt that the former Prime Minister was convinced that the loan was vital for Britain's recovery, and that he used every ounce of his immense moral authority to encourage American approval.[28] As the attitude of Congress was so much in doubt, the administration was forced to advance arguments designed to swing reluctant Congressmen. They had to represent that America had made a good bargain at Britain's expense – which inevitably caused resentment in Britain. There was some temptation to argue that the loan was necessary to counter Russian designs, and bring Britain to America's side. This argument was very much a two-edged sword. Henry Wallace supported the loan. Asked whether he thought its purpose was to bring about a military alliance between Britain and his own country, Wallace replied that if he thought that was the purpose, he would have opposed the loan.[29] In the event, most of the doubtful people did what was required of them, and this probably tipped the scales. At last, in May, the two Houses of Congress approved the loan; but in neither was the vote overwhelming. Despite Vandenberg, the Republican minority split two to one against it – and a substantial number of Southern Democrats voted with them. The United States was inevitably led to think of financial policies in a Cold War context, while the Soviet Union became more and more eager to set up its own dependents as an economic bloc to rival the Americans.

In the second half of 1946, the public controversy between former Allies continued to deepen. James Byrnes delivered an extremely important speech at Stuttgart on 6 September, which set many hares running in different directions. In the presence of various military, diplomatic and political luminaries, the Secretary of State made it plain that the United States had no intention of withdrawing her military presence: 'As long as an occupation force is required for Germany, the army of the USA will be part of that occupation force.' He delivered the *coup de grâce* to any lingering idea of the 'Morganthau Plan': the Germans should be encouraged to 'win their way back to an honourable place among free and peace-loving nations'. Byrnes favoured the early re-establishment of a central government for the vanquished Reich. He came out clearly against the French plan to detach the Ruhr and Rhineland – although he favoured their claim to the Saar. While Byrnes accepted the view that Poland should receive territorial compensation from Germany, he refused to underwrite the full current Polish claim. The extent of Poland's acquisitions, he explained, 'must be determined when the final settlement is agreed upon'.

Some effects of this speech were predictable. The French were bitterly shocked that the Americans repudiated their own more covetous designs – and a powerful argument exists for the view that the substantial Communist gains in the November elections were an expression of this disappointment. There can be no doubt that Byrnes's attitude to the new Polish frontier was deeply resented in that country.[30] Poles of all shades of opinion were conscious of the need to find space for their compatriots from the east; and the Secretary's speech can hardly have improved the already frail prospects of Mikolajczyk.

The Stuttgart speech derived further importance from the contrasting tone of another delivered soon afterwards. On 12 September, Henry Wallace spoke in New York. The speech was not conceived as a *riposte* to Byrnes – it had been drafted long before the Secretary of State spoke – but the differences between them were widely noted. Wallace was by no means uncritical of Russia – a fact which caused visible annoyance among a section of his audience – but the general tone was expressly opposed to 'getting tough' with the Soviet Union, and the former Vice President indicated his view that the Russians should be allowed a free hand in eastern Europe. The speech was far from friendly to Britain: 'the British imperialistic policy in the Near East alone, combined with Russian retaliation, would lead the United States straight to war unless we have a clearly defined and realistic policy of our own'.[31] What gave the speech peculiar significance, however, was the fact that the President himself seemed to be implicated in Wallace's views. During the next few days it became clear that Truman had had a preview of the speech, which he had considered in detail and approved *in toto*.[32] The American press and public saw the speeches of Byrnes and Wallace as completely contradictory. The Secretary of State, currently attending the Peace Conference at Paris, and Senator Vandenberg, who accompanied him, were both acutely embarrassed, not to say confused. Truman explained to Wallace that the Secretary of State 'had been giving him hell',[33] and that Byrnes – not unreasonably – blamed the President rather than the Secretary of Commerce. Wallace complained in reply of the current 'bipartisan' foreign policy, declaring that the Democrats must break free from an alliance with the Republicans, whom he accused of 'warmongering against Russia'. Wallace appears to have convinced himself that the true author of current American foreign policy was Vandenberg, rather than Byrnes.[34] In the end, however, the President made it clear that Wallace must cease speaking on foreign policy. After a couple of days for further reflection, Truman suddenly resolved to dismiss Wallace – which he did in a letter so maladroitly drafted, and at such a 'low level', that Wallace himself, as an act of kindness, persuaded the President to rephrase it.[35]

The British *Annual Register*, calmly reviewing events of the year long afterwards, described Truman's handling of the whole Wallace affair as 'inept in the extreme',[36] and it is difficult to dissent from that judgement. The American people appear to have concurred; for at the Congressional elections of 5 November, the Republicans seized control of both Houses. Thus Truman was in a most unhappy situation: a Democratic President, universally regarded as a compromise between the better, but conflicting, claims of Byrnes and Wallace, faced by a hostile Congress on the 'right' and sapped by Wallace and his associates on the 'left'. As recently as September 1946, Truman had told Wallace that he still believed that a great loan to Russia could be piloted through Congress at a later date.[37] Whether this view was realistic, even in the old Congress, appears most doubtful; but in the new one it was absolutely out of the question.

Nor did the disastrous Congressional elections end the political misfortunes of Harry Truman. However uncomfortable his relations may have been with 'Jimmy' Byrnes, the Secretary of State was the strong man of the administration. At the time of the elections, Byrnes was on point of resignation. As far back as April, he had received a medical report indicating heart disease, and wheels were set in motion for selecting a successor.[38] Happier professional opinions followed, and Byrnes remained to see matters through the Peace Conference. Shortly after the November elections he decided to retire, although no immediate announcement was made. Finally, in January 1947, General George Marshall became Secretary of State.

The significance of this appointment would prove enormous. Marshall, a man of immense dignity and reserve, was almost an American equivalent of the Duke of Wellington in the decades after Waterloo: a military figure of exceptional distinction and capacity, who entered politics half-unwillingly, whom most 'middle of the road' opinion regarded as a patriotic judge rather than a political advocate. Like Wellington, Marshall was able to carry men who would normally have been political opponents into courses of action which appeared necessary for the common good, while he did not possess Wellington's abrasiveness which encouraged bitter feelings among opponents. As we shall see later, both the President and the American nation would soon have good reason to rejoice at the apparent disaster of Byrnes's departure.

The confused American furore over mixed financial, military and international questions was soon paralleled in Britain. Two issues were closely connected. In October, the British Cabinet had decided to make military conscription permanent – a conclusion towards which their American counterparts had been gravitating reluctantly about a year earlier.[39] Such a decision, reached so soon after the end of the war, scarcely suggested that feelings between the victors were good; but, strangely, the main subject of attention was a more general and less tangible question.

On 29 October 1946, twenty-one Labour MPs sent a letter to Attlee, declaring themselves 'increasingly perturbed by the trend of the Government's foreign policy'[40] and urging the Government to 'provide a genuine middle way between the extreme alternatives of American "free enterprise" economics and Russian totalitarian socio-political life'. These MPs were not figures on the crypto-Communist ('crypto') wing of the party – a fact which gave their arguments special weight. It is significant, however, that British dissidents over foreign policy on this and future occasions were usually disposed to blame the United States for tendencies they disliked; while the American foreign policy dissidents like Wallace were usually disposed to blame Britain.

This line of complaint soon led to something much more formidable than a genteel letter to the Prime Minister. On 12

November, Labour backbenchers tabled two amendments to the Address – one opposing peace-time conscription, the other critical of the government's foreign policy. Both amendments – but particularly the latter – gained adherents in the days which followed. Richard Crossman, publicist and future Cabinet Minister, acquired special prominence among the foreign policy rebels, but it would be wrong to see him as the definitive leader; for the movement acquired its own momentum. The government noted with some relief that the rebels did not propose to press matters to a division; but the Prime Minister was particularly piqued to find that a number of Parliamentary Private Secretaries to Ministers had added their names.[41] A report in the Communist *Daily Worker* even claimed that three senior Ministers were encouraging the rebels behind the scenes. This statement was wrong in at least one of the cases.[42] Attlee remonstrated severely with the signatories, but the revolt continued. When a division was pressed, the Government applied a three-line whip for the 'No' lobby. Well over a hundred Labour MPs pointedly abstained on the foreign policy issue, and nearly as many on conscription.

Dalton wrote after the division that 'there is no doubt that there is deep concern in a wide and sensible section of the [Labour] party – in addition to a few professional grumblers, or real cryptos, or disappointed office seekers'.[43] Perhaps he should have added to the list a small number of more or less strict pacifists. The real importance of this revolt, as with the Wallace saga in the United States, lies not merely in its immediate political importance, but in the way in which it demonstrates a widespread and genuine unquiet which pervaded large sections of the population.

Concern of a different kind was felt on both sides of the Atlantic by the acknowledged 'experts' – professionals especially concerned with foreign policy. There was much doubt about Russia's objectives, both in the long and in the short term. In February, George Kennan, American Chargé in Moscow, sent an important and influential despatch, arguing that the Soviet leadership had 'learned to seek security only in patient but deadly struggle for the total destruction of rival power, never in compacts and compromises with it'.[44] A very different interpretation was provided the following month by Kennan's British counterpart, F. K. Roberts, who argued that 'there is nothing in internal conditions within the [Soviet] Union which might encourage a return to the old revolutionary traditions'.[45] The picture which derived from interviews with Soviet spokesmen was no more clear. Both countries appointed new Ambassadors to the Soviet Union soon after these messages were sent, and the new men sought elucidation from Stalin himself. Neither General Bedell Smith nor Sir Maurice Peterson really got much further than to discover that the

Russians were currently interested in expansion towards the Dardanelles. Stalin said that he had no other aspirations; but various European statesmen had said similar things in the previous decade.[46] Much less anodyne were meetings which American and British diplomats had with Maxim Litvinov – a man currently out of favour, but with great experience and well-liked in the West. Litvinov suggested that decisions taken after the war were adverse to friendly cooperation with the Western Democracies: concluding that 'the best we could hope for was an armed truce'.[47]

Yet, as the year wore on, the Americans in particular began to draw baleful conclusions from the general drift of events. Documents circulated by the State Department in May noted an accumulating mass of evidence which suggested that the Soviet Union had moved from its wartime position of international collaboration, towards a revival of 'the Marxist hypothesis of the inevitability of conflict between the Soviet state and the Capitalist world'.[48] The author concluded that it was likely that 'the Soviets have embarked on a policy of aggrandizement which will be contained only by the limitations of Soviet power or eventually by armed resistance on the part of other major Powers in areas where they feel their vital interests to be endangered'. A gloomy prospect indeed, just a year after V.E. Day! President Truman appointed a Special Counsel, Clark M. Clifford, to report fully on the situation. His analysis was immensely depressing.[49] The Soviet leaders – the argument ran – were indeed guided by a philosophy which held that prolonged peace was impossible, and were currently preparing for the forthcoming clash in a variety of ways: isolating Soviet citizens from foreign influences; maintaining armed forces much larger than true defence required; expanding wherever possible into new areas of control; acting through international organisations, not to foster the ostensible objectives of those organisations but to frustrate possible resistance to Soviet expansion; fostering internal disruption and external disputes affecting other countries.

Not all informed opinion in the West took such a bleak view. The danger of war was slight, argued F. K. Roberts, 'if Britain and America are strong and if they stand together'. Yet he and most others accepted that peril lay if 'the Kremlin should doubt our will or our ability to resist over issues which we could not in effect allow to pass unchallenged'.[50] Senator Vandenberg, who also did not believe that war would come if the Western Democracies acted with 'firmness but with patience', added: 'If we *are* in such danger, the continuing appeasement merely postpones and multiplies the hazard.'[51] Whether one believed, on balance, that war was inevitable or that peace could be preserved, here was a policy on which most men in the West could agree.

Before the year was out, some evidence began to appear which confirmed that this was both the wisest and the safest approach for the West, and that Russia was likely to react to the new determination by backing down. A story passing through rather indirect channels told that Maurice Thorez paid a secret visit to Moscow shortly after the French Communists recorded their impressive gains at the November elections. On his return, the French Communist leader told his principal followers that 'the Soviet Union is not prepared for war and its military preparations will not be completed for a number of years'.[52] Hence they 'should not advance too rapidly and above all else must not endeavour to seize power by force since to do so would probably precipitate an international conflict from which the Soviet Union could hardly emerge victorious'. On this view, the overriding Soviet concern would be to consolidate power in places where the Western Democracies would be unlikely to intervene – rather than make dangerous bids elsewhere. It is certainly consistent with what happened soon afterwards in France itself.

If these explanations were even approximately correct, then the message for Western statesmen was one of mixed joy and sorrow. If they exhibited firmness, they could, without war, prevent further territorial advances by Russia or by Communists acting under Russian instructions. Yet they could do nothing to rescue the peoples already behind the Iron Curtain, or to generate truly friendly relations with the Soviet Union. No doubt Russia would repeatedly test the determination of the Western Democracies. She would seek every opportunity to drive wedges between them, and play on suspicions and fears within each. The alternative to all-out surrender was not a 'hot war', but a long 'cold war' which would test everyone's nerves to the limit.

13

Moment of Truth

'[Bevin] There was no hope of reaching a satisfactory settlement either by agreement among the four Great Powers or through the UNO and . . . resolute action must be taken to counter the Soviet threat to western civilisation.' Cabinet Minutes, 5 March 1948. C.M.(48)19. CAB 128/12.

'[Chamberlain] said that he had now come definitely to the conclusion that Herr Hitler's attitude made it impossible to continue to negotiate on the old basis with the Nazi regime . . . No reliance could be placed on any assurances given by the Nazi leaders.' Cabinet Minutes, 18 March 1939. Cab.12(39). CAB 23/98.

Those major events of 1947 which signalled the growing estrangement of the Great Powers and their rapid drift into what was undeniably a 'Cold War' situation must be set against the background of other events in countries under Russian domination, and particularly those of central and eastern Europe; for the news which filtered into the Western Democracies from those places profoundly influenced their judgement about Russia's intentions, and therefore about the policies which were necessary to counter those intentions. Just as honest indignation at the treatment meted out to victims of Nazism played at least as large a part as self interest in rallying the British and American people against Hitler, so also were they stirred by indignation and pity, at least as much as self interest, in their growing antagonism towards the Soviet Union.

Broadly, the story of events in lands under Soviet control was a continuation of trends already observed in the previous year and earlier: the gradual tightening of the Communist grip; active suppression of individuals and organisations who provided possible nuclei of future opposition. There were considerable local variations, and in some countries at some times there was even a brief relaxation of that grip, which was soon applied again more tightly than before. Poland was an example of this. The January election produced its predicted result: by fair means or foul, the Communist-dominated coalition secured a large majority. Thereafter, a wide amnesty was proclaimed, and some 33,000 people are said to have taken advantage of it.[1] Some evidence received in the first part of the year suggested that the government was – as Polish governments went – not unpopular.[2] Certain Socialists appear to have believed that it would be possible for their own party to 'reassert its independence' within the foreseeable future.[3] Right at the end of 1947, a British Minister who had just returned from Poland claimed that he 'saw no evidence of domination by the USSR', and also that the 'various parties in the government, whether Communist or otherwise, definitely put country first'.[4] This, however, was the conclusion of a brief, official visit – and he had doubtless seen what his hosts wanted him to see. Other reports from Poland, particularly in the second half of the year, told a very different tale. Mikolajczyk had been returned to the Sejm in the January elections; but he was promptly dropped from the Government. In October, he made urgent contact with the American Embassy, reporting news that there were plans to seize him and bring him to trial on some political charge. Urgent discussions took place as to how Mikolajczyk might be spirited out of Poland. Bizarre suggestions were advanced, including one proposal that he should be smuggled out of the country in a coffin.[5] Eventually, a truck driver was equipped with 500,000 zloty for bribery, if required, and charged to convey Mikolajczyk to Gdynia. The driver later told how his vehicle was stopped and searched, while 'he held the money in one hand and a monkey wrench in the other, prepared to use either if necessary'. Neither aid to persuasion was required. Mikolajczyk was safely embarked at the port, and later reappeared in Britain, then in the United States.

Bevin circulated a report to the Cabinet in November, which suggested that the persecution of Mikolajczyk had been the prelude to a much wider policy. 'Mikolajczyk's party, which is believed to represent about 80 per cent of the people, has been broken up, the right wing Socialists await trial, the Government Socialists have endorsed the Cominform declaration; the Roman Catholic Church is the last, but still formidable, organised opponent of Communist rule.'[6] Reviewing events of 1947, the American Chargé in Warsaw declared that, in the course of the year, 'the Communists had made almost incredible advances in their march towards complete control.'[7]

Accounts which emerged from Romania showed not even a temporary relaxation in the Communist grip. Iuliu Maniu, leader of the Peasant Party, was arrested, like a great many lesser critics of the Government. In November, he was 'tried' and sentenced to solitary imprisonment for life. 'All legal opposition,' wrote Bevin soon afterwards, 'has now been eliminated, the Government has recently been purged of all but Communists and their puppets by the dismissal of the Foreign Minister and his fellow-Liberals and the fusion of the Government Social Democrats ... The police and strong-arm men among whom many of Horia Sima's Iron Guards, the former Nazi spearhead in Romania, have been enrolled, becomes ever more efficient and powerful.'[8] The anomaly of a King as head of a Communist state could not long be maintained, and some people thought that Michael might take occasion of a visit to Britain as suitable opportunity to go into exile. The King was made of sterner stuff, and returned to Romania. This set his Government the minor embarrassment of devising excuses to depose him – an operation which was concluded by the end of December.

The Western Democracies had deferred recognition of the Bulgarian Government in the vain hope of some face-saving gesture. Early in 1947 they decided that none would come, but they edged towards recognition all the same. To add to their humiliation, restoration of diplomatic relations coincided closely with the persecution of Nikola Petkov, leader of the Agrarian Party and by far the most celebrated critic of the Communists. Petkov was seized in June, charged with plotting a *coup d'état*: an unlikely crime, surely, at a time when the Red Army was still in occupation of the country. He was brought to trial, and, in September, executed. The period around Petkov's arrest also coincided with suppression of the last vestiges of Bulgarian freedom. The two surviving Opposition newspapers disappeared during the spring; and in the next couple of months twenty thousand people – most of them anti-Communist – were called up for service in the labour corps[9] – as their stint of penal servitude was euphemistically described.

In Hungary the Smallholders Party – despite the overwhelming popular vote it had received – was in a demoralised condition by the beginning of 1947. The Communists, familiar with the technique of picking off unimportant Smallholders deputies, compelling the removal of their Parliamentary immunity, and thereafter bringing them to stage 'trials', moved against larger prey. In February 1947, they demanded removal of immunity from Bela Kovács, former Secretary-General of the Smallholders Party. For once, the party refused; but this difficulty was overcome by the Red Army, which arrested him.[10] For a long time, the world heard nothing of Kovács. In May, Prime Minister Ferenc Nagy departed for a fortnight's holiday in Switzerland. As he was preparing to return, Nagy was warned that Kovács – who had been held incommunicado for three months – had signed a deposition implicating Nagy and others in 'conspiracy against the Republic'.[11] Nagy took the hint, and fled to the United States. A new Smallholder Prime Minister was produced, and the Coalition continued in office; but the Smallholders Party was still further demoralised. In this atmosphere it was possible to coerce the Assembly to enact a law 'to protect the Republic' whose scope could be almost limitless. This measure prescribed punishment up to death for 'anyone who publishes true or false reports which would harm the reputation at home or abroad of the Hungarian Republic'.[12]

New elections were due in Hungary in August. Strangely, British and American diplomatic reports of conditions during the election period are in considerable conflict.[13] British accounts suggest the election was conducted in reasonably fair conditions. American diplomats, by contrast, told of disqualifications on a huge scale, for most frivolous reasons: Jews accused of belonging to Nazi organisations; old women charged with being prostitutes; working people arraigned as owners of great landed estates, and so on. They also reported massive personation of electors, and other abuses. The very disparity between these Western accounts is significant, for it shows how internal conditions in Hungary made it impossible to discover what was going on.

The Communists emerged from the elections as the largest single party; but their vote was only just over 22 per cent, so this was scarcely a great victory. What was more important, the coalition in which the Communists participated won an almost 2:1 majority over a fragmented opposition. The official Smallholders Party was nearly quartered, but a separate group of Smallholders existed outside the coalition. A great variety of other political groups emerged, all with perceptible representation. From the Communist point of view, the principal *desideratum* had been achieved: all possible organised opposition to their operations had been broken up almost beyond belief; and a small but cohesive and well-disciplined party was henceforth destined to rule Hungary – though it was still convenient to maintain the façade of a coalition, nominally led by a Smallholder. Consolidation of Communist power did not take place until the following year; but an American diplomatic report of October 1947 referred gloomily to ' "realists" in Hungary who . . . have held that Hungary cannot survive without making a compact with the Soviet Union', and to the 'growing number of persons who, weary of the chaos and lack of direction of the traditional Hungarian parties and their leaders and despairing of any concrete support from the West, accept with resignation the Communist leadership'.[14]

In some parts of eastern Europe, there were signs that Social Democrats were regrouping in the course of 1947; but this was really little more than preparation for a last stand against the Communists. 'The Social Democrats' attempts at resistance are, I fear, rather unlikely to succeed', wrote Bevin about Hungary.[15] In

Czechoslovakia, the Socialists were reported in May to have 'become quite independent'[16] and the influence of their pro-Communist leader Fierlinger was declared to have 'declined enormously'. In November, the Czech Socialists became bolder still, and actually threw Fierlinger and his associate Erban from leadership; but the Communists meditated a terrible revenge, which they would wreak on the country the following year.

But the sweep of events in eastern Europe was generally towards total Communist domination. The question in 1947 was whether the democracies would – or could – respond in time to save their foothold in western Europe. In March, Jefferson Caffery, American Ambassador in Paris, decided that – on balance – it was unlikely that the Communists would take over France; but he appeared far from certain on the matter.[17] A few weeks later, diplomatic reports from Italy told the State Department how far Communists had already succeeded in undermining commercial morale: 'Population generally and particularly more responsible banking and industrial leaders have lost confidence entirely in the Government and are afraid to venture upon new and expanded enterprises. A flight from the lira is beginning; rise in spiral inflation is unchecked.'[18] Sir Archibald Clark-Kerr had been moved from Moscow to Washington, and elevated to the peerage as Lord Inverchapel. In March 1947, he wrote to Attlee that 'many intelligent Americans ask whether even the British Isles can indefinitely remain proof against Soviet blackmail. As yet there is fortunately little or no disposition to answer this alarmist question in the negative.'[19] Yet the fact that the question could even be asked is a terrible reflection on the deterioration which had taken place in the previous couple of years.

The military situation was no more encouraging than the diplomatic. Although the West still retained its monopoly of the atomic bomb, nobody could know how long that monopoly would last, and the number of troops whom they could set against the Russians was woefully inadequate. At the beginning of February 1947, the British, Americans and French together had only 529,000 troops on foreign soil in Europe, against 1,110,000 from the Soviet Union.[20] And how many could be mobilised within the Soviet Union itself?

Prospects on the economic front were equally bleak. Britain had by far the strongest economy of the major countries in western Europe; but her weakness was apparent enough. A combination of world price rises and the side effects of an appalling winter had greatly reduced the value of the highly controversial American loan. Hugh Dalton, Chancellor of the Exchequer, sounded repeated warnings to his Cabinet colleagues about the great speed with which this money was disappearing. In March he concluded that – at current rate of spending – it would be exhausted by February 1948.[21]

The first real stand against the rising Communist menace was made over Greece and Turkey. Neither was a very attractive proposition. The parliamentary delegation which visited Greece late in 1946 had presented an ambiguous view about the balance of right and wrong between contending terrorist units of varying political complexions. Greek politicians were a thoroughly unimpressive body of men, no whit better than their predecessors twenty-four centuries earlier – and weak, corrupt governments followed each other in bewildering succession. The country was more or less ripe for a Communist take-over. In February, British diplomats on the spot anticipated an imminent collapse. 'I do not believe that [the Americans] could have come in after a collapse,'[22] wrote one of those diplomats not long afterwards. 'So the Middle East would have gone behind the iron curtain, and such of our friends here . . . as could not get away to Egypt would have been done in.' What all this would have meant, not just for the unfortunate individuals concerned, but for prestige and influence of the Western countries throughout the world, is easy to imagine.

Turkey had been neutral until practically the end of the war, despite many blandishments; and people recalled with bitterness that this neutrality had prolonged the war considerably, and cost many Allied lives. The Turkish Government was a dictatorship, with little to be said in its favour. For some time there had been moves by the Soviet Union in favour of what was called, in diplomatic terms, 'revision of the Montreux Convention'. This meant that a new regime should apply to the Bosporus-Dardanelles, under which all nations except those actually bordering the Black Sea should be excluded from passage, while defence of the Straits themselves, which had formerly belonged exclusively to Turkey, should be shared henceforth with the Soviet Union.[23] Stalin made no secret of the fact that Russia's immediate aspirations included possession of a base on the Straits.[24] Russia would be authorised to introduce her armed forces into the area, no doubt with the ostensible aim of sharing control with Turkey; thereafter, those troops could easily be employed to secure mastery over Turkey. Russia would thereby acquire a certain foothold on the Mediterranean, would be set in a convenient position to exercise control over Greece, and would be able thereafter to spread havoc in the Near and Middle East. This could easily lead to domination of the oil wells, and ultimately to control over the great countries of Asia.

Britain, now near the end of her tether, was in no position to do much about all this. It is surely a mark of her decline in power and morale that most of the Cabinet documents of the time are preoccupied with her own immediate problems – diplomatic, military and economic – rather than with the wider questions of Western defence. On 30 January 1947, the Cabinet – following advice from the Chiefs of Staff and Foreign Secretary – decided to reduce British forces in Greece to a single brigade, which would itself remain only until Russian troops had been withdrawn from Bulgaria.[25] Unless the Americans could be persuaded to take over Britain's responsibilities, the prospects of keeping Communism from Greece were vanishingly small. Even if Greek Government troops could temporarily repel the insurgents, these could easily escape over any of the three northern frontiers, to regroup, rearm and return when the moment was ripe.

The Americans soon heard rumours of the impending British withdrawal. On 21 February, they were told officially. A formal memorandum was presented to the State Department, admitting that Britain could no longer defend the Governments of Greece or Turkey. On the same day, Dean Acheson, Under-Secretary of State, sent Marshall a gloomy appreciation of 'the probability of an imminent economic and financial collapse' – noting that 'the morale of the ill-equipped Greek army was at low ebb'.[26] The key to the preservation of both countries was economic rather than military.

When water is pouring through the breach and the whole dyke threatens to collapse, a man has little choice into which hole he must thrust his arm. Morally, economically, militarily and diplomatically, there had been many places which deserved defence better than Greece and Turkey. But those other places had already fallen. Would this immediate challenge be accepted? On 27 February 1947, Marshall and eight leading Congressmen – four from each party – met with the President. The Secretary of State gave a clear lead: 'Our choice was either to act or to lose by default.' The President emphatically concurred: the others did not dissent. On 7 March, the American Cabinet met. Truman told them that he proposed to ask Congress for a $250 million loan for Greece, $150 million for Turkey: furthermore, that 'this would be only a beginning'.[27]

Proper minutes of American Cabinet meetings were not kept during this period, but a rather scrappy record in the papers of the President's Appointments Secretary gives some impression of the atmosphere of that crucial meeting.[28] The lead appears to have been taken by Dean Acheson, who pointed out that 'complete disintegration of Greece is only a matter of weeks', although 'Turkey is much better off' and 'a good risk if peace is maintained'. 'If we go in,' argued Acheson, 'we cannot be certain of success in Middle East and Mediterranean. If we do not go in there will be collapse in these areas.' The possibility that economic involvement might create a military risk was admitted, but the likelihood discounted. This contemporary record does not suggest that any member of the Cabinet dissented from the line of conduct proposed; but it upholds the President's later assertion that there was widespread feeling among his colleagues that reform of the Greek Government was essential if the money was to be set to useful purpose.[29]

On 12 March, the President promulgated before Congress what became known as the 'Truman Doctrine': 'it must be the policy of the United States to support free peoples who are resisting attempted subjugation by armed minorities or by outside pressure'. Specifically, he asked Congress to authorise the proposed loans, and also to grant authority to send American civilians and soldiers. While the lumbering procedure for legal authorisation was in progress, Truman charged his 'official family' to devise whatever means could be employed without special Congressional authority to assist Greece and Turkey meanwhile.

The first attack on the 'Truman Doctrine' came from Henry Wallace, who broadcast the following night. The money, Wallace declared, was 'a down payment on an unlimited expenditure aimed at opposing Communist expansion'. The Greek loan was 'a military subsidy to the Greek Government to continue its efforts to stamp out all opposition'. The President was criticised for not acting through the United Nations: 'If Greece is in danger, let the United Nations tell us the facts and recommend action. America will do what the United Nations recommends.'[30] In the course of April, Wallace visited London and set forward the same arguments with equal force: 'The world is devastated and hungry, the world is crying out, not for American guns and tanks to spread more hunger, but for American plows and machines to fulfil the promise of peace.'[31] If the situation in Greece and Turkey could have been taken in isolation, out of its wider context, and if the United Nations had not been hamstrung by the 'Great Power Veto', then there would have been much force in Wallace's argument. Alas, the operative facts were against him. The former Vice-President's speeches, and particularly his pronouncements in foreign countries, were counter-productive in the charged atmosphere of the time, and generated the most furious criticism against their author.

Wallace was by no means the only American politician who opposed the loans to Greece and Turkey on such grounds. The irrepressible Senator Claude Pepper of Florida spoke in similar language. Senator Joseph O'Mahoney wrote to the President, declaring that the proposed loan to Greece was 'likely to lead to war', and claiming that there was a 'substantial opinion' among his Senatorial colleagues to similar effect.[32]

Truman was more vulnerable to attack from other quarters. America had just devoted money on an unprecedented scale to the cause of Allied victory; would any further spending encompass financial ruin, thus destroying her capacity to help anybody over anything? John Foster Dulles, himself a future Secretary of State, had a very different outlook from Wallace on almost everything; but he also declared that he had 'never been very keen' about the new loans – 'and I think it needs considerable overhauling to be workable. The Soviet Union with very little expense and effort can bleed us badly in Greece.'[33] The more strictly isolationist argument also had force. If America was embarking on a general policy of containment of Communism, there were risks that war might one day break out where her own vital interests were not involved.

Other currents also ran against the 'Truman Doctrine'. A vociferous body of opinion in the United States felt extremely bitter about British policies in Palestine, and complained that the President's proposals involved an American decision to underwrite British commitments. Bevin – perhaps desiring to take a 'patriotic' stand, perhaps wishing to hold off his own 'left-wing' critics, perhaps at times out of sheer pique – had not always been averse to pulling feathers from the eagle's tail, and to making anti-American statements which reverberated damagingly across the United States. The 'China lobby', whose chief exponent was Admiral Leahy, argued that 'a stable non-Soviet government in China is of much more importance to America than the Mediterranean states'.[34] If Chiang was being urged to unite with Communists, then why finance the Greeks and Turks to fight the Communists? The real answer, which nobody liked to give, was that the scale of support required to save China at that stage was perhaps more than America could provide, and certainly more than Congress would authorise, while the money needed to save Greece and Turkey was not an impossible sum. This serves to remind us of an aspect of the 'Truman Doctrine' which has perhaps not attracted as much attention as it deserves. The President's decision was, in practice, not merely a decision to take a stand against Communist expansion – but a decision to take that stand first in Europe rather than in Asia.

In the end, the President won his point. In April and May, the two Houses of Congress each provided majorities in the region of 5:2 in favour of Truman's recommendations; and the majorities were clear in both parties. These decisions by no means ended the Communist threat – particularly in Greece. The aid provided was economic, and for many months the military issue remained in doubt; in October the British Cabinet Defence Committee described the military outlook at 'gloomy'.[35] Relief would eventually come, but from a source which nobody anticipated in 1947. Thus the American decision effectively set geographical limits to the Communist tide in Europe.

The cue was followed very quickly. Most countries of western Europe at that time had coalition governments which included Communist members. Whatever the reason for this may have been at first, Communists were retained into 1947 not because other politicians were impressed with their positive usefulness. In March 1947 the Communists nearly left the French Cabinet, but relented. The American Ambassador, Caffery, declared that the other parties were 'vastly relieved' at the decision 'because they feared that if [Communists] left the Government they might make all government impossible by ... a series of strikes all over the country'.[36] The situation in France was further complicated by the position of de Gaulle, whose temporary withdrawal from the centre of affairs was related to an evident intention that he would later return with much more power. Other politicians were deeply conscious of the attractive force which the General might exercise on their own supporters, and of the likelihood that French politics could soon become a battleground between de Gaulle and the Communists, with all other parties crumbling away.

When the French Communists attempted simultaneously to promote political strikes and retain their places in the Government, this was too much for Premier Ramadier. In May 1947, he managed to drive the Communists from the Government, and to form a coalition without them. This was a tremendously risky experiment, and even Ramadier's own Socialist Party gave him only a bare majority for making it. There was virtual certainty that – if the experiment failed – the pro-Communist wing of the Socialists would take control of the party: which would mean a massive addition to an already huge and menacing Communist party. Of the various perilous courses open to Ramadier, the one he took was, nevertheless, the safest, and Caffery was convinced that 'the President's policy towards Greece and Turkey was probably one of the decisive factors'[37] in enabling him to make it. If the Americans were prepared to back the Greek Government against Communist insurrection, then they would presumably back the French as well – and so, for the first time since 1945, the anti-Communist French politicians thought it was worth making a stand.

Almost at the same time, and probably for similar reasons, the Italians also threw the Communists from their Government. The Ministry formed by Christian Democrat de Gasperi was a bizarre mixture of his own followers, the Communists, and Communist-inclined Socialists.[38] As in France, the Communists were attempting to run with the hare and hunt with the hounds. In the judgement of the American Ambassador, they were 'doing everything possible outside and within the Government to bring about inflation and chaotic economic conditions'. De Gasperi wished to broaden his government by incorporating members of moderate political groups, but was under strong pressure from the left not to do so, and he greatly feared the chaos which might result if he made the attempt. As in the French crisis, the United States appears as the *deus ex machina*. Marshall assured the Italian Ambassador that de Gasperi could 'count on the strong moral support of the United States and that we will make a serious effort to assist Italy in meeting her essential financial needs'.[39] De Gasperi was at last strong enough to establish a government without Communists.

For the time being at least, the breach had evidently been plugged; but the dyke walls of Europe required more permanent repairs; and these Europe was in no condition to provide from her own resources. 'The recovery of Europe,' Marshall broadcast to his country on 28 April, 'has been far slower than had been expected . . . The patient is sinking while the doctors deliberate. Whatever action is possible . . . must be taken without delay.'

The United States had long been making loans and grants to Europe and to other parts of the world on an unprecedented scale: no less than $15,000 million in the two years immediately following the war.[40] In the spring of 1947, a Treasury official noted, programmes totalling $1850 million were before Congress, and a further programme for $540 million was being prepared.[41] The well-being of innumerable potential recipients, the interests of the American taxpayer, the likelihood or otherwise of a future trade recession, plus wider problems of international security, all required that such massive subventions should be allocated according to some kind of preconceived policy, not merely distributed haphazardly to whatever claimant happened at a particular moment to make a strong and immediate case for a loan or gift.

A body called the Policy Planning Staff received the task of working out the main features of the Government proposals. The Chairman was George Kennan, former Chargé at Moscow. Kennan argued that 'further Communist successes would create serious danger to American security' – yet, nevertheless, 'American effort and aid to Europe should be directed not to the controlling of Communism as such but to the restoration of the economic health and vigor of European society'.[42] Thus America's overriding concern should be removal of economic and social conditions which breed Communism and other forms of totalitarianism, and the establishment of a Europe equipped with moral and material resources adequate to meet such threats. Kennan urged American policy makers to remove the widespread notion that the United States was merely reacting to Communist pressure, and the connected view that the 'Truman Doctrine' was 'a blank check to give economic and military aid to any area of the world where the

Communists show signs of being successful'.

On 5 June, Marshall developed these views in a speech at Harvard:

> Our policy is directed not against any country or doctrine but against hunger, poverty, desperation and chaos. Its purpose should be the revival of a working economy in the world so as to permit the emergence of political and social conditions in which free institutions can exist.

Curiously, this speech attracted little immediate world attention. Bevin, however, had been tipped off in advance as to its importance, and made immediate contact with his counterpart, Georges Bidault of France. They soon decided that the 'initiative must be taken by the European governments outside the framework of the United Nations, since to remit the task of preparing the plan to the Economic Commission for Europe could only result in delay'.[43] Bidault, very conscious of domestic pressures within France, insisted on an approach to the Russians as well.

The Americans had been conscious from the start that there was no device by which they could legitimately exclude Russia if she chose to participate: yet they were conscious that 'the thing would be unworkable' in that event – if for no other reason than because the sum which would then be required would be too large for the Administration to hope to get from Congress. But at the turn of June to July, the meeting *à trois*, on which Bidault insisted, took place. Molotov opened by suggesting 'that we should first ask the United States to state the amount, conditions and probability of aid, [and] refused to consider any course except that of presenting the United States with a statement of each country's requirements'. This attitude would, beyond doubt, have been completely unacceptable to the United States, who were most anxious to promote positive cooperation among the Europeans, not a mass of separate demands. Molotov's position hardened, if anything, as discussions proceeded. At last the talks broke down, and Bevin made no attempt to conceal relief:

> I am confident that our conversations were doomed from the start in the sense that there was never any prospect of getting Soviet collaboration except on M. Molotov's unacceptable terms. Moreover, had the Russians decided to come in, even on our terms, the opportunities which they would have had to delay and obstruct would have been almost unlimited . . .

Thus Molotov had over-reached himself with his truculence. In the unlikely event that Russia genuinely desired to participate, he effectively shut the door in his own face. If Russia sought to sabotage this or any other American scheme for European recovery, then he abandoned the possibility of employing those delaying tactics at which he was past master. Nor did Molotov improve his case when, on the last day of the triple meeting, he resorted to threats – telling the two other Foreign Ministers that if they accepted the American offer 'that action would have grave consequences. It would result not in the unification and reconstruction of Europe but in a division into two groups.'[44] Bevin and Bidault probably had decided that the eventuality which Molotov was threatening had already come about; the effective choice for Europe was between cooperation with America on the lines Marshall was suggesting, or collapse into chaos from which Russia would be the only beneficiary.

Now that Russia had withdrawn, Britain and France were free to act. Invitations were sent to all other European countries, save Spain. In the first half of July, all the countries of western Europe accepted. Poland and Czechoslovakia seemed disposed to do likewise, although Russia's other dependants refused. Then the Poles, obviously under orders from Moscow, withdrew their tentative acceptance. Soon afterwards, the Czechs did the same, in circumstances which made the origin of their reluctance even more evident. The original decision in favour of participating – or at least discovering what the Americans might have to offer – apparently derived from Beneš, who persuaded his colleagues to apply, making the reservation 'that if they found the program was directed against Russia they would withdraw'.[45] Klement Gottwald, the Communist Premier, promptly departed for Moscow, fairly confident that the Russians would authorise this acceptance, which had already been publicised. Gottwald then had an alarming interview with Stalin, as a result of which he telegraphed Prague, demanding withdrawal of the acceptance. His colleagues duly complied.[46]

The Americans also received information which suggested that Hungary had wished to participate. The Smallholder and Social Democratic parties, who together formed a vast majority in the Assembly, each decided in favour. Thereupon the Communists and the Russians told them that if they did so, the country's reparations bill would be increased by $100 million: futhermore, that there would be no further return of Hungarian prisoners of war. The following morning, the Hungarian assembly voted against acceptance.[47] Thus the three countries of eastern Europe which were in Russia's military orbit but not yet completely under Communist political domination, had all wished at least to discover what the American offer might be, but were forbidden to do so by the Soviet Union.

The sixteen countries which evinced continuing interest in the

Marshall proposals worked with considerable alacrity. An initial report was produced in the middle of September. The countries set out the measures which they proposed to take in order to secure internal stabilisation; indicated their production targets; explained how they would ensure free flow of goods and labour, and the full use of European resources, and what they would do to meet special problems presented by their balance-of-payments deficit with the American continent. The United States Government, seised of this information, began to prepare Bills for Congress. At the end of 1947, everybody knew that a long and tough struggle was bound to follow before Congressional approval could be secured – but there was a substantial chance that the United States would provide assistance on a scale adequate for the western Europeans to rehabilitate themselves. Yet any hope that the Russians or their satellites would also participate, had been effectively destroyed. The military and diplomatic and political iron curtain was now accompanied by an economic iron curtain as well. Russia might plunder her satellites, or she might try to set them up after her own fashion, or she might do something in between; what she would not do was allow them to retain and strengthen economic bonds with the West.

Thus were the countries of western and eastern Europe drawing apart in the course of 1947; and the word 'Allies' acquired a note of bitter irony. Even the interest which had drawn together the erstwhile comrades-in-arms – the 'common hate', as Churchill called it – proved more divisive than unifying. The process of finally ratifying peace treaties with Italy and the 'minor enemies' went on without further incident. In practice, the reparation terms exacted from the east European countries tied them indissolubly to the Russian economy, while the 'Free Territory of Trieste' appeared on the map, as visible monument of the incapacity of Allies to agree even on a dividing line between their interests.

So far as the great, central question of Germany went, the sometime Allies got no further than defining their differences. At the beginning of the year, it had been possible to believe that they were playing the ancient game of bluff – delaying, haggling, even blackmailing each other, no doubt, but all of them anxious to reach a settlement and prepared to make compromises in order to do so. The Council of Foreign Ministers held two long, weary sessions: for seven weeks in the spring, and for another three in the late autumn. All that emerged was a general feeling that it was pointless to go on further. The tedious, but apparently 'negotiable', questions of eastern frontier, reparations and occupation costs paled before the fundamental dispute. This was posited as an argument on whether a German central government should be set up before peace treaty discussions opened (as the Russians proposed), or vice versa, and on the kind of relationship which would eventually subsist between the Länder and the central government. But there was vastly more behind these issues than matters of procedure or constitution. Bevin put his own gloomy analysis in a memorandum circulated to the Cabinet not long after the collapse of the second set of negotiations.[48] The Russians, contended the Foreign Secretary, were applying to eastern Germany a technique essentially similar to that which had long been used in their east European dependencies: a

consistent policy of suppression of freedom of the individual . . . discrimination against . . . non-Communist political parties, beginning with the Social Democrats, the incarceration of political opponents in the same concentration camps as were used by the Nazis, the forced deportation of labour to the USSR, the re-arrest of prisoners of war returning to the Soviet zone from the west, political discrimination in the distribution of economic resources, and an extreme form of centralisation of all types of public authority under the domination of the Socialist Unity Party

– the product of a shotgun marriage between Communists and East German Social Democrats. That was bad enough; but, as Bevin went on to argue, all British information indicated not merely that Russia proposed to push this policy to its very limits, but also 'if possible extend their political and economic system into the western zone with the object of winning Germany over to Communism and so undermining one of the principal policies of the Marshall Plan'. In order to achieve this, the Russians would

bind the other three Powers to a joint policy in Germany as a whole, which would in practice have allowed them a free hand to operate directly and through German Communist stooges in the western zone, while at the same time they prevented, on grounds of military security, any penetration either political or economic, of the eastern zone by the Western Powers.

Marshall's views were similar. On return from the Foreign Ministers' Conference, he told the American Cabinet:

Soviets want a form of Government in Germany to which they can dictate. US and France opposed. Soviets are taking reparations out of Germany out of current production in Soviet zone. They are putting nothing into Soviet zone. They account for nothing. We can only estimate the amount. Molotov devoted most of his time to propaganda speeches. They were filled with lies, and accusations of what the US was getting out of Germany.[49]

Thus by the end of 1947 the patience and tolerance of Britain and the United States had been stretched to the limit, and they were in no mood to make any further concessions to Russia. What is more remarkable is that France was reacting in the same way. Until 1947, she had sought to act as a bridge between Russia on one side and the Anglo-Americans on the other – particularly in matters affecting Germany. Whether realistically or not, the French feared attack by the Red Army;[50] but the increasing American involvement in Europe gave them hope of support in that event. Less speculative was the internal problem presented by a large and menacing Communist Party: a problem which did not disappear when Communists left the Government. Such weighty considerations made the French unwilling to participate in the 'zonal fusion' which the Anglo-Americans accomplished at the end of 1946. A year later, however, there was little practical difference between France and the Anglo-Americans on German questions. To some extent, this shift was perhaps influenced by the way in which the French zone was turning from an economic asset to a liability; but the more fundamental reason was a growing fear that Russia would come to dominate the whole of Germany unless the Democracies pulled together.

As a sort of epilogue to the year, the Russians took occasion in October to establish the 'Cominform' – the 'Communist Information Bureau'. The dissolution of the old Comintern in 1943 was taken by many in the West as an earnest of Russian goodwill. The Cominform was a new organ of international subversion, with no meaning save as a device for enabling Communists everywhere to learn from each other's experience and perfect their techniques for winning power. If there was one incident which should be considered a 'declaration of Cold War', this was it. 'Information' which the new Bureau would transmit to Communist parties outside the Soviet Union would be, for all practical purposes, commands from Moscow. Granted the now undeniable fact that Russian Marxists believed that they were engaged in a life-and-death struggle with all Capitalist Powers, the general nature and purpose of those commands was clear. In the countries of central and eastern Europe, where Communists were dominant but not yet in absolute control, the Communists would be instructed on how to destroy the remaining vestiges of opposition. In the rest of the world, the Communists would be told how best to undermine existing governments, and how to frustrate resistance which might be offered against the worldwide march of Communism.

14

Cold War

'Hindsight now indicates that attention by us to the political aspects of the war might have given us control of central Europe at a nominal cost.' Laurence A. Steinhardt to Marshall, 30 April 1948. FRUS 1948 IV, p. 747 seq.

'It can hardly be doubted that the liberation of Prague and as much of the territory of western Czechoslovakia as possible by the Allies might make the whole difference to the post-war situation in Czechoslovakia and might well influence that in nearby countries. If the Western Allies play no significant part in Czechoslovakia's liberation, the country may well go the way of Yugoslavia.' Sir Orme Sargent to Churchill, 22 April 1945. PREM 3/114/3A, fo. 103.

In the beginning of 1948, hundreds of millions of people at each extreme of the Eurasian landmass seemed likely to come under Communist rule within a very short time. Nobody in the West seems to have taken a very emphatic and conscious decision as to which parts of that area were 'vital' to the non-Communist countries and which were not; but the United States administration largely followed the guidance of a Policy Planning Staff Paper communicated to Marshall by George Kennan in February 1948.[1] The United States – so the argument ran – was much over-extended in relation to Asia. Nothing America could do would prevent the peoples of Asia from developing new political forms, and the process 'cannot be a liberal or peaceful one'. During that process, it was probable that many people would fall for varying periods 'under the influence of Moscow'. Japan and the Philippines were the only large territories in the area vital to American Pacific defence, and both must be preserved. Meanwhile, American commitments to China must be liquidated, and the United States recover its 'position of detachment and freedom of action'. In another document, written a fortnight later, Kennan argued that Korea should 'be evacuated as soon as possible'[2] – a piece of advice which was certainly not taken. It was events, however, which soon focused the main attention on Europe.

With Finland as the only large exception, those countries which had lain in the path of the Red Army were virtually written off – not only by the Western Democracies, but by the indigenous peoples themselves. Nowhere was this more plainly shown than in the Czechoslovak crisis of February 1948, and its immediate aftermath.

The precarious and exact balance between Communists and their fellow-travellers on one side and anti-Communists on the other, could not long persist in the Czech Cabinet. We have already noted the restiveness which Social Democrats felt towards Zdenek Fierlinger. The general view in the West was that the elections scheduled for May would result in a substantial erosion of Communist strength. Apparently, the Communists thought the same; for otherwise they had no reason to take the action they did, when it would have been easier to await the verdict of the voters. Like the Nazis in Austria in 1938, the Czech Communists ten years later were not disposed to leave matters in such hands.

The crisis came with little warning. On 20 February, a dispute turning on Cabinet control of the police resulted in twelve non-Communist Ministers tending their resignations to President Beneš. Gottwald, the Communist Prime Minister, declared that the Ministers who resigned 'have handed themselves to me on a golden platter'.[3] This was bad and inept enough; but the situation was made far worse by the fact that the two democratic politicians who enjoyed real prestige were, for different reasons, disabled from effective action. Beneš was suffering from acute arteriosclerosis:[4] a condition likely to impair judgement, and one which contributed to his death later in the year. Foreign Minister Jan Masaryk, who enjoyed a prestige only a little less than Beneš himself (for he was not only a considerable statesman in his own right, but also son of the founder of the Czechoslovak state), disabled himself, for he remained largely passive throughout the crisis. It is likely that Masaryk's inaction led many of his admirers to the view that no particular action was required of them either.

The tendered resignations were not accepted for five days. During that period, the Communists staged mass demonstrations. On 23 February, 'Action Committees' came into existence, and Trade Union militia paraded with rifles. At last, on 25 February, Beneš accepted the resignations, and commissioned Gottwald to form a new Ministry – which he promptly did. Masaryk was still included; but most of the others were Communists or 'fellow-travellers'.

Two features of the *coup* are particularly remarkable. In the first place – as the American Ambassador observed several weeks afterwards – 'there was no direct evidence of Soviet interference'.[5] Of course, the Russians knew what was happening and approved; very likely they had counselled and advised the Czech Communists throughout; but the fact remains that it was Czechs and not Russians who executed the *coup*. In the second place,

> . . . With the exception of a few students, not a single person from the President of the Republic down to the humblest citizen even uttered a public word in defense of their political liberties.[6]

Three days elapsed before the firearms appeared; and when they did appear, nobody tested whether they were loaded. There was no attempt to invoke assistance from the West, even though the American zone of Germany adjoined Czechoslovakia. After the event, many Czechs indicated that their eventual salvation would come from a war between the United States and the Soviet Union. Not surprisingly, the Americans did not feel disposed to oblige.

Jan Masaryk was bitterly criticised by many people for his weakness in the crisis. He told the British he had thereby saved fifty people from the Communists, and claimed to the Americans that the figure was five times as great – surely a considerable disparity. On the night of 9–10 March, Masaryk fell to his death from a window of the Czernin Palace. The facts are, even to this day, obscure; but two explanations were predictable from the outset. The Czech Government declared it was suicide; the Czech opponents of Communism said it was murder. This is not the place to sift conflicting evidence; suffice to observe that either Masaryk was murdered, or else he was convinced that the remainder of his existence in a Communist Czechoslovakia would be worse than death. Both explanations underscore the ruthlessness of the new régime.

The Czechoslovak elections, which had been scheduled for May before the *coup* took place, went ahead as planned, but with one significant variation: the electors had one list of candidates set before them, and no opportunity of expressing disapproval save by the perilous expedient of tendering a blank ballot paper – which, they had been pointedly advised, would be 'tantamount to treason'.[8] On the official figures, about 11 per cent of the voters eventually exhibited that degree of courage.

Events in Czechoslovakia provided the clearest and most dramatic indication to date of the implacable determination of the Communists, and the impossibility of securing any durable compromise with them. Czechoslovakia was an Allied country; a state which had deliberately bent its foreign policy to please Russia for many years; which had foregone the tangible economic advantages of the Marshall Plan in 1947, at Russia's behest. The *coup* was a naked demonstration of force, whose sole possible object was to forestall the free vote of the Czechoslovak people.

In Hungary too, the final suppression of liberty took place in 1948; but the process was a good deal messier, less dramatic and clear-cut, than in Czechoslovakia. The Smallholders Party had already been shattered and demoralised before the year began; so the Communists now applied similar techniques to the Social Democrats and the smaller 'National Peasant' Party. At the beginning of 1948, some leaders of the Social Democratic Party came under heavy Communist fire for their allegedly 'anti-Soviet' attitude. In February, a Social Democrat Minister assured a British diplomat that his party proposed to deal with the situation by expelling the individuals concerned from the party's Central Committee, thus disarming criticism and prolonging resistance to the more serious Communist demand, which was fusion of the two parties.[9] Needless to say, this expedient was completely counter-productive. Very soon, a 'liaison committee' was set up, and by the middle of June amalgamation of Socialists and Communists was complete. Before the year was out, the resulting 'United Workers' Party' was already in process of actively purging its right wing. The National Peasant Party, and the shattered remnants of the Smallholders Party, were also required to conduct purges. By the end of the year, there were still a few members of the Government who did not carry the 'United Workers' label; but there was no single individual who was in any way resisting the Communist line.[10] Hungary, like Czechoslovakia, was now a Communist state.

Western politicians ceased to delude themselves as to the reality of the danger which now confronted the whole of Europe. 'Resolute action must be taken to counter the Soviet threat to Western civilisation,'[11] Bevin told the British Cabinet on 5 March, even before the death of Masaryk. 'The Cabinet should have an appreciation of the military strength needed to support diplomatic action . . . and of the defence measures needed if that policy failed to prevent war.' The language and the atmosphere of that Cabinet were very similar to those of Chamberlain's Cabinet nine years earlier, when Ministers took stock of the situation resulting from Hitler's seizure of Prague. All talk of compromise or deals with the aggressor had vanished. Nothing could be done to save what remained of liberty behind the Iron Curtain, and everyone knew that it was impossible to reverse the Communist tide within the countries already lost. Now statesmen were determined that – whatever the price – Communism should advance no further in Europe.

The military position was precarious, even desperate. At the moment when the Communists seized Czechoslovakia, the Americans had three and a half divisions in Germany, the British had two and a half. Even these were scattered, and engaged mainly in occupational and police duties. The French had fewer than six divisions in their own country, the Low Countries very little. As Dean Acheson observed later, 'the Western Union was a complete shell: there was nothing whatever to that, except a group at Fontainebleau, and the only activity that occurred there was the continuing battle between Montgomery and de Lattre and no progress of any sort in any field whatever'.[12]

How – if at all – might western Europe be defended? The vital economic underpinning which derived from Marshall's proposals – the European Recovery Program, as it became known – had a fairly smooth course through Congress. Most of the Republican 'heavyweights' backed the proposals – the main exception being ex-President Hoover. The necessary legislation was eventually enacted in April 1948. Meanwhile, frantic attention was given by the American administration to the preparation of a Military Assistance Program. Yet, as matters stood in the spring of 1948, even this kind of defensive arrangement could not be pressed too hard or too fast. While the European Recovery Program was still before Congress, Marshall decided that its fate would be endangered if military questions were raised simultaneously.[13]

Most critical of all questions still facing the sometime Allies collectively was the fate of Germany. The British, at any rate, seem to have regarded as decisive the failure of the Council of Foreign Ministers at the end of 1947, and concluded that in all probability no solution could be worked out based on real cooperation between Russia and the West. At the beginning of 1948, Bevin circulated a memorandum on the subject to his Cabinet colleagues.[14] 'It should be clearly known in Germany and elsewhere,' declared the Foreign Secretary, 'that the guiding principle of British policy towards Germany is that H.M. Government will not be a party to creating a situation which can be used to bring about gradually a Communist-controlled Germany on the pattern of . . . eastern Europe.' A 'stable, peaceful and democratic Germany' should be set up as speedily as possible, by four-Power agreement if one could be secured, but, much more probably, by agreement between the Western countries. The Anglo-American economic arrangements in their two zones should be extended; and in the course of the current year elections should take place in Germany for bodies 'exercising most of the functions of a Government and Parliament'. First the Americans and then the French should be approached in order to secure their cooperation.

The proposed inclusion of France was highly significant. Bevin noted that 'one of the principal results of the Council of Foreign Ministers (and of other recent events in France) is that the French have now finally ceased their attempt to act as a bridge between the Soviet Government on one hand and the Americans and ourselves on the other in German matters'. There were still considerable differences between France and the Anglo-Americans: notably, the French wanted Germany to become a good deal more decentralised than the British and Americans thought desirable or possible, and they still hankered for international control of the Ruhr; but these differences were not incapable of resolution. The French, as we have seen, feared an attack by the Red Army; and this emphasised the need for some kind of common defence, involving the United States. The British Government therefore made a secret approach to the Americans, proposing a joint Anglo-American commitment to go to war against an aggressor in western Europe.[15] The American response on matters of military defence was very similar to their response on economic matters. Let the Europeans themselves take the initiative and agree on some collective policy. Then let them approach the United States for assistance.[16]

In March 1947, Britain and France had concluded a mutual defence alliance – the Treaty of Dunkirk. A year later, with the American view in mind and with vivid memory of the Czech *coup*, they had extended the alliance to include the Benelux countries, and envisaged that Italy might eventually be included as well. At this point they felt justified in approaching the Americans.[17] Hopes of United States participation were fulfilled; and in the summer, negotiations commenced for the establishment of what eventually became the North Atlantic Treaty Organisation.

All this was vital to defence against any future attack from the East; but it did not of itself resolve the problem of Germany. The French concern to keep Germany weak could well lead to a situation in which the three western zones were more or less demilitarised, while the Russians would be free to encourage the Germans within their own zone to develop a strong military establishment. The French view made perfect sense if the likely aggressor was Germany, but no sense at all in the current situation. As Marshall pointed out, Germany could not possibly be a threat to anyone so long as the country remained under military occupation.[18] That occupation – so far as the Western Allies were concerned – was likely to prove 'of unforeseeable and indefinite duration'.[19] The Americans would certainly not authorise reunification with the Russian zone 'under conditions which are likely to being about effective domination of all Germany by the Soviets'.[20]

In the latter part of April, discussions on the linked questions of Germany's future and the general defence of western Europe commenced in London – involving Britain, France, the Benelux countries and the United States. The British, at any rate, were both surprised and delighted at American willingness to participate, and to authorise indefinite military occupation of Germany by their own forces.[21] Yet French attitudes to Germany's future remained a serious stumbling-block to any common policy, and at one point the British Cabinet was seriously considering the possibility that France might have to be excluded altogether from the Anglo-American plans. Fortunately, this risk was averted, and eventually the Western countries agreed on a plan to set up a federal state in western Germany. It appears that the reticence of the French Government was not based on any real opposition to this policy, but on the fear that any such proposals would be defeated in the Chamber of Deputies. This peril was narrowly averted; the London Conference recommendations were upheld by 300 votes to 286, with Communists and Gaullists voting against them.

These London discussions played a substantial part in the development of the most dangerous crisis since the war. The situation of Berlin was, from every point of view, anomalous. The city still had a unified local government, despite the presence of the four occupying Powers. From its geographical situation, it would appear to be the natural capital of eastern Germany, now that the western part of the country was developing on different lines. The Russians were obviously unhappy about the continued presence of the Western Allies in the city, and it was predictable that efforts would soon be made to dislodge them. The operative questions were what these efforts would be, and to what extent the Western Allies would resist them. The British position – so far as the Americans could determine it – was that a direct Soviet military attack on Western positions would constitute a *casus belli*; but it was far from clear whether the British would go to war if the Russian pressure was of a different – though equally effective – kind.[22]

In the early part of 1948, the Russians committed a number of relatively minor acts of harassment against the Western Allies in Berlin, particularly against their transport communications with the city. Most dramatic of these incidents was a collision near Berlin between a passenger aeroplane and a Russian fighter. By late April, the Americans were convinced that the Russians were seeking to bring about final collapse of the Four-Power *Kommandatura* in Berlin, but 'in circumstances so obscure that the break-up cannot be laid to them'.[23] The Americans were not willing to allow this to happen, and the Russians were forced to make a dramatic withdrawal from the meeting of Allied commandants in the middle of June – followed by a formal withdrawal from participation in Four-Power control a fortnight later.

Next phase in the Berlin crisis derived indirectly from the plans of the Western Allies to unify their own zones in Germany. One feature of this unification which did not attract exceptional attention during the preliminary discussions was the introduction of a new currency for western Germany, in succession to the old Reichsmarks which circulated throughout the country. This was announced on 18 June, only two days after the effective collapse of the Berlin *Kommandatura*. This currency reform provided the Russians with a perfect excuse for further interruption of most kinds of traffic into Berlin – the argument being that this was necessary in order to prevent introduction of the new western currency into the city. The Soviet commander now produced a new currency reform for Greater Berlin; to which the Western countries retorted by ordering the municipal government not to apply this order in their own sectors, meanwhile informing the local authorities that they had no intention of introducing the new West German currency into the city.

At this point a new suggestion was advanced by one of the Russian officers. This was declared to be 'strictly personal', but bore all the marks of a Soviet Government 'kite'. Could existing zonal boundaries be adjusted, in order to eliminate friction? The Americans at once perceived this as a hint that the Western countries should abandon Berlin and receive other places in return – perhaps Saxony and Thuringia, which the Americans and British had originally occupied.[24]

On 24 June, the Russian blockade of land communications to western Berlin, across the Soviet zone, became practically complete; and the situation was exacerbated further by cutting off electricity supplies, which came largely from the eastern part of the city.

There were considerable pressures within the Western countries for some kind of withdrawal from Berlin. Communists and 'fellow-travellers' could easily point out the inherent risks of war, and appeal to a mixture of apprehension, honest pacifism, and residual pro-Russian feeling. 'No war over Berlin' made much sense to many people who were by no means Communists. There was also considerable apprehension in diplomatic circles that the Western Allies were being engineered into a situation both absurd and dangerous. Byrnes – as Truman noted at the time – 'wants to hedge – he always does. He's constantly sending me alibi memos which I return with directions and the facts.'[25] Luckily for the world, Byrnes was no longer in charge of American foreign policy. There were many others who showed reservations and doubts about the determination now evinced by Marshall and the President. An official at the Quai d'Orsay 'stated that France was committed to follow the lead of United States and the United Kingdom at Berlin, [but] that he personally believed that a serious error had been committed by the Western Powers ... by overstressing the importance of remaining in Berlin and announcing that we would remain there at all costs'.[26] The American Ambassador in Moscow contrasted the 'present hysterical outburst of humanitarian feeling' about the political fate of the Berliners with the inconvenient recollection 'that just $3\frac{1}{2}$ years ago I would have been considered a hero if I had succeeded in exterminating those same Germans with bombs'.[27] The Ambassador was acutely conscious of the risks attached to an 'exposed salient' like Berlin which, it was patent to all, could not possibly resist a military attack.

But Berlin had acquired a symbolic importance transcending all other considerations. The United States political adviser in Germany told Marshall that 'if we docilely withdraw now, Germans and other Europeans would conclude that our retreat from western Germany is just a question of time. United States position in Europe would be gravely weakened.'[28] The matter was discussed at the highest level with the President and a firm decision taken late in June to remain in Berlin, and supply the city, if necessary, as a beleaguered garrison.[29]

The Americans were by no means clear as to what extent the primary Russian aim was to force the Western Allies out of Berlin, and to what extent they were merely using the Berlin question as a device to compel other concessions over Germany.[30] A long meeting between Bedell Smith and Stalin elicited the Soviet reply that their overriding objection was to the establishment of a West German government which would effectively vitiate any possibility of a future government for Germany as a whole.[31] The Berlin problem would disappear if Germany were united. Stalin indicated that he desired a meeting to discuss all the wider questions of Germany's future; but this must be contingent on the Western Allies halting their plans for establishment of a West German government. Everybody was really back to the old question of what the political orientation of a united Germany was likely to be; and whether the long-term risks of a Communist-dominated Germany were even more alarming than the current risks over Berlin.

Nevertheless, the interview with Stalin seemed to justify further negotiations. A familiar pattern developed. Matters were remitted to Molotov, in whose hands futile discussions took place. Stalin was interviewed again; the Western Allies again felt rather encouraged; whereupon matters reverted to Molotov, and again no one made any progress. Molotov was patently acting with Stalin's authority, and probably under Stalin's orders, so, clearly, the whole operation was a waste of everybody's time. The Western Allies, however, were by now taking measure of the Russians, and were not disposed to let everything turn on negotiations in which their adversary's interest lay in protracting discussions and inhibiting action. Long before these futile talks had even begun, Britain and America had inaugurated what was to prove the most remarkable feature of the crisis; and they continued to act without reference to temporary encouragements or discouragements.

Discussions within the British Cabinet on 25 June[32] led to the conclusion that it was impossible to force the Russian blockade by rail, while to convoy lorries would require a major military operation, which was out of the question. Conversations between Truman and General Clay at a rather later date produced similar conclusions.[33] What both Governments considered feasible – at least on a short-term basis – was to bring supplies to Berlin by air. The service advisers of both Governments were very far from convinced that this 'Air Lift' could be mounted on a large enough scale to supply the city over a protracted period.[34] There was a risk that the Russians might intercept planes; but the general view was that such action would constitute an act of war, and would be started only if Russia had resolved upon war in any case. The balance of evidence made this seem an unlikely contingency. Thus on 26 June the Berlin Air Lift commenced; and within the next few days both Anglo-Saxon countries had made public statements of their intention to remain in Berlin, from which retraction was impossible. During the ensuing weeks, the Air Lift was very rapidly stepped up. By the latter part of August, the daily supplies amounted to 3300 tons, of which about a third was carried in British planes. Before the middle of September it stood around 4000 tons: very close to the quantities required to meet all the city's needs, even in winter.[35] The whole massive operation was conducted in a spirit of grim, even desperate, determination by both British and Americans. 'There could be no question of yielding to Soviet pressure; if the Western Allies were forced out of Berlin the prospect of Western Union would be fatally weakened,' declared Bevin in June. 'To yield to Soviet pressure there would lead to further withdrawals by the Western Allies and in the end to war', was the consensus of Cabinet opinion a month later. 'This government is prepared to use any means that may be necessary' to supply Berlin, Marshall wrote to the Ambassador in London, in a context which made it clear that the Secretary of State did not exclude war from his contemplation.[36]

Although the city virtually split in two during the Air Lift, the operation undeniably paid off. On 22 October, General Clay reported that the German people had turned against Communism and towards the West; and in the first month of the new year came indications that Russia was prepared to negotiate an end to the blockade. War had not been courted, but the risk of war had been coolly faced; and thereafter the risk that war would break out in Europe began to abate.

On the other side of the world, a situation had been developing throughout the post-war period which had curious parallels with that in Germany. In Korea, as we have seen, an arbitrary line had been drawn for immediate military purposes. As in the German case, there is no reason for thinking that any of the Allies contemplated for a moment that it would acquire more than ephemeral significance. As early as autumn 1945, the Americans sought to eliminate the Korean barrier by agreement with the Russians, and bring about political and economic unification of the country. After two years of discussions, however, it eventually became evident that further talks would be futile.[37] In November 1947, the General Assembly of the United Nations called for free elections throughout the country, under international supervision; but the Soviet authorities refused United Nations agents access to the part of the country which they controlled. Elections were nevertheless held in the south, and in August 1948 a government was set up; whereupon American military occupation ceased. Meanwhile, the Russians had set up their own satellite government in the north: which, as Dean Acheson explained, 'has never been willing to give its subjects an unfettered opportunity, under the scrutiny of an impartial international agency to pass [judgement] upon its claims to rule'.[38] There was a curious contrast with the situation in Germany; for in Germany the Russian view had been that elections should precede Allied withdrawal, and in Korea it had been the reverse. The reasons in both cases were clearly related to calculations of future developments. In Germany, the Russians needed time to strengthen Communist hold on the east, and to subvert the west, before they would allow a united government. In Korea, the Russians were organisationally ahead of the Americans. What industry there was in Korea was located in the north, and the Russians had available a large body of Koreans who had long lived in Siberia. The south was agricultural, in a parlous condition both politically and militarily, and with few people capable as yet of providing leadership to the country. The practical result was the same in Korea and in Germany: division of the country into two, one part looking to Russia and the other to America.

Meanwhile, China proceeded in her own direction. Whatever doubts Americans and Russians may have felt about the two sides in the civil war, and whatever their long-term wishes for the country may have been, neither was in much position to control events, which took their own course. By the late summer of 1946, the American Cabinet was told that 'the extreme conservatives in China ... have strong influence in the nationalist group', and had 'successfully prevented the ratification of the agreement proposed by General Marshall'.[39] From this point forward, matters went from bad to worse. Civil war became more and more sharp, and by the latter part of 1948 there was no reasonable doubt that the Communists were soon going to win it. It was possible, however, to dissociate events in China, to an extent, from the Cold War; though manifestly there was some relation between the two.

During the course of 1948, there were many signs that the peoples of Britain and America, and most of western Europe, were rallying behind the new, firm, foreign policies epitomised in the personalities of Ernest Bevin and George C. Marshall respectively. The massive doubts about foreign policy which had prevailed in Britain at the end of 1945 were by no means confined to 'fellow-travellers'. Three years later, the picture had changed beyond recognition. With the exception of a couple of Communists, and well under a dozen Labour MPs who, for practical purposes, adopted the Communist position, the British Parliament was united; and attitudes among the nation as a whole were approximating to a similar measure of unanimity.

In the United States, the position appeared briefly to be radically different. The activities of Henry Wallace were far more embarrassing for the American administration than the antics of Communists and crypto-Communists were for the British. Not one of the British intransigents could lay any claim to the rank of a major statesman, or any impressive record of achievement in any other field of public activity. Wallace certainly was a major statesmen, and in different circumstances would have made a perfectly credible President. His views on domestic policy were attractive to many 'New Dealers' who were far from satisfied with the Truman administration. If he had kept his political head, he would have been a much greater force still. When he chose not merely to criticise the Truman Doctrine of 1947, but to do so through speeches made abroad, he upset people with whom he had much in common: Eleanor Roosevelt, widow of the President; the publicist Walter Lippmann; senators like William Fulbright.[40]

Wallace provides a remarkable example of a man whose ideology had nothing in common with Communism who came under strong, though temporary, influence from Communists and 'fellow-travellers'. He was a deeply religious man, whose outlook on economic and political matters would have fitted well with that of a British Liberal in the years shortly before 1914; but his most frequent British correspondent during 1947–8 was the 'crypto-Communist' Labour MP, Konni Zilliacus. Others with a similar outlook found it useful to cultivate Wallace. In the middle of 1947, he backed the Marshall Plan; then he swung violently against it. Somebody had to make the pun that the Marshall Plan was a 'martial plan': in fact it was Wallace who did so. At the end of 1947, Wallace's judgement slipped further still. He announced his intention to stand for

Presidency in the forthcoming year, and a 'Progressive Party' was conjured up in support of his claims. Perhaps nobody believed that he would win; but most early estimates predicted a vote of several millions.

As 1948 advanced, public opinion polls became increasingly discouraging for Wallace's campaign; but one thing seemed clear to most political commentators. He would take enough votes from Truman to turn a Republican win from a likelihood to a certainty. To make the President's position even worse, Truman faced a revolt on the 'right' as well as one on the 'left'. Primeval Southern Democrats, who found Truman's racial tolerance unsupportable, organised what were officially called 'State Rights Democrats', but were universally known as 'Dixiecrats'. They too promoted a candidate for the Presidency.

Yet, in the end, Truman won an incredible triumph. More than 24 million people supported him, against fewer than 22 millions for the Republican Dewey, and around a million each for Wallace and the 'Dixiecrat' Thurmond. More to the point, Truman had a convincing majority of the electoral college, and there was no question of negotiating concessions to either of the smaller parties. Thereafter, the Progressives, and the foreign policy attitudes with which they were linked, rapidly became insignificant in American politics. Parenthetically, we may observe that Wallace himself eventually broke with the Progressive Party, and by 1950 his outlook had changed so profoundly that he supported the United Nations defence of South Korea.

Even the Russians made the best of a bad job with Wallace's decisive defeat. Having long contended that there was nothing to choose between Democrats and Republicans, Soviet propaganda executed a sharp U-turn after the election, applauding Truman's return to office as an indication that the American people had rejected the 'frankly reactionary and most aggressive program . . . of Republican Party and Dewey'.[41]

The year 1948 was seen by many to bring the Allies close to a new war over Berlin, and it certainly signalled a great unification of public opinion in western Europe and North America. It also witnessed another effect, also closely related to the Cold War situation. The Western Allies had long been deeply concerned by the equation between Communism and the aspirations of the Soviet Union. Some people argued that this equation would not always be exact, and we have already noted the scathing views Stalin is alleged to have held about the Chinese Communists. Such arguments, however, looked very much like wishful thinking. If China was poised to go Communist; if western Europe was still by no means secure from Communism; if the growing movements for national independence in European colonies like French Indo-China and the Netherlands East Indies were under substantial Communist influence: then where could the limits be drawn? The United States and Britain were certainly interested in the kind of internal political system which those countries might develop; but this was not their primary concern. What worried them most was the prospect that practically all the Eurasian landmass might soon become an integral part of the Soviet Union, for all practical purposes. The likelihood that this would involve a rupture of commercial and other relations with the great bulk of mankind was alarming enough to trading nations like the Anglo-Saxon countries; but more alarming still was the fear that Communism would seek at all times and by all means to subvert the rest of the world as well. Marxists made no secret of the view that the whole world, and not just part of it, must eventually go Communist, and that every effort should be made to expedite that process. Russian nationalism, or Russian imperialism, was not different in kind from other European imperialisms which had been defeated in the past; but if it was exactly coterminous with political Communism, then the threat was greater than any which had previously been faced.

First sign of a crack in this fearful monolith appeared in what might seem the unlikeliest place of all: Yugoslavia. This was the one place in the Soviet empire outside Russia itself where there was fair reason for thinking that an honest poll of the people would deliver a majority for Communism.

For the latter part of 1947, Marshal Tito had not been granting political interviews to foreign diplomats. Then, on 3 January, he received the American Ambassador, who derived the firm impression that the Russians could not, or would not, supply the mechanical equipment Yugoslavia required for the current Five Year Plan.[42] In the middle of June appeared the first tiny act of defiance ever shown by a Soviet satellite. A Danubian Convention had been planned for Belgrade in July, to consider matters of common concern to the riparian countries. Suddenly, the Russians proposed that it should be held in some other Danubian country; but the Yugoslavs openly demurred.[43] People suddenly recalled that in January the Russians had rebuked both Yugoslavia and Bulgaria for proposing a federation between their two countries. The Bulgarians had recanted; the Yugoslavs had remained silent.

At the end of June came further signs of a split between Russia and Yugoslavia. Representatives of most of the larger European Communist parties were summoned to a meeting of the Cominform, to consider the affairs of the Yugoslav Communist Party. The Yugoslavs were invited, but refused to attend. Thereupon the Cominform passed a resolution criticising the Yugoslavs for an

unfriendly policy towards the Soviet Union, and for sins against
Marxist theory and practice. So, far from making the abject
apologies expected of them, the Yugoslavs issued a public statement
repudiating the charges. More astonishing still, they proceeded to
level sharp counter-charges against the Soviet Communist Party.

During the next few weeks, a number of features in the Yugoslav
situation began to emerge. On the issue of the Danubian Convention
itself, Yugoslavia won her point, for the meeting was held in
Belgrade. Within Yugoslavia, there was no sign of internal
disruption, and it appeared that most of the local Communists
accepted the Titoite position on its merits, quite apart from the local
constraints set upon them. The country showed no resilement from
the Communist position: indeed, at least one American observer
perceived a shift to the 'left'. Yet, in her international dealings,
Yugoslavia was visibly seeking reconciliation with the West.
Considerable interest was evinced in the Marshall Plan. An
agreement was concluded with the United States, settling various
financial claims. Before the split with Russia, the Greek guerrillas
had been able to escape across the Yugoslav frontier when
hardpressed by Government forces – then to rest, and re-enter
Greece elsewhere. They were even acquiring machine guns and
mortars from that source. When a 'rebel' Greek Government was set
up in the more inaccessible parts of the country, it had obtained
substantial help from the Yugoslavs. Now such assistance was
completely cut off, and the Greek rebellion was brought under
control.[44]

The Yugoslav precedent of revolt from Soviet control was not
followed successfully by other European satellites of the Soviet
Union, save for the insignificant and inaccessible Albania; but an
American Policy Planning Staff paper, produced as early as 30 June
1948, and bearing signs of the hand of George Kennan, recognised its
true significance: 'The aura of mystical omnipotence and infallibility
which has surrounded the Kremlin power has been broken.'[45]
Thereafter Marxism, like other philosophical doctrines, became a
matter for argument, not a matter of revealed truth.

Before 1948 was out, signs appeared which suggested that
disagreements between Communist states might perhaps work
positively to the advantage of the West – indeed, they might in some
ways facilitate true reconciliation with both competing groups of
Marxists. The 'Free Territory of Trieste' had been established as a
sort of legacy of the Venezia Giulia dispute. Part was under Yugoslav
administration, part under Western administration; but lip service
was paid to the principle that a Governor should be appointed
acceptable to both sides. There was no sign that such a remarkable
individual would ever appear, and in the spring of 1948 the Western

Allies proposed that the whole territory should be returned to Italy. They could not have anticipated an eager acceptance of such a suggestion by the Soviet Union, but the approach might have some propaganda value with the Italians. The predicted Russian rebuff, however, did not occur; and soon afterwards the world heard of the dispute between Tito and the Kremlin. Within the Free Territory, extreme acrimony prevailed between pro-Kremlin and pro-Tito Communists. The Yugoslav zone was progressively integrated into Yugoslavia itself, and large numbers of Italian refugees poured into the western zone. The Russian attitude to Trieste now began very subtly to shift. Nobody doubted that Russian support for the Yugoslavs was a very serious political liability for the Italian Communists. This was a price Russia might be prepared to pay if Yugoslavia were her own satellite; but certainly not if Yugoslavia was in full revolt from the Kremlin. Nobody could foresee, right to the end of 1948, where that revolt would end, and Russia had no incentive to make a total *volte face* over Trieste; but the potential existed, and would later become a reality.

Much more important, the developing story of Yugoslavia's revolt bore obliquely on the greater events which were already foreshadowed. China, as we have repeatedly observed, was poised to go Communist. This likely development was certainly not viewed with any pleasure in the United States; indeed, there is much to be said for the view that the hostile reaction of America on the matter did her a great and unnecessary measure of damage in future international dealings. Yet the story has another side to it. An exceedingly influential paper by Kennan, masked by the transparent pseudonym 'X', appeared in the journal *Foreign Affairs* in July 1947. Kennan there promulgated the doctrine which became familiar as 'containment'. The meaning of 'containment' is far from clear, and Kennan himself later qualified much of his own argument.[46] One point, however, emerged very clearly from the 'X' article: that Chinese Communism would not provide an accretion of massive strength for the Soviet Union. The Yugoslav precedent would be repeated on a far greater scale at a much later date.

The Cold War was by no means over at the end of 1948: indeed, relations between the West and the Soviet Union would in many respects continue to deteriorate right down to the death of Stalin in 1953; and even in our own day, full reconciliation has not been achieved between Russia and the West. Yet by the end of 1948 there were already indications that it would not develop into full-scale conflict. Bedell Smith, in a despatch from the American Embassy in Moscow just before Christmas, recognised several signs which suggested that the danger of war between Russia and the West was receding – if, indeed, it had ever been a very real danger. The split between Tito and Stalin would hardly have been allowed to take place if either man considered that war would soon break out against the West. The process of agricultural collectivisation was being pressed hard in the Baltic States, and was meeting with strong resistance; but this fact was not deterring the authorities in the satellite states from undertaking a similar process. There were many other signs suggesting that Russia and her dependencies were undertaking programmes designed to strengthen them in the long run – but of a kind which could not fail to produce short-term weakness. These were not the actions of a state which anticipated a major war at an early date.[47]

15

The Lessons

'... "Why, 'twas a very wicked thing!"
  Said little Wilhelmine.
"Nay ... nay ... my little girl," quoth he,
  "It was a famous victory.

"And everybody praised the Duke
  Who this great fight did win."
"But what good came of it at last?"
  Quoth little Peterkin.
"Why that I cannot tell," said he,
  "But 'twas a famous victory." '

Robert Southey, *The Battle of Blenheim.*

On 14 February 1938, a remarkable correspondence was published in *Pravda*, official organ of the Communist Party of the Soviet Union. The interrogator was an unknown individual named Ivan Ivanov; the respondent, Stalin. The context of that correspondence gave it peculiar significance. Stalin was approaching the end of what was perhaps the most bloodthirsty purge of real or imaginary enemies which the world had ever seen in any country at any time. Many of those enemies were designated 'Trotskyites'. The chief ostensible issue of Marxist theory between Stalin and Trotsky was whether socialism could be built in one country (as the Stalinists claimed), or whether (as Trotskyites held) world revolution was essential first. In a crucial passage of the letter to Ivanov, Stalin declared:

This is what Lenin said concerning the matter. '... the existence of the Soviet Republic alongside the imperialistic states for a prolonged period of time is unthinkable. In the end of ends, either the one or the other will be victorious. And while this end approaches, a number of most terrible clashes between the Soviet Republic and the *bourgeoisie* are inevitable ...' ... Simply and

strongly   spoken,   but   honestly   and   truthfully,   without
embellishment, as Lenin was able to speak . . .¹

The word 'imperialist' was of somewhat uncertain meaning, but
certainly covered (for example) Britain and France, as well as
Germany, Italy and Japan.

In one sense, perhaps, this correspondence is not remarkable at
all. There is nothing in Stalin's letter which constituted an addition
to Marxist philosophy. The particular quotation we are considering
was the expression of ideas foreshadowed in the writings of Marx
himself, and which were present in a developed form in the works
attributed to Lenin and Stalin. One could provide dozens of similar
utterances with equal authority, all to the same effect. Yet in another
sense the statement was very remarkable indeed: and that was in its
timing. The Communists in Russia and in other countries had for
some years been bending their main efforts to the task of persuading
non-Communists to join them in establishing 'popular fronts',
which should cover the widest possible range of Communist,
Socialist, Liberal and even moderate Conservative opinion. These
'popular fronts' were ostensibly designed to counter the internal and
international activities of 'fascists'. In order to establish 'popular
fronts', the Communists were anxious to demonstrate the essential
moderation of their outlook. If, in such circumstances, the Soviet
dictator was prepared to promulgate a message which could hardly
fail to revive the quiescent fears of many people whom he desired to
attract into the 'popular fronts', then he may be presumed to have
meant what he said.

Stalin, of course, was not proclaiming that the Soviet Union
proposed itself to inaugurate the 'terrible clashes' which must
precede the final proletarian victory. There was also a possibility that
some, at least, of the clashes would take place between rival
'imperialists', and would not directly involve the Soviet Union at all.
Indeed, much could be said for the view that the dominant aim of
Soviet foreign policy in the 1930s was to bring about exactly that
result.

Still less did Stalin's statement imply that the Soviet Union
proposed to involve itself in conflicts in order to produce
'ideological' results. After the period of the Russian revolutionary
wars, there was little evidence to show that the Soviet Government
would willingly sacrifice one soldier or one kopek for the cause of
anybody else's revolution. In that sense, Russia was behaving – and
would continue to behave – in the tradition of aristocratic
diplomacy: completely selfish, completely ruthless, completely un-
ideological, in pursuit of objectives which would have been
thoroughly familiar to Catherine or Metternich or Talleyrand or

Palmerston. Ideology might indeed be invoked in pursuit of those objectives: to rouse the enthusiasm of Russian nationals; to sap the will of others who might oppose Russian aspirations; but this use of ideology as a diplomatic weapon was just like Russian behaviour, and the behaviour of other states, long before 1917. Just so did Russians of the Tsarist period find pan-Slavism a useful weapon to embarrass Austria or Turkey; to assist their designs towards the Mediterranean, or to weld non-Russian Slavs within their Empire in loyalty to the Romanovs. Just so was Russia's self-appointed task as protector of the Eastern Christians a useful weapon when dealing with Turkey. In that sense, ideology could be conjured up or abandoned whenever it suited the purpose of the Russian Government to do so. Pan-Slavism could be soft-pedalled when Russia sought rapprochement with Austria; Armenian Christians could be left to their fate when the Tsar's government was not currently ready to take over the lands in which they lived. These precedents were followed by Stalin. When Germans invaded the Soviet Union, and it was plain that a great many Soviet citizens would not fight with zest in defence of Communism, the old Russian nationalism was revived in its place. When it occurred to Stalin that the Orthodox Church might help rally the people against the German invader, no scruples about Marxist atheism inhibited him from giving his best encouragements to their efforts.

The external policy of Stalin's Russia was just as cynical, just as un-ideological. In the period immediately preceding September 1939, Stalin decided that he wished to bring the Baltic area and eastern Poland under Soviet control. He was willing to do a deal with Britain and France under which the Allies would acknowledge Russia's right to interfere in neighbouring countries, in return for support against Germany. The British, however, were not prepared to dispose of the interests of the people concerned in such a manner.[2] Hitler, on the other hand, had no scruples about it; so Stalin concluded a 'Non-Aggression Pact' with the Nazis, which gave him what he wanted. This was done in full knowledge that the Nazis would greatly expand their own area of control as part of the deal; and that a major European war would probably result. Later, when the thieves fell out, Stalin successfully persuaded more tolerant governments in Britain and (ultimately) America, to acknowledge for all practical purposes what he had sought several years earlier.

The opportunism continued. Observing Yugoslavia in 1943, Stalin had no more sympathy for Tito than for Mihajlović; not the least concern about whether or not the people of the country were to enjoy the putative benefits of Communism after the war. Although he was in no position to render significant military aid to any Yugoslavs until a late stage of the war, yet his diplomatic assistance might well have helped the British when they were trying to secure full backing for Tito. In the event, Stalin was more or less passive for a long time. He finally supported Tito – but only because Tito seemed likely to give better value in fighting the Germans, and thus marginally reduce Russia's own losses. For comparable reasons of military and diplomatic strategy, Stalin alternately encouraged and snubbed EAM in Greece. When there were signs that the Americans desired to assist the subject-peoples of European empires to gain independence after the war, the Russians did not lift a finger to assist that 'struggle against imperialism' which was to form such a fruitful source of Communist propaganda a few years later. Russia's attitude to the Chinese Communists changed from time to time; what did not change was her desire to dominate as much of China as she could. We have already noted the rampant imperialism of the secret deal at Yalta; and the well-founded American suspicion that what Russia desired from the Chinese civil war was not outright victory for one side or the other, still less reconciliation between the two – rather, that the country should remain weak and divided for as long as possible. All this, of course, did not inhibit Stalin from drawing what propaganda and other advantages he could from the situation when eventually the Chinese Communists triumphed. All the burning ideological causes of the 1940s, for which so many of Russia's young and enthusiastic admirers sacrificed so much, counted for nothing to the scheming old tyrant in the Kremlin.

In the limited sense which we have just considered – but only in that limited sense – Stalin's policy may justly be seen as a mere projection of the policies of the Tsars. Russia desired to expand for reasons which have always prompted strong nations to expand: desire for raw materials and markets; desire for land; fear that others might preempt her claim and exclude her; to secure an advantageous military position; perhaps at times because of sheer megalomania, or the inherent difficulty of applying brakes to a machine which has acquired its own momentum.

Like all expanding Powers, Russia had to invent excuses for her aggression; for people will only rob with real enthusiasm when they have first convinced themselves that this robbery is subserving some high moral purpose. One excuse came readily to hand: she had no natural frontiers. Thus, Russia's existing possessions at any given moment would always seem to require external defence: a consideration which has repeatedly brought her into conflict with neighbours. To Russians, such conflicts have always been seen as essentially defensive in purpose: to her neighbours as unprovoked aggression.

To that extent, the expansion of Stalin's Russia, and the reactions of others to that expansion, all followed a very familiar pattern. Yet there was another respect in which Russian expansion was unique; for it was linked to Marxist doctrine, which confidently predicted that the political system embodied in Russia would eventually conquer the world. We have already seen that Stalin, like all Marxist thinkers, believed that prolonged coexistence between Communist and non-Communist societies was impossible, and that the issue between the two would eventually be decided by war. Belief in the inevitability of conflict is likely to be self-serving. A person who holds it will inevitably interpret the behaviour of his perceived enemy in the worst possible light. If he sees some opportunity of improving his own strategic position, or of making a preemptive strike, then he will naturally avail himself of the advantage.

The most crucial question facing the Western Democracies in their dealing with Russia throughout the 1940s was whether the view of Soviet policy and anticipations which had been stated so lucidly and on the highest possible authority as recently as 1938 had been abandoned or not. If it had been abandoned, then there was no apparent reason why Russia and the democracies could not cooperate to the full, both in the war against Germany and in the post-war period. No doubt there were fields in which interests conflicted; but these were of small account by comparison with the fields where their interests were the same.

But if, on the other hand, Russia's general view had not been abandoned, but had merely been set in cold storage until Hitler was beaten, then the Western Democracies were surely set on enquiry as to the policy they ought to pursue. They might – for example – consider that there was little or nothing to choose between Nazi Germany and Communist Russia, for each was a thorough-going tyranny which sought total destruction of the democratic states. In that event, the logical course for the Western Democracies to follow might be to stand more or less aside while Russia and Germany fought each other – meanwhile reserving enough strength to deal with the survivor. Alternatively, the Western Democracies might consider that there were good and sufficient reasons for strongly preferring Russia to Germany in the current conflict. In that event, they might well cooperate to the full with Russia in the common war against Germany; but they would also employ every available device, military and diplomatic, to ensure that Russian power was extended no further than was absolutely necessary after the war; and they would take the closest possible counsel together in all matters touching on Russia.

Roosevelt and Churchill were receiving constant warnings about Russian designs from their own diplomatic officials, and from other Allied Governments, most particularly the Poles. Even clearer warning came from the writings of Stalin himself: documents much more lucid than *Mein Kampf*, which many men had foolishly ignored in earlier days. Both leaders felt occasional sharp doubts in the light of particular events as to whether full cooperation with Stalin would be possible after the war, or perhaps even during the war itself.

Against the weighty evidence which suggested that the leopard had in no way changed his spots, there were serious arguments which disposed Churchill and Roosevelt towards close cooperation with Stalin; even concession of their own or other people's interests to his demands. Strongest of these arguments was the view that victory in the current war, and the future security of mankind, both depended on cooperation between the Big Three. If concessions would indeed keep mankind at peace for the rest of history, then perhaps they represented a small price to pay. The operative question, however, was whether concessions by the West would produce that effect – or whether they would be counter-productive, as concessions to Hitler had been.

Other arguments were used to buttress the case for concessions. First, chronologically, was the argument that if concessions were not made by the West, Russia would conclude a separate peace with Germany. This argument was used to a great extent both in Britain and in America around 1942, but it was still occasionally employed even into the second half of 1943. Yet it was never very convincing. Stalin had proved conclusively enough in 1939 that he was perfectly willing to make peace with the Nazis on suitable terms; it was Germany who broke the agreement. While the Nazis were advancing, the terms which they would have exacted would assuredly have produced total destruction of the Soviet regime and the deaths of its leaders – if not on German insistence then at the hands of the Russian people themselves. Once the Germans were retreating, the Soviet leaders had no cause to make peace with them. A compromise peace between Germany and Russia was only likely to arise in conditions of military deadlock. Yet even if we discount such considerations, it is vital to remember that Russia's requirements were essentially military, not diplomatic. A Second Front in the West, or delivery of great quantities of weapons, might conceivably reduce the prospect of a Russo-German peace – though even that was unlikely. What was completely unbelievable from the start was that diplomatic concessions, such as acknowledgement of the Russian position in the Baltic States or eastern Poland, could possibly exert any significant weight in the matter.

The second line of supporting argument appeared later. In January 1944, Churchill wrote to Eden of 'the deep-seated changes which have taken place in the character of the Russian State and Government', and of 'the new confidence that has grown in our hearts towards Stalin'[3] – admitting that both had exerted an effect on his own attitudes. Yet this argument was also of doubtful force. Whether Russia's leaders had undergone a fundamental change of heart or not, it was predictable that the Russian Government would try to make itself reasonably amenable to the West during the period of common conflict against Germany. If the external ambitions which we have been discussing were still entertained, they would assuredly be dissembled. Stalin, in his language to Roosevelt and Churchill, might talk toughly; but he would talk the language of an Ally who shared the most vital interests in common with them, not the language of an enemy who proposed eventually to destroy them both. During the war-time period, internal oppression in the Soviet Union would also certainly be relaxed – partly to engender sympathy in the West, but mainly in order to persuade the Soviet people, who had suffered so much under Stalin, that it was worth making common cause with their Government against the German invader. Thus the superficial 'evidence' of a change of heart in Russia, which influenced Churchill so much around 1943, would have appeared in any event, and gave no indication whatever about Russia's ultimate objectives.

Our present study suggests that the deep questions about Stalin's long-term objectives were never properly and calmly examined by the most senior policy makers during the war-time period. Documents which bore on the matter certainly emerged in abundance from the Foreign Office and the State Department; but we have no indication that the question was really thought through exhaustively at the highest level. Churchill and Roosevelt – men whose reputations had been built on the validity and ruthless logic of their warnings about Nazi Germany – stood in the vanguard of those who accepted the bare word of Stalin as assurance for the future, and refused to make the cool examination which the occasion demanded. Both men seem to have decided their future policy towards Russia mainly on the basis of their personal encounters with Stalin, who – like Hitler – possessed an almost infinite capacity to switch on charm as the occasion demanded. All was effectively staked on the guess that a deal could be made, and would be honoured: that Stalin had abandoned all he ever said about the future world revolution, and Russia's likely part in it. The Western leaders never considered properly what objective tests might be applied to test the matter, or what consequences were likely to follow if the preferred view proved wrong. Statesmen should not be blamed lightly for taking wrong decisions, but it is more difficult to acquit them from blame for brushing aside evidence available to them.

Because Churchill and Roosevelt wielded exceptional power and influence during the war, their personal foibles were of great value to Stalin in advancing his own purpose. Roosevelt reached the thoroughly rational conclusion that a world where political, economic and personal freedom were universal would be incomparably happier and more secure than one in which they were very limited. He perceived, with equal rationality, that the ideology of Nazi Germany was wholly inconsistent with the system which he desired to prevail. He then made the gigantic leap in the dark of assuming that Stalin hated Hitlerism for the same reasons that he did; and that Stalin's aspirations for the future of the human race were broadly similar to his own. On a famous occasion, the President revealed this clearly in a discussion with William Bullitt. Like Joseph Davies, Bullitt had been Ambassador to the Soviet Union; but he had returned with diametrically opposite conclusions. An article by Bullitt, written some years afterwards, quoted the President:

> Bill, I don't dispute your facts, they are accurate . . . I don't dispute the logic of your reasoning. I just have a hunch that Stalin is not that sort of man . . . If I give him everything I possibly can and ask nothing from him in return, he won't try to annex anything and will work with me for a world of democracy and peace.[4]

The pointers, alas, suggest that the word 'hunch' was not ill-chosen. Roosevelt's 'hunch' about Stalin was not based on careful analysis and study, drawing to the full on informed opinion, but on unreasonable pride in his own judgement.

Roosevelt has nevertheless been pilloried too harshly by some commentators – who, one feels, were often more anxious to draw morals applicable to current politics than to assess the past objectively. He does not emerge from our story unscathed: His *hubris* brought the rewards which *hubris* usually does; his behaviour towards colleagues left much to be desired; and he had a disposition to set immediate interests before long-term ones. Yet in the early part of the period of study, he appears rather well. When Churchill had already bent reluctantly to pressure from Eden and the Foreign Office over recognition of Russia's position in the Baltic States, Roosevelt perceived that deep principles were at stake; and when he saw that it was no longer possible to defend those principles he did at least evince compassion for the individuals who were likely to suffer, and tried to win a refuge for them in the United States. It is quite likely that the President's reluctance to abandon Polish interests was influenced to no small degree by knowledge that there were millions of Polish votes in his own country; but he continued to show concern for those interests even when he had no immediate need for Polish votes.

With Churchill, the story was different. Many have commented on the facility with which the extreme anti-Bolshevik of 1919 could turn into the staunch advocate of a close Russian alliance, and then into the Fulton orator of 1946. The one thing which never changed was his absolutely implacable hatred of Nazism. This would have been wholly praiseworthy if it had led him to discern the loathsome features of Nazism, wherever they existed in the world; but unfortunately it disposed him to adopt the 'one-war-at-a-time' mentality, and not properly to consider whether different policies might reduce the danger that another Hitler should confront mankind, even before the original was dead. Yet there is nothing about Churchill which suggests a self-seeking hypocrite; at every turn there are all the marks of passionate sincerity in his new convictions. Right at the root of Churchill's character was a deep psychological need to be at the very thick of some conflict or other: to devote every ounce of energy to that conflict, and to ignore all other considerations, however vital for the future. It was agony to him that he could do little to assist the great and decisive battles which were being played out on the Soviet plains in 1942 and 1943: that a Second Front at that time would have been an act of futile suicide; that he must even suspend the Arctic convoys. By a strange and archaic logic, which he may not have understood fully himself, Churchill sought to discharge the moral debt which he felt to the Soviet people in the only way which came to his mind: by backing the political aspirations of their Government, at the expense of so many other peoples. This fits in well with the corporate ethic which was deeply ingrained in men of the Prime Minister's class and generation. Stalin, however, was neither a liberal like Roosevelt nor the product of a Victorian public school like Churchill. He probably did not understand their motivations at all, or wrongly construed them as mere rationalisations of weakness.

A complex mixture of these personal considerations and perceived national interests made it all too easy for Stalin to play off Britain and the United States against each other. If America dragged her feet over acknowledgement of Russia's Baltic conquests; if Roosevelt strove to retain the city of Lwow for Poland or demurred at the prospect of a Balkan carve-up, then Britain could be used in the matter. Conversely, Roosevelt would blithely issue a statement on the Second Front in 1942 which was bound to embarrass Britain. Although Churchill soon saw that Stalin had hoodwinked everybody else at Yalta, first the dying Roosevelt temporised, and then Harry Truman sent Hopkins to make further concessions in Moscow. When Churchill, warned by British diplomats of the damage which would follow if the Russians took Prague, tried to persuade the Americans to make a swift dash for central Europe in the crazy last few days of war, they would not oblige. While British and Americans wrangled for weeks over the ideal arrangement in Venezia Giulia, Tito was able to establish himself in an impregnable military position. Once we bring de Gaulle and the French into the story, the potentialities for Russian mischief are multiplied again. Not only were the British and the Americans at loggerheads, but there were great power-struggles over France within both of those countries, while de Gaulle was not unwilling to play from time to time on Russia's side in order to win small and doubtful advantages for France. Other states were used in the process of general disruption among the democratic Allies. The Poles, the only people of eastern Europe who could hope to form a nucleus of resistance against Soviet westward expansion, were broken into fragments: and the Western Allies assisted actively in the process of breaking them. Beneš of Czechoslovakia was willing to be used as a catspaw, in the hope of winning some benefits from Russia. He lived just long enough to see the result of his brittle cleverness, in the final destruction of his country's liberty. 'Divide and rule' was indeed the order of the day, and remained so until Ernest Bevin and George Marshall were able to guide their countries' foreign policies in a spirit of harmony and true cooperation.

Many have suggested that Russian ascendancy over central and eastern Europe was the inevitable product of the victories of the Red Army; that Britain and America merely authorised a process which they were powerless to prevent. Our present study does not confirm that view. The first major acknowledgement of Russian conquests over unwilling people was the *de facto* British recognition of her position in the Baltic States. This was effectively granted in the spring of 1942, at a time when the territories concerned were in German occupation and when the Russian army was in full retreat. Indeed, the argument for that recognition was posited on the proposition that Russia *was* weak, and might otherwise compound with the Germans. The second great step – tacit acknowledgement of the Curzon Line as future frontier for Poland – was already being prepared long before the first returning Red Army soldier set foot in pre-1939 Poland; for the Western Allies were already disposed to abandon much, if not all, of the eastern moiety of the country.

Yet is it true to say that Russia would have taken all of those lands for herself sooner or later; that the Western acknowledgement may have been premature, but was inevitable at some time or other? This is by no means clear. Until a very late stage of the war, Russia was – from a military point of view – a suppliant. There was a great deal that the West could have done to keep her in line. Much of the material which Russia was receiving in Lend-Lease could have been set at the disposal of the Western Allies themselves, or at the disposal of non-Communist insurgents in Europe. The 'Second Front' could have moved earlier and faster if America had not sent such massive help to the Soviet Union. Long before the Warsaw rising, the Poles pleaded for more material help from America:[5] and there is something to be said for the view that allocation of such assistance could have proved of crucial importance in helping the Poles to play a more effective part in freeing their country from the Germans – and thereafter preserving its independence from the Russians. Mihajlović in Yugoslavia suffered, as did the Poles, from shortage of arms from the West; and there can be little doubt that he would have rendered them better assistance if he had been better supplied. Thus the Western Allies were giving great quantities of material to Russia and to pro-Communist insurgent forces, at a time when there were other ways in which some, at least, of that material could have been used, which would also have assisted in bringing about the defeat of Germany. It would surely have been wise if closer consideration had been given to the likely long and short-term results which would have flowed if the support had been given differently, and distributed with the conscious object of not merely helping to win the war swiftly, but also of shaping the post-war world.

Yet it would be quite wrong to imply that everything was more or less determined by the end of the war, that it was already clear in general terms where the line would be drawn between Communist and non-Communist states. That line might very easily have come to be drawn hundreds of miles either to the east or to the west. Russia's behaviour even towards Romania in the latter part of 1945 was not the behaviour of a victor who was absolutely confident of his own strength: rather the Russians acted as if it was of considerable importance to them to carry America in what was being done. This state of affairs was brought out even more strikingly in Bulgaria. Right at the last moment, Maynard Barnes – misunderstanding his instructions from Washington – called for postponement of an obviously faked election. The Russian puppets drew back, even though this involved a considerable loss of prestige. Not until the Russians felt confident that the State Department would not interfere were matters again allowed to proceed. In Hungary, the situation was even more remarkable. The Russian commander wanted the 1945 elections to be held on a 'government list' system – in which case eventual Communist domination would have been more or less assured. Hungarian politicians themselves, apparently with little encouragement from outside, refused to play that game; and the Russians accepted their refusal with good grace. If the great Smallholders majority which was recorded soon afterwards had been backed financially and morally by the Americans during 1946, the economic collapse might well have been averted, and the country would have had a good chance of emerging with established democratic institutions. It is even more likely that events could have run differently in Czechoslovakia. The Red Army was withdrawn from most of the country soon after the war. What demoralised Czech democrats, and made the 1948 *coup* possible, was the feeling that they had been abandoned by the West.

It is no less likely that events could have taken a very different course in Poland. When Truman stood up to Molotov in the famous first interview, and when he refused thereafter to submit to Soviet blackmail and recognise the Lublin régime in time for the San Francisco meeting of the United Nations, the Russians acted like men who had been bluffing, and whose bluff had been called. Only afterwards was Harry Hopkins sent to Moscow for another disastrous piece of 'personal diplomacy'; and it was only after Byrnes had become Secretary of State that the Hopkins deal over Poland was endorsed at Washington.

The present author suspects, but cannot prove, that Byrnes's own approach played a very large part indeed in the tragic story of eastern Europe. We have seen that he had a reputation as a compromiser among friends and foes alike, even before he took on his vital office. Perhaps the most striking feature of events in 1946, by comparison with the very beginning of the Truman period and the period from 1947 onwards, is not the vigour of Communist pressure but the weakness of American reaction to that pressure. There is surely a lingering suspicion that a kind of personal deal – perhaps no more than a 'nod and a wink' – was done between Byrnes and Molotov towards the end of 1945, as a result of which Soviet ascendancy in what are today the 'Iron Curtain' countries was acknowledged; and perhaps even Truman himself was not kept properly informed.

In fact, the more closely one examines the aftermath of war in eastern Europe, the more questions are posed. The old type of economic order was doomed, whatever happened. The operative question in 1945 was what should succeed it. There was also much doubt about the future political order. Only Czechoslovakia had a highly-developed democratic tradition, although others had had experience of democratic forms to a limited extent. Yet, on the other hand, they were not – on Marxist theory – 'ripe' for Communism. Communist parties in eastern Europe had been very weak before the war. In some countries they were illegal, but doubtless existed to a limited extent underground. The Polish Communist leaders had been invited to the Soviet Union, and there quietly liquidated. Where Communist parties were lawful, as in Czechoslovakia, they were not very effective. If Stalin was looking for Communist revolutions in European countries in the immediate aftermath of war, then France, Italy, Spain and – above all – Germany, must have seemed far better propositions. Nor did the economic resources and potentials of the east European countries add much to the Soviet Union itself.

It is impossible to know for certain what vision the Russians had in the moment of victory of the immediate future of the eastern European countries. We have noted that there was a formal agreement with Britain that Romania, Bulgaria and Hungary should pass into the Soviet sphere of influence, but this did not logically imply that they must have Communist governments, any more than the allocation of Greece to the British sphere of influence implied that she must have a Westminster-type democracy. Stalin certainly complained about the way in which Germany had used eastern Europe as a corridor into Russia in both world wars, and was anxious for full military protection against a repetition. In that cause Russia had full moral backing from Britain and America, who also had suffered much from German aggression. What worried Russia most about the countries of eastern Europe was not their strength but their weakness.

To that statement there is one great exception: Poland. While a very weak Poland could serve as a corridor for the Germans, a very strong Poland would pose a different threat. No serious Polish politician wanted any territory east of the Riga Line; but a strong Poland would block any westward extension of Russian influence. Hence the Russians were anxious to discourage a Polish-Czech federation, to push Poland westwards and embroil her permanently with Germany, and to break Polish morale by frustrating the Warsaw rising. Thus the Russians were more disposed to exert their military might for political purposes in Poland than in most of eastern Europe. Elsewhere, they were probably disposed to allow matters to develop in their own way – no doubt giving 'guidance', but without forcing the pace. Why bother if Hungary elected Smallholders, or if Maynard Barnes was fastidious about free elections in Bulgaria, or if King Michael of Romania stood up to Peter Groza? If western Europe and the Soviet Union were both Communist, then eastern Europe must soon follow. Russia could reasonably anticipate a chain of events in which her own direct role would be minimal and (save perhaps in Poland) of a kind to which America could raise little technical objection.

There was much reason for thinking that events would follow roughly that course, when Roosevelt announced at Yalta that the Americans would leave Europe within a couple of years, he expressed no more than what everybody expected. The last thing the Americans wanted was to keep soldiers stationed thousands of miles from home, where no 'vital' strategic or economic interests seemed threatened. If the Americans had indeed left when they expected, then nobody else was in a position to resist Communist takeovers in western Europe. As to the idea of 'Western Union' between European states – an idea which bemused the Foreign Office and the Quai d'Orsay – Molotov even told the British that he had no objection to it. Churchill seems to have taken in the danger of American withdrawal far earlier and far more clearly than any other major Western statesman.

With their eyes on western Europe, the Russians may very well have been willing to trade the liberties of eastern Europe with the Americans in return for advantages of a more tangible kind: specifically, for a large low-interest loan from the United States. On at least one occasion, Molotov actually teased the Americans for their apparent reluctance to bargain. What the Russians almost certainly did not realise was the radically different nature of relations between the executive and the controllers of public finance in America from those prevailing in their own country. If an American pointed out that no President or Secretary of State could guarantee Congressional support on some important matter like a Russian loan, the Russians probably disbelieved him. Even the British, who were used to a much closer partnership between Parliament and Ministers, probably had considerable difficulty in appreciating the problems which an American Executive encountered in 'selling' major economic policies to Congress. To make matters more difficult still, the Russian way of doing business was first to show that they could wreak injury if they chose, and then to talk of deals. How could the Russians hope to understand that the American public, as reflected in Congress, would note the injury and then eschew the deal with righteous anger? Whatever might have been the tangible advantages of a deal whereby Russia undertook good behaviour in return for a monetary bribe, such an arrangement was out of the question; and the Russian attempt to bring it about led straight to the Cold War.

The American public reacted to the increasing Russian 'misbehaviour' not merely by rejecting deals, but by organising resistance. The 'Truman Doctrine' – Marshall Aid – and later the North Atlantic Treaty Organisation and permanent American commitment on the European continent, were all part of a natural American reaction. Instead of leaving western Europe to its own devices, as they had fully intended, the Americans found themselves from 1947 onwards treating the area as a vital element of their own security. Instead of treating eastern Europe as a military bastion against Germany, which for other purposes could be left largely to its own devices, the Russians found themselves actively controlling the politics and economics of the area. The nature of diplomacy abhors a power vacuum.

It is instructive to observe the process by which the countries of eastern Europe became Communist states. The only place where the Red Army was used to a great extent to destroy political opposition was Poland. Elsewhere, the Red Army doubtless helped the process of economic disruption by living off the land, and thus encouraged conditions in which Communism could thrive; while the presence of Russians in the background encouraged Communists and demoralised the opponents of Communism. Yet in most of eastern Europe it was the local Communists, and not the Russians, who actually frustrated possible developments towards democracy, and set up the Communist state. The Red Army was scarcely required to fire a shot in anger outside Poland. The success of Russia's work depended on confusion, division, absence of fixed purpose and pusillanimity among the local opponents of Communism, and lack of leadership from the great democracies. In such circumstances, tiny, but well-trained and carefully guided cadres of Communists were able to take over country after country.

By early 1947, when Marshall at last replaced Byrnes, Romania and Bulgaria were already, in effect, Communist states, and the processes of disintegration and demoralisation had gone beyond the point of no return in Poland, Hungary and Czechoslovakia. The issue by then was not whether any stand could be made in countries which Russia had occupied at the end of the war, but whether all Europe would be lost. Greece and Turkey, Italy and France – all were menaced in different ways, and their politicians were under sore temptation to establish makeshift agreements with a Communist enemy which they knew in their hearts to be implacable. Although men sometimes spoke of the danger of a Red Army attack, the real threat was much more the menace of economic chaos, which would be exploited to the uttermost by men whose political theory taught them that chaos was an essential condition precedent for the 'inevitable' revolution. Defeat of Communism turned on the willingness of the United States to assist actively in reestablishing the economies of the threatened states of Europe.

There were several distinct considerations which could very easily have persuaded the Americans to act differently. It was impossible for them to save both western Europe and China, and there were many Americans for whom eastern Asia seemed the more vital interest. Any policy designed to preserve either of those places required the use of economic measures in a manner which could not be justified readily on economic grounds alone, save as a very long-term consideration. Massive investment for reasons which were in part political required formal abandonment of isolationism, and presented some apparent risk of war. Considerable restraint was demanded from the Republican majorities in Congress to abstain from rocking the Administration's boat. Perhaps George Marshall was the only man who could have exerted the necessary authority.

At no point during the whole story which we have studied was there any positive indication that Russia was prepared to engage in any sort of hot war with the West. Yet a new and very serious danger of war was beginning to appear. The course of events in 1946 must have suggested to the Russians that the West was in process of total collapse: that the predictions of Marx and his successors were being vindicated: that the historical process which they believed to be inevitable would complete itself within a very few years. Then came the unexpected rally: first over Greece and Turkey; then, a few months later, the Marshall Plan. This was an economic effort, however; had the West sufficient determination to resist the show of military force? Berlin was the test. The West was by no means united. Substantial voices were being raised, even in America, in favour of temporising or withdrawal; but the United States decided to make a stand. Bevin rallied the British Cabinet, and the French had no alternative but to fall in line. For all the heart-searchings over Berlin, there was no evidence at any time that Russia would assert her claims by arms – or, indeed, that she would have resisted a determined effort by the Anglo-Americans to force their way by arms to the beleaguered city. Yet the Berlin blockade, and the determination of the Americans not to allow the Western Allies to be shifted from the city at any price, proved the decisive turning-point. It was the turning-point not only for the security of western Europe against Communist pretensions, but also for halting the drift of events which – if unchecked – would have led inevitably to an all-out shooting war at a later date.

The enormous advances registered by Communism during the period of this present study depended far more on the weakness of morale in the democracies than on either the strength of the Red Army or the persuasiveness of Marxist ideology. Nobody ever tested how strong the Red Army was; but Soviet behaviour whenever Russia was faced, or seemed to be faced, by determined resistance does not suggest that the Soviet Union itself felt much confidence in its invincibility. As for the intellectual strength of Marxist ideology, the successes as well as the failures of Communists during the period around the end of the war both underscore the essentially unsatisfactory nature of that analysis. Marx taught that feudal societies must pass through a capitalist phase on their passage to socialism. Yet, with the very doubtful exception of Czechoslovakia, the 'Marxist' revolutions of the twentieth century have all taken place in societies which were much more feudal than capitalist in character. The advanced capitalist societies of western Europe, which on Marxist theory were 'ripe' for revolution, were indeed shaken in the immediate aftermath of 1945; but they have since become stabilised. So far from producing a vast, alienated 'proletarian' class with no interest in the preservation of the society within which it lived and everything to hope from its destruction, they have developed a standard of living which is not only higher, but also more broadly based, than in any earlier society. The places where social revolutions have occurred, and where they continue to occur to this day, are places with peasant economies, not places with capitalist economies.

Marxists and supporters of Capitalism alike could profitably ponder that fact. Marxists might ask whether they have been attacking the wrong enemy; whether the source of poverty is to be found in the land system rather than in Capitalism; and whether a free Capitalist economy is not in truth the best friend of labour. Conversely, the supporters of Capitalism might consider whether they have been manoeuvered into a false position in the years since 1945, in underwriting societies where there has been a naked confrontation between a small landowning class and a great, impoverished, landless majority. Such societies are necessarily unstable in the modern world. If the people living in those societies believe that only Communists are prepared to redress their poverty, then they will sooner or later go Communist. The revolutions which will be launched in order to produce this effect will be exceedingly unpleasant for all who dwell in the regions directly affected, and they will probably be followed by a very long period of political tyranny. They will also be accompanied by renewed outbreaks of the Cold War, affecting the major countries of the world.

Bibliography

UNPUBLISHED PAPERS

Abbreviations refer to location of papers

Dean Acheson papers, HSTL
C. R. (Earl) Attlee papers, ChC
Earl of Avon (Anthony Eden) papers, UB; PRO
A. A. Berle papers, FDRL
Ernest Bevin papers, ChC
Cabinet papers, PRO
C. M. Clifford papers, HSTL
M. J. Connelly papers, HSTL
Hugh (Lord) Dalton diary, LSE
J. E. Davies papers, LC
Foreign Office papers, PRO
Harry L. Hopkins papers, FDRL
Cordell Hull papers (micro.) LC
H. L. Ickes papers LC
Kolko papers, LSE. These are photocopies of papers from various US
    archives, deposited by Joyce and Gabriel Kolko.
Premier papers, PRO
F. D. Roosevelt papers, FDRL
Sir Orme Sargent papers, PRO
State Department papers, NA
Edward R. Stettinius papers, UV
Viscount Thurso (Sir Archibald Sinclair) papers, ChC
Harry S. Truman papers, HSTL
Henry A. Wallace papers, UI
Edwin H. Watson papers, UV

ChC = Churchill College, Cambridge. FDRL = F. D. Roosevelt Library, Hyde
Park, New York. HSTL = Harry S. Truman Library, Independence,
Missouri. LC = Library of Congress, Washington, D.C. LSE = British Library
of Political and Economic Science, London School of Economics.
NA = National Archives, Washington, D.C. PRO = Public Record Office,
Kew, Surrey. UB = University of Birmingham. UI = University of Iowa, Iowa
City. UV = University of Virginia, Charlottesville, Va.

PUBLISHED WORKS

Acheson, Dean, *Present at the Creation: My Years in the State Department* (New York: Norton, 1969).

Adams, Henry H., *Harry Hopkins* (New York: Putnam, 1977).

Alperovitz, Gar, *Atomic Diplomacy* (London: Secker and Warburg, 1966).

Annual Register.

Avon, Earl of (Anthony Eden), *The Eden Memoirs:* II The Reckoning (London: Cassell, 1965).

Bohlen, Charles E., *Witness to History 1929–1969* (New York: Norton, 1973).

Byrnes, James F., *Speaking Frankly* (London & Toronto: Heinemann, 1947).

Cadogan, Sir Alexander, *The Diaries ... 1938–1945*, Ed. David Dilks (London: Cassell, 1971).

Churchill, Winston S., *The Second World War*, 12 vols (London: Cassell, 1964).

Congressional Record.

Curry, George. See Ferrell, Robert H. (ed.).

Davis, Lynn E., *The Cold War Begins: Soviet-American Conflict over Eastern Europe* (Princeton, NJ: Princeton U.P., 1974).

Divine, Robert A., *Foreign Policy and US Presidential Elections 1940–1948* (New York: New Viewpoints, 1974).

Documents on American Foreign Relations (Princeton, NJ: Princeton U.P.).

Douglas, Roy, *The Advent of War 1939–40* (London: Macmillan, 1978).

Farnworth, Beatrice, *William C. Bullitt and the Soviet Union* (Bloomington & London: Indiana U.P., 1967).

Ferrell, Robert H. (ed.), *The American Secretaries of State and their Diplomacy* (New York: Cooper Square). Vols XII, XIII: Julius W. Pratt: *Cordell Hull* (1964); vol. XIV: Richard C. Walker: *E. R. Stettinius Jr.*, and George Curry: *James F. Byrnes* (1965); vol. XV: Robert H. Ferrell: *George C. Marshall* (1966).

Foreign Relations of the United States (Washington, D.C.: Department of State).

Freeland, Richard M., *The Truman Doctrine and the Origins of McCarthyism* (New York: Knopf, 1972).

Gladwyn, Baron (H. M. G. Jebb), *The Memoirs of Lord Gladwyn* (London: Wiedenfeld & Nicolson, 1972).

Harriman, Averell, *America and Russia in a Changing World: A Half Century of Personal Observation* (Garden City: Doubleday, 1971).

Harvey, John (ed.), *The War Diaries of Oliver Harvey* (London: Collins, 1978).

Horowitz, David, *The Free World Colossus* (New York: Hill & Wang, 1971).

Hull, Cordell, *The Memoirs of Cordell Hull*, vol. II (London: Hodder & Stoughton, 1948).

Kennan, George F., *Memoirs 1925–1950*, vol. II (Boston: Little Brown, 1967).

Macmillan, Harold, *The Blast of War 1939–1945* (London: Macmillan, 1967).

Pratt, Julius W. See Ferrell, Robert H. (ed.).

Sherwood, Robert E., *The White House Papers of Harry L. Hopkins*, vol. II (London: Eyre & Spottiswoode, 1949).

Taylor, A. J. P., *Beaverbrook* (London: Hamish Hamilton, 1972).

Taylor, A. J. P., *English History 1914–1945* (Oxford: Clarendon Press, 1965).

Truman, Harry S., *Memoirs*; vol. I: *Year of Decisions*; vol. II: *Years of Trial and*

Hope (New York: Doubleday, 1956).

Vandenberg, Arthur H., Jr. (ed.), *The Private Papers of Senator Vandenberg* (Boston: Houghton Mifflin, 1952).

Walker, J. S., *Henry A. Wallace and American Foreign Policy* (Westport & London: Greenwood Press, 1976).

Walker, Richard C. See Ferrell, Robert H. (ed.).

Walton, Richard J., *Henry Wallace, Harry Truman and the Cold War* (New York: Viking Press, 1976).

Westerfield, H. B., *Foreign Policy and Party Politics: Pearl Harbor to Korea* (New Haven & London: Yale U.P., 1955).

Wilmot, Chester, *The Struggle for Europe* (London: Collins, 1952).

Woodward, Sir Llewellyn, *British Foreign Policy in the Second World War*, 5 vols (London: HMSO, 1970–76).

ABBREVIATIONS USED IN THE NOTES

AAB	A. A. Berle Papers
ATLE	C. R. (Earl) Attlee Papers
BEVIN	Ernest Bevin Papers
CA	Confidential Annexe
CAB	Cabinet Papers
CF	Confidential File
CH	Cordell Hull Papers
CMC	C. M. Clifford Papers
DA	Dean Acheson Papers
ERS	Edward R. Stettinius Papers
FDR	F. D. Roosevelt Papers
FO	Foreign Office Papers
FRUS	*Foreign Relations of the United States*
HAW	Henry A. Wallace Papers
HLH	Harry L. Hopkins Papers
HLI	H. L. Ickes Papers
HST	Harry S. Truman Papers
JED	J. E. Davies Papers
MJC	M. J. Connelly Papers
MR	Map Room Papers
NA	State Department Papers (National Archives)
PREM	Premier Papers
PSF	President's Secretary's File
SD	State Department
THRS	Viscount Thurso (Sir Archibald Sinclair) Papers
WM	War Minutes

Notes

For abbreviations please see previous page

1 APPEASEMENT

1 Bohlen, C. E., *Witness to History 1929–1969* (New York: Norton, 1973) p. 123.
2 SD memo., 4 February 1942. FDR/PSF 68.
3 Ibid.
4 Eden memo., Conversations with Stalin 16–20 December 1941. FO 371/32879, fo. 10 et seq.
5 Ibid.
6 SD memo., 4 February 1942, supra.
7 WM 131(41), 19 December. CA CAB 65/24.
8 SD memo., 4 February 1942, supra.
9 Churchill to Eden, 8 January 1942. PREM 3/399/6, fo. 87.
10 Churchill to Attlee; to Curtin, 20, 27 December 1941, ibid., fos 85, 86.
11 Eden to Halifax, 10 February 1942. PREM 3/395/12, fo. 276 et seq.
12 Ibid.
13 Memo. of conversation between Halifax and Welles, 18 February 1942. NA NND 730,032, box 2562.
14 NA NND 730,032, box 2582.
15 Memo. of conversation between Halifax and Welles, 20 February 1942, ibid.
16 Halifax to Eden, 21 February 1942. PREM 3/395/12, fo. 270 et seq.
17 Eden to Churchill, 6 March 1942. PREM 3/395/12, fos 256–7.
18 Churchill to Roosevelt, 7 March 1942. PREM 3/395/12, fos 256–7.
19 Memo. of conversation ..., 30 March 1942. FRUS 1942 III, p. 536 et seq.
20 Ibid.
21 SD memo., 4 February 1942, supra.
22 Halifax to Eden, 2 April 1942. PREM 3/399/8, fo. 200 et seq.
23 Berle diary, 4 April 1942. AAB 214.
24 Welles to Berle, 4 April 1942. FRUS 1942 III, p. 541.
25 Dominions telegram, 15 April 1942. FO 371/32879, fo. 113A.
26 Beaverbrook memo., 18 February 1942. PREM 3/395/12, fo. 28. See also Taylor, A. J. P., *Beaverbrook* (London: Hamish Hamilton, 1972) p. 510 et seq.
27 Beaverbrook to Eden, 3 March 1942. FO 954/25A, fo. 38.
28 Ibid. See also Beaverbrook to Churchill, 17 March 1942. PREM 3/399/9, fo. 220 et seq.

29   Churchill to Hopkins, 19 March 1942. HLH 136.
30   Butler to Eden, 13 March 1942. FO 954/25A, fo. 55 et seq.
31   Cazalet to Eden, 17 April 1942; Nicolson to Eden, 24 April; Simon to Churchill 8 May. FO 954/25A, fos 102 et seq., 122, 162 et seq.
32   Cooper to Eden, 22 April 1942. FO 954/25A, fo. 112 et seq.
33   Harvie Watt to Churchill, 24 April 1942. PREM 3/399/8, fos 175–6.
34   Second meeting ... 21 May 1942. PREM 3/399/4 & 5, fo. 36 et seq.
35   Churchill to Eden, 6 October 1943. PREM 3/399/6, fo. 92.
36   See, in particular, Second Meeting, 21 May 1942, supra.
37   Churchill, W. S., *The Second World War*, vol. VII (London: Cassell, 1964) p. 308.
38   Press release, 11 June 1942. FRUS 1942 III, pp. 593–4.
39   Harvey, John (ed.), *The War Diaries of Oliver Harvey* (London: Collins, 1978) p. 132.
40   Pratt, J. W., *Cordell Hull*, vols VII & VIII of Ferrell, R. H. (ed.), *The American Secretaries of State and their Diplomacy* (New York: Cooper Square, 1964) p. 609.
41   Churchill to Roosevelt, 14 July 1942. HLH 136.
42   Churchill, op. cit. vol. VIII, p. 61,
43   Churchill to Roosevelt, 31 October 1942. HLH 136.
44   Dalton diary, 6 April 1943.
45   Churchill to Eden, 16 January 1944. PREM 3/399/6, fo. 81.
46   Harriman to Roosevelt, 5 July 1943, FDR/PSF 49.
47   Dubrow memo., 3 February 1944. FRUS 1944 IV, p. 813 et seq.

2 TEHRAN

1   See: 'The Eastern Frontier of Poland' (F. K. Roberts) 16 March 1942, FO 371/38279; Temperley, H. W. V., *A History of the Peace Conference of Paris*, vol. VI, (Oxford, 1924) p. 268 et seq.; FRUS 1919 (Paris PC XIII, p. 793; FRUS 1944 III, p. 1218 et seq., and refs.
2   O'Malley to Eden, 29 April 1943. FO 371/34571, fo. 174 et seq.
3   FO to Moscow, 7 March 1944, and refs. PREM 3/355/9, fo. 641.
4   Eden to Dormer, 22 January 1943. FO 954/19B, fo. 476.
5   Sikorski to Churchill, 9 February 1943. FO 371/34563, fo. 141 et seq.
6   O'Malley to Churchill, 26 March 1943. FO 371/34566, fo. 109.
7   Savory to Eden, 8 March 1943. FO 371/34565, fo. 108 et seq.
8   Berle diary, 13 March 1943. AAB 214.
9   PSP communiqué, 5 March 1943, FO 371/34567, fo. 109 et seq.; PSP to Attlee, 10 January 1944. FDR/PSF 66.
10   Conversations between Eden and Polish Ministers 3 March 1943. FO 371/34565, fo. 37 et seq.
11   Raczynski to Cadogan, 1 April 1943. FO 371/34567, fo. 184.
12   O'Malley to Eden, 1 April 1943. FO 371/34557, fo. 109 et seq.
13   Welles-Ciechanowski conversations, 8 April 1943. FRUS 1943 III, p. 120 et seq.
14   Sargent memo., 15 April 1943. FO 371/34568 fo. 78 et seq.
15   Ibid.

16 Ibid., marginal comment.
17 Avon, Earl of (Anthony Eden), *The Eden memoirs:* II *The Reckoning* (London: Cassell, 1965) p. 289.
18 WM 52(43), 12 April, CAB 65/34.
19 Churchill memo., 15 April 1943. FO 371/34566, fo. 108 et seq.
20 O'Malley to Eden, 24 May 1943. FO 688/31; FDR/PSF 52.
21 Clark-Kerr to FO, 21 April 1943. FO 371/34569, fo. 28.
22 Halifax to FO, 22 April 1943. FO 371/34569, fo. 64.
23 Stalin to Churchill, 21 April 1943. CAB 66/36, fo. 171 et seq.
24 Churchill to Stalin, 24 April 1943, ibid.
25 Churchill to Stalin, 25 April 1943, ibid.
26 Stalin to Churchill, 25 April 1943, ibid.
27 Clark-Kerr to FO, 26 April 1943 (2 telegrams). FO 371/34669, fos 158, 160.
28 Roosevelt to Stalin, 26 April 1943. FRUS 1943 III, p. 395.
29 WM 59(43), 27 April. CAB 65/34.
30 WM 65(43), 7 May. CAB 65/34.
31 Dalton diary, 16 September 1943.
32 Dalton diary, 4 February 1943.
33 Berle diary, 12 January 1943. AAB 214.
34 WM 89(43), 28 June. CAB 65/43.
35 Eden memo., 28 September 1943. CAB 66/41.
36 Eden to Dormer, 8 June 1942. FO 954/19B, fo. 451.
37 Eden to Dormer, 20 August 1942, ibid.
38 Clark-Kerr to FO, 25 October 1943. PREM 3/114/2, fo. 20.
39 Eden memo., 28 September 1943. CAB 66/41.
40 For text, see FDR/PSF 40.
41 Churchill to Roosevelt, 6 January 1944. PREM 3/355/7, fo. 313.
42 Sargent to Eden, 27 January 1944. FO 954/4A, fo. 37.
43 Memo of conversation ..., 7 May 1943. FRUS 1943 III, p. 52 et seq.
44 Eden memo., 23 August 1943. FO 954/2, fo. 50.
45 Ickes diary, 29 August 1943. HLI 18.
46 Thurston to Hull, 17 December 1941. FDR/PSF 31.
47 Eden memo., 5 October 1943. CAB 66/41.
48 Eden to O'Malley, 7 October 1943. PREM 3/355/5, fo. 204 et seq.
49 Hull to Roosevelt, 23 November 1943. FDR/PSF 65.
50 Eden to FO, 6 November 1943. PREM 3/355/5, fo. 220.
51 Harriman to Roosevelt, 5 November 1943. FRUS 1943 III, p. 589 et seq.
52 Eden to O'Malley, 18 November 1943. PREM 3/355/5, fo. 200.
53 Hull to Biddle, 25 November 1943. FRUS 1943 III, p. 486 et seq.
54 Dalton diary, 21 December 1943.
55 Churchill, *The Second World War*, ibid., vol. X, p. 17.
56 See, for example, Harriman to Roosevelt, 5 July 1943. FDR/PSF 49.
57 Ickes diary, 1 January 1944. HLI 19.
58 Dalton diary, 21 December 1943.
59 Bohlen, C. E., *Witness to History 1929–1969*, ibid., p. 151.
60 Dalton diary, 21 December 1943.
61 Schoenfeld to Hull, 13 January 1944. FRUS 1944 III, p. 1225 et seq.
62 WM 169(43), 13 December. CAB 65/36.

63 Churchill to Eden, 20 December 1943. PREM 3/355/6, fo. 237 et seq.

3 WARSAW

1 Hull to Harriman, 15 January 1944. FRUS 1944 III, p. 1228 et seq.
2 O'Malley to Eden, 22 January 1944. FO 954/20A, fo. 14 et seq.
3 WM 11(44), 25 January. CA CAB 65/45.
4 Cadogan note for Churchill, 21 January 1944. PREM 3/355/7, fo. 399 et seq.
5 WM 21(44), 15 February. CA CAB 65/45.
6 Churchill to Stalin, 18 February 1944. PREM 3/355/8, fo. 372 et seq.
7 See Mikolajczyk to Roosevelt, 18 March 1944. FDR/PSF 66.
8 Mikolajczyk to Eden, 17 January 1944. PREM 3/355/7, fo. 266.
9 WM 16(44), 7 February. CA CAB 65/45.
10 WM 23(44), 21 February. CA CAB 65/45.
11 Churchill to Roosevelt, 5 February 1944. PREM 3/355/5, fo. 544 et seq.
12 Harvey, J. (ed.), *The War Diaries of Oliver Harvey* (London: Collins, 1978) 28 February 1944.
13 Romer to O'Malley, 20 June 1944. PREM 3/355/12, fo. 932 et seq.
14 Stettinius to Hull, 12 June 1944. FRUS 1944 III, p. 1281.
15 Churchill to Roosevelt, 27 June 1944. PREM 3/355/12, fo. 910.
16 Churchill to Stalin, 20 July 1944. PREM 3/355/12, fo. 887 et seq.
17 FO report, 25 July 1944. PREM 3/355/12, fo. 870 et seq.
18 Stalin to Churchill, 23 July 1944. PREM 3/355/12, fo. 881 et seq.
19 Churchill to Roosevelt, 11 August 1944. PREM 3/355/12, fo. 827.
20 Eden to Churchill, 16 August 1944. PREM 3/355/12, fo. 817 et seq.
21 Ibid.
22 Harriman to Hull and Roosevelt, 4 August 1944. FRUS 1944 III, p. 1305 et seq; FDR/PSF 66.
23 Eden to Churchill, 16 August 1944; Stalin to Churchill, 8 August. PREM 3/355/12 fos 817 et seq, 838 et seq.
24 Memo., Warsaw rising, 30 September 1944. PREM 3/352/11, fo. 306 et seq.
25 Harriman to Roosevelt and Hull, 17 August 1944. FDR/PSF 66.
26 Ibid.
27 Harriman to Roosevelt and Hull, 10 August 1944. FDR/PSF 66.
28 Churchill/Stalin correspondence, 4, 5 August 1944. PREM 3/403/2, fos 14, 13.
29 WM 103(44), 9 August. CAB 65/44.
30 Churchill to Stalin, 12 August 1944. PREM 3/403/2, fo. 8. Much of the correspondence about the rising is also to be found in FDR/PSF 66.
31 Memo., Warsaw rising, supra.
32 See WM 117(44), 5 September. CA CAB 65/47.
33 Ibid.
34 Stalin to Churchill, 17 August 1944. PREM 3/403/2, fo. 8 et seq.
35 Roosevelt and Churchill to Stalin, 20 August 1944. PREM 3/403/2, fos 5, 4; FDR/MR 31.
36 Harriman to Roosevelt, 15 August 1944. FDR/PSF 66.

37 Stalin to Churchill and Roosevelt, 23 August 1944. PREM 3/403/2, fo. 2.
38 WM 106, 112(44), 14, 29 August. CAB 65/43.
39 WM 111(44), 28 August. CA CAB 65/47.
40 Eden to Churchill, 22 August 1944. PREM 3/355/12, fo. 812 et seq.
41 Churchill to Eden, 23 August 1944. PREM 3/355/12, fo. 811.
42 Dalton diary, 6 September 1944.
43 Churchill to Eden, 13 September 1944. FO 371/39499.
44 Polish Government statment: report from Bor, transmitted 14 September 1944. FO 371/39497, fo. 137.
45 WM 130(44), 2 October. CA CAB 65/48.

4 TOLSTOY

1 Matthews to Hull, 5 January 1943. FRUS 1943 II, p. 969.
2 Eden to Rendel, 11 December 1942. FO 954/33B, fo. 369.
3 MacVeagh's report ..., 3 August 1944. ERS 216.
4 Matthews to Hull, 5 January 1943, 24 February, 23 March. FRUS 1943 II, pp. 969, 975 et seq, 984 et seq.
5 Winant to Hull, 30 June 1943. FRUS 1943 II, p. 1015.
6 FO to Washington, 7 December 1943. PREM 3/510/10, fo. 281.
7 Roosevelt to Churchill, 23 October 1943. FO 954/33B, fo. 394.
8 Fraleigh to Berry, 22 November 1943. NA NND 739,032 box 2532.
9 FO to Stevenson, 21 December 1943. FO 954/33B, fo. 399.
10 Eden to Churchill, 28 December 1943. PREM 3/511/2, fo. 115.
11 Churchill to Tito, 8 January 1944, ibid., fo. 42 et seq.
12 WM 5(44), 11 January. CA CAB 65/45.
13 Stettinius to Winant, 29 February 1944. FRUS 1944 IV, p. 1351 et seq.
14 Principal Yugoslav problems. FRUS 1945 (Confs), p. 262 et seq.
15 Chapin to Hull, 7 May 1944. FRUS 1944 IV, p. 1364.
16 Peter II to Roosevelt, 17 April 1944. FRUS 1944 IV, p. 1359 et seq.
17 Winant to Hull, 13 September 1944. FRUS 1944 IV, p. 1405.
18 MacVeagh report, supra.
19 Harvey, ibid., p. 320.
20 Churchill to Roosevelt, 23 June 1944. PREM 3/355/12, fo 937 et seq.
21 Eden to Clark-Kerr, 18 May 1944. PREM 3/66/7, fo. 240 et seq.
22 Churchill to Roosevelt, 31 May 1944. PREM 3/66, fo. 236 et seq.
23 Halifax to FO, 31 May 1944. PREM 3/66/7, fo. 233 et seq.
24 Roosevelt to Churchill, 11 June 1944. PREM 3/66/7, fo. 220.
25 Churchill to Roosevelt, 11 June 1944, ibid., fo. 224 et seq.
26 Roosevelt to Churchill, 13 June 1944, ibid., fo. 221 et seq.
27 FO to Moscow, 8 July 1944, ibid., fo. 196 et seq.
28 Eden to Churchill, 8 August 1944, ibid., fo. 189.
29 Ickes diary, 4 June 1944. HLI 20.
30 For aspects of the Vice-Presidential question, see HLI 20, passim; Wallace diary, 2 February 1946. HAW 38.
31 Bohlen to Hopkins, 3 October 1944, HLH 335; Sherwood, White House papers ... II, p. 825.
32 Bohlen to Hopkins, 3 October 1944, supra.

33 Roosevelt to Stalin, 5 October 1944. PREM 3/434/8, fo. 79.
34 Record of meetings ... PREM 3/434/2.
35 Ibid.
36 Sargent to Eden, 12 October 1944. PREM 3/66/7, fo. 177.
37 Churchill memo., 12 October 1944, ibid., fo. 185 et seq.
38 See PREM 3/434/2; Churchill to Attlee, 17 October 1944, PREM 3/434/8, fo. 188 seq; Eden to Churchill, 26 January 1945, PREM 3/51/3, fo. 10 et seq.
39 Bohlen, *Witness to History 1929–1969*, ibid., p. 163.
40 Harriman to Roosevelt, 10 October 1944. FDR/MR 32.
41 Baruch to Roosevelt, 23 October 1944. Edwin H. Watson box 11.
42 Maclean to Churchill, 28 October 1944. PREM 3/512/10 and FRUS 1945 (Confs), p. 251 et seq.
43 Record of conversation, 17 November 1944. PREM 3/512/10.
44 Churchill to Wilson, 20 November 1944, ibid.
45 Eden to Churchill, 23 November 1944, ibid.
46 Churchill to Eden, 1 January 1945. PREM 3/510/2, fo. 260.
47 Churchill note, 8 January 1945 (misdated 1944). PREM 3/513/2, fo. 206.
48 Record of conversation, 9 January 1945, ibid., fo. 195 et seq.
49 Peter II press communiqué, 11 January 1945, ibid., fo. 164 et seq.
50 WM 4(45), 11 January. CA CAB 65/51.
51 Principal Yugoslav problems, FRUS 1945 (Confs), p. 262 et seq.
52 WM 7(45), 22 January. CA CAB 65/51.
53 Churchill to Stalin, 23, 27 January 1945. FO 954/34B, fos 261, 270.
54 Churchill to Eden, 2 March 1945. FO 954/34B, fo. 279 et seq.
55 *Times*, 4 December 1944.
56 Leeper to Eden, 15 January 1945. PREM 3/213/4.
57 Churchill to Hopkins, 14 December 1944. HLH 337.
58 TUC Interim report ..., PREM 8/49.

5   THE LATIN WEST

1 Churchill to Macmillan, 26 December 1943. PREM 3/182/3, fo. 82.
2 Cole memo. on N. Africa, 26 January 1943. Hull reel 35.
3 Hull to Cole, 28 March 1944. FRUS 1944 III, p. 659.
4 See Pratt, J. V., *Cordell Hull*, vol. XII of Ferrell, R. H. (ed.), *The American Secretaries of State and their Diplomacy* (New York: Cooper Square, 1964) pp. 533–41.
5 Macmillan, H, *The Blast of War 1939–1945* (London: Macmillan, 1967) pp. 356–7.
6 Ickes diary, 9 January 1943. HLI 18.
7 US policy towards France, 15 July 1943. PREM 3/181/6, fo. 32 et seq.
8 Swope to Hopkins, 12 July 1943. HLH 153.
9 Hull-Churchill conversation, 13 May 1943. FRUS 1943 II, p. 115.
10 WM 75(43), 23 May. CA CAB 65/38.
11 Eden: The French C.N.L., 2 July 1943. CAB 66/38.
12 Berle diary, 8 June 1943. AAB 215.

13 Roosevelt to Churchill, 17 June 1943. PREM 3/181/12; FRUS 1943 II, p. 155 et seq.
14 Churchill to Roosevelt, 21 July 1943. PREM 3/181/2, fo. 67 et seq.
15 Ickes diary, 15 August 1943. HLI 18.
16 Churchill to War Cabinet, August 1943. PREM 3/363/10.
17 Macmillan: The road to recognition, 27 August 1943. PREM 3/181/4, fo. 5 et seq.
18 Hull to Roosevelt, 10 May 1943. FRUS 1943 II, p. 113 et seq.
19 Churchill to Eden, 21 December 1943. PREM 3/182/3, fo. 131.
20 Churchill to Macmillan, 26 December 1943, supra.
21 Churchill to Eden, 19 January 1944. PREM 3/182/3, fo. 61.
22 Stettinius to Hull, 11 February 1944. ERS 218.
23 Stimson Record ..., 14 June 1944; notes after talk with Hull, 20 June 1944. Stimson mss, box 411. Kolko.
24 Cooper to FO, 8 April 1944. PREM 3/182/1, fo. 30.
25 WM 74(44), 7 June. CA CAB 65/46.
26 Stimson Record ... and notes ..., supra.
27 Ickes diary, 2 April 1944. HLI 19.
28 Chapin to Hull, 10 June 1944. FRUS 1944 III, p. 704 et seq.
29 Chapin to Hull, 11 June 1944, ibid., p. 706 et seq.
30 Eden to Churchill, 12 September 1944. PREM 3/182/4, fo. 88.
31 Ickes diary, 2 July 1944. HLI 20.
32 Churchill to Stalin, 25 November, 1944. PREM 3/173/1, fo. 16.
33 Stalin to Churchill, 2 December 1944, ibid., fos 44–5.
34 WM 161(44), 4 December. CAB 65/44.
35 Churchill to Macmillan, 3 November 1943. PREM 3/243/8, fo. 650.
36 Macmillan to FO, 3 November 1943. PREM 3/243/8, fo. 644.
37 Hull to Chapin, 25 January 1944. FRUS 1944 III, p. 1007 et seq.
38 Churchill to Wilson, 20, 21 February 1944; Roosevelt to Churchill, 11 February. PREM 3/243/6, fos 471, 468, 510.
39 Roosevelt to Churchill, 13 March 1944; Churchill to Roosevelt, 15 March. PREM 3/243/8 fos 344 et seq, 330.
40 Chapin to Hull, 11 March 1944. FRUS 1944 III, p. 1041 et seq.
41 Charles to FO, 21 April 1944, PREM 3/250/3, fo. 157 et seq; Chapin to Hull, 11 March, FRUS 1944 III, p. 1041 et seq.
42 Churchill to Eden (recorded telephone message), 10 June 1944. PREM 3/243/12, fo. 883.
43 Attlee to Churchill, 13 June 1944. PREM 3/243/12, fol 846.
44 Roosevelt to Churchill, 15 June 1944. FRUS 1944 III, p. 1133 et seq.
45 Churchill to Eden, 20 June 1944. PREM 3/243/12, fo. 783–4.
46 Franco to Templewood, 18 October 1944 (trans.). PREM 8/106.
47 Attlee: Policy towards Spain, 4 November 1944. PREM 8/106.
48 Selborne: Policy towards Spain, 14 November 1944, ibid.
49 Eden to Halifax, 9 November 1944, ibid.
50 Churchill to Eden, 10, 18 November 1944, ibid.
51 Eden to Churchill, 17 November 1944, ibid.

6 YALTA

1 Churchill to Mikolajczyk, 7 October 1944. PREM 3/355/13, fo. 1124 et seq.
2 Churchill to Attlee, 10 October 1944, ibid., fo. 1117.
3 Eden to Churchill, 11 October 1944, ibid., fo. 1102 et seq.
4 Eden to FO, 14 October 1944, ibid., fo. 1069 et seq.
5 Eden to FO, 15 October 1944, ibid., fo. 1056.
6 Churchill to Attlee, 17 October 1944, ibid., fo. 1028 et seq.
7 Ibid.
8 Eden to FO, 15 October 1944, supra.
9 Churchill to Attlee, 17 October 1944, supra.
10 Harriman to Roosevelt and Hull, 23 November 1944. FDR/PSF 66.
11 Eden to FO 14 October 1944. PREM 3/355/13, fo. 1067A et seq.
12 Churchill to the King, 15 October 1944. PREM 3/434/8, fo. 107 et seq.
13 Eden to Cadogan, 19 October 1944. PREM 3/355/13, fo. 1012 et seq.
14 WM 143(44), 1 November. CA CAB 65/48.
15 Stettinius to Roosevelt, November (?) 1944. FDR/PSF 68.
16 Eden to Clark-Kerr, 24 November 1944. FO 954/20B, fo. 350.
17 WM 157(44), 17 November. CA CAB 65/48.
18 Roberts minute, 4 December 1944. FO 954/20B, fo. 353 et seq.
19 Churchill to Roosevelt, 17 December 1944, ibid., fo. 368.
20 Stettinius Record, 16 December 1944. FRUS 1945 (Confs), pp. 434–5.
21 WM 169(44), 15 December. CA CAB 65/48.
22 See Schoenfeld to Stettinius, 21 December 1944. FDR/PSF 66.
23 Stettinius press statement, 18 December 1944. HLH 337.
24 WM 142(44), 30 October. CA CAB 65/48.
25 Eden: The Polish Provisional Government, 22 January 1945. CAB 66/61.
26 FO to Moscow, 30 January 1945. PREM 3/144/3A, fo. 156; Eden to Churchill, 18 January. FO 954/4A, fo. 41.
27 WM 7(45), 22 January. CA CAB 65/51.
28 Ibid.
29 Eden to Churchill, 28 January 1945. FO 954/20B, fo. 396.
30 Eden to Churchill, 1 February 1945, ibid., fo. 399 et seq.
31 Stettinius to Johnson, 10 October 1948. ERS 278.
32 Cadogan diaries, p. 709.
33 See Adams, H. H., *Harry Hopkins* (New York: Putnam, 1977) p. 370 et seq.
34 Cadogan diaries, pp. 709, 695.
35 For current of Cabinet opinions, see CAB 65/51, passim.
36 'Argonaut' 1, 11 February 1945. PREM 3/51/4; CAB 66/63.
37 WM 22(45), 19 February. CA CAB 65/51.
38 'Argonaut', supra.
39 WM 18(45), 12 February. CAB 65/49; CA CAB 65/51.
40 WM 22(45), 19 February. CA CAB 65/51.
41 Agreement ... 1 February 1945. FRUS (Confs) p. 984.
42 Bohlen, C. E., *Witness to History 1929–1969*, ibid., p. 186.
43 Cadogan diaries, p. 718.

7 DISILLUSION

1   Schoenfeld to Roosevelt, 17 February 1945. FRUS 1945 v, p. 122.
2   Arciszewski to Gvt Delegate, 24 February 1945. CAB 66/62.
3   Fraser to Churchill, 20 February 1945. PREM 3/356/4, fo. 127 et seq.
4   Churchill to Fraser, 22 February 1945 (draft). PREM 3/356/4, fo. 124 et seq.
5   WM 22(45), 19 February. CA CAB 65/51.
6   R. R. Stokes and two ILP members, as well as two 'right-wing independents', supported the Amendment.
7   Churchill to Clark-Kerr, 28 February 1945. PREM 3/356/9, fo. 844.
8   Churchill to Roosevelt, 28 February 1945. PREM 3/356/9, fo. 844.
9   Ibid.
10 Churchill to Roosevelt, 10 March 1945, mentions another Minister who actually resigned, but does not name him. PREM 3/356/9, fo. 812.
11 Cong. Rec. 62 part 2, p. 1618 et seq.
12 Fortnightly survey, 20 February 1945. ERS 389.
13 Princeton survey, fortnightly survey, 20 March 1945, ibid.
14 Cong. Rec. 62 part 2, p. 1701.
15 Churchill to Clark-Kerr, 28 February 1945. PREM 3/356/9, fo. 844.
16 See, for example, Churchill to Clark-Kerr, 28 February 1945; to Roosevelt 8 March, ibid., fos 844 et seq., 814 et seq.
17 Harriman to Stettinius, 27 February 1945. FRUS 1945 v, p. 129 et seq.
18 Churchill to Roosevelt, 8 March 1945. PREM 3/356/9, fo. 814 et seq.
19 Churchill to Roosevelt, 13 March 1945. PREM 3/356/9, fo. 766; FRUS 1945 v, p. 158 et seq.
20 Churchill to Roosevelt, 8 March 1945. FDR/MR 31.
21 Churchill to Roosevelt, 13 March 1945, supra.
22 Eden to Churchill, 24 March 1945. PREM 3/356/9, fos 722–3.
23 Churchill to Eden, 24 March 1945. PREM 3/356/9, fo. 718 et seq.
24 Stettinius Record, 11–17 March 1945. ERS 245.
25 Churchill to Roosevelt, 27 March 1945. FDR/MR 23.
26 Roosevelt to Churchill, 29 March 1945. CAB 66/64.
27 Stettinius Record, 18 March–7 April 1945. ERS 245.
28 Eden to Churchill, 2 April 1945. FO 954/20C, fo. 513.
29 Moscow to FO 3 April 1945. FO 954/20C, fo. 520 et seq.
30 Harriman to Stettinius, 4 April (2), 6 April 1945. DFR/PSF 68.
31 Stettinius Record, 8–14 April 1945. ERS 245.
32 Truman to Churchill, 13 April 1945. FRUS 1945 v, p. 211 et seq.
33 Sargent to Churchill, 7 May 1945. PREM 3/356/7, fo. 475 et seq.
34 Moscow to FO 12 April 1945. PREM 3/356/7, fo. 485.
35 WM 50(45), 24 April. CA CAB 65/52.
36 Truman, H. S., *Memoirs*; vol. I: *Year of Decisions* (New York: Doubleday, 1956) p. 85.
37 Memo. of meeting ..., 23 April 1945. HST/PSF 187.
38 Churchill to Cranborne, 3 April 1945. FO 954/20C, fo. 531.
39 Memo. of meeting ..., 23 April 1945, supra.
40 Eden: Dissolution of the Polish National Council, 29 March 1945. CAB 66/64.

41　Maclean: … situation in Yugoslavia, February 1945. PREM 3/513/5.
42　Dalton diary, 13 February 1945.
43　Henderson minute, 8 May 1945. PREM 3/114/3A, fos 58–9.
44　Dalton diary, 15 March, 5 April 1945.
45　Dalton diary, 5 April 1945.
46　FO to Moscow, 13 April 1945. PREM 3/114/3A, fo. 111.
47　Sargent to Churchill, 22 April 1945, ibid., fo. 103.
48　Cadogan diaries, p. 735.
49　Churchill to Sargent, 25 April 1945. FO 954/4A, fo. 55.

8　STOCKTAKING

　1　Kirk to Stettinius, 20 February 1945. FRUS 1945 IV, p. 1103 et seq.
　2　Grew to Kirk, 28 February 1945, ibid., p. 1107 et seq.
　3　Churchill to Eden, 11 March 1945. PREM 3/513/6, fo. 10.
　4　Churchill to Eden, 18 April 1945, ibid., fo. 8 et seq.
　5　Kirk to Stettinius, 7 April 1945. FRUS 1945 V, p. 1119.
　6　Stevenson to Macmillan, 28 April 1945. PREM 3/495/6, fo. 127.
　7　Sargent to Churchill, 28 April 1945, ibid., fo. 125 et seq.
　8　Churchill to Truman, 27 April 1945. FRUS 1945 IV, p. 1125.
　9　Grew to Harrison, 29 April 1945, ibid., p. 1126 et seq.
10　Memo. of telephone conversation, 30 April 1945, ibid., p. 1129 et seq.
11　Truman to Churchill, 30 April 1945. PREM 3/495/6, fo. 113.
12　Matthews to Grew, 2 May 1945. FRUS 1945 IV, pp. 1132–3.
13　Grew to Truman, 4 May 1945, ibid., p. 1136 et seq.
14　Grew to Truman, 10 May 1945, ibid., p. 1151 et seq.
15　Macmillan to FO, 14 May 1945. PREM 3/495/7, fo. 12.
16　Churchill to Sargent, 14 May 1945. PREM 3/513/9, fo. 8.
17　… Committee of Three, 8 May 1945. FRUS 1945 IV, p. 1145 et seq.
18　FO to Belgrade; Macmillan to FO, 10 May 1945. PREM 3/495/7, fo. 124; 121 et seq.
19　Grew to Truman, 10 May 1945. FRUS 1945 IV, p. 1151 et seq.
20　Memo. of conversation …, 10 May 1945, ibid., p. 1154.
21　Macmillan to FO, 14 May 1945, supra.
22　SHAEF to AGWAR, 15 May 1945. PREM 3/495/7, fo. 2.
23　Grew to Patterson, 14 May 1945. FRUS 1945 IV, p. 1161.
24　Patterson to Stettinius, 25 May 1945, ibid., p. 1175.
25　Churchill to Fraser, 22 February 1945 (draft). PREM 3/356/4, fo. 124 et seq.
26　WM 39(45), 3 April. CA CAB 65/52.
27　Dalton diary, 16 May 1945.
28　Churchill to Truman, 12 May 1945 (no. 1). PREM 3/495/7, fo. 57 et seq.
29　Churchill to Truman, 12 May 1945 (no. 2), ibid., fo. 52 et seq.
30　Truman to Churchill, 14 May 1945, ibid., fo. 486.
31　Ickes diary, 2 June 1945. HLI 21.
32　Truman to Churchill, 9 May 1945. PREM 3/430/1, fo. 114 et seq.
33　Morrison to Attlee, 11 May 1945; Attlee to Morrison, 12 May (no. 2). BEVIN 3/3, fo. 12.

34 Churchill to Attlee, 18 May 1945. ATLE 2/2, fo. 24 et seq.
35 See Churchill to Attlee, n.d., but after 20 May 1945. Ibid., fos 27–8.
36 For position for Gwylim Lloyd George see Sinclair to Davies, 3 December 1945 (copy). THRS 1945.
37 CM 6(45), 8 June. CAB 65/53.
38 Attlee to Churchill, 8 June 1945. ATLE 2/2, fo. 25.
39 Westerfield, H. B., *Foreign Policy and Party Politics: Pearl Harbor to Korea* (New Haven & London: Yale U.P., 1955), pp. 184–5.
40 Ickes diary, 28 April 1945. HLI 21.
41 Many noted this trait. See Ickes diary, 7 July 1945, HLI 21; Curry, G., *James F. Byrnes*, part of vol. XIV of *The American Secretaries of State and their Diplomacy*, ibid., p. 167 (re. Vandenberg); Truman, *Memoirs* file, 19 July 1948, HST/Post-Presidential 3.
42 Memo of conversation ..., 15 May 1945. FRUS 1945 (Potsdam 1), p. 12 et seq.
43 Hopkins to Truman, n.d., HST/MR (Top Secret), box 3.
44 Truman to Churchill, 1 June 1945. PREM 3/356/13, fo. 1157 et seq.
45 Clark-Kerr to FO, 16 July 1945. PREM 3/356/14, fo. 1180.
46 Truman, longhand notes, 22, 23 May 1945. HST/PSF 333.
47 23 May, ibid.
48 Davies to Truman, 12 June 1945. FRUS 1945 (Potsdam 1), p. 64 et seq.
49 Davies notes, 26 May 1945. JED 17.
50 *Times*, 18 December 1945.
51 *Times*, 23 May 1945.
52 FO to 'Terminal', 21 July 1945. PREM 3/66/9, fo. 301 et seq.
53 Prague to FO, 6 June 1945. PREM 3/114/3A, fo. 41 et seq.
54 CM (45)18, 7 August. CAB 128/1.
55 Harriman to Byrnes, 3 July 1945. FRUS 1945 IV, p. 519 et seq.
56 See Stettinius to Harriman, 12 April 1945. FRUS 1945 V, p. 1219 et seq.

9 POTSDAM

1 Roosevelt to Churchill, 29 February 1944. ERS 218.
2 Churchill to Roosevelt, 19 November 1944. FRUS 1945 (confs), pp. 286–7.
3 Roosevelt to Churchill, 20 November 1944, ibid., p. 287.
4 See Matthews memo. 20 September 1944. FRUS (confs), p. 134 et seq.
5 Byrnes, J. F., *Speaking Frankly* (London & Toronto: Heinemann, 1947), p. 181.
6 Eden to FO, 7 February 1945. PREM 3/192/2, fo. 19.
7 Attlee to Churchill, 9 February 1945, ibid., fo. 16.
8 Protocol ..., 11 February 1945, ibid., fo. 6.
9 WM 18(45), 12 February. CA CAB 65/51.
10 Memo. of conversation, 4 February 1945. ERS 276.
11 Shortly before his death in 1972, Eisenhower told Lord Home that there were two reasons: the political directive, and the not insuperable problem of distance. Information from Lord Home.
12 Churchill, *The Second World War*, vol. XII, ibid., p. 292.

13 Churchill, op. cit., p. 298.
14 Spain: memo. by Russian delegation, 19 July 1945. PREM 8/106.
15 Private talk, Churchill–Stalin, 18 July 1945. PREM 3/430/6, fo. 45 et seq.
16 Ibid.
17 See, for example, Dalton diary, 29 May (?) 1945, 25 July.
18 Meeting, Attlee–Bevin–Stalin, 28 July 1945. PREM 3/430/9, fo. 297 et seq.
19 See Dalton diary, 27, 28 July 1945.
20 Ickes diary, 14 November 1945. HLI 21.

10   TUBE ALLOYS

1 … situation in China, n.d. FRUS 1945 (confs), p. 351 et seq.
2 Third Secretary memo., 23 January 1943. FRUS 1943 (China), p. 193 et seq.
3 F.E. Affairs memo., 11 February 1943. FRUS 1943 (China), p. 205 et seq.
4 Vincent to Hull, 30 March 1943. FRUS 1943 (China), p. 221.
5 Gauss to Hull, 14 October 1943. FRUS 1943 (China), p. 351.
6 Stimson to Marshall, 29 November 1945. Stimson mss 428. Kolko.
7 Memo. to President, 20 August 1945. Locke B6–42, box 2. Kolko.
8 Wallace diary, 6 November 1945. HAW 13.
9 Memo. to President, 20 August 1945. Locke, supra.
10 Hurley to Truman, 18 (?) May 1945. HST/MR 3.
11 Memo …, 20 August 1945, supra.
12 Wallace diary, 6 November 1945. HAW 13.
13 Cadogan diaries, p. 715; Stettinius to Johnson, 9, 10 October 1948, ERS 278.
14 Churchill to Dominion PMs, 5 July 1945. PREM 3/397/5, fo. 191 et seq.
15 Ibid. For text of secret agreement of 11 February 1945, see FRUS (confs), p. 984.
16 Harriman to Truman, 3 July 1945. HST/MR 3.
17 Clark-Kerr to Eden, 18 July 1945. PREM 3/397/5, fo. 180.
18 Halifax to Churchill, 13 May 1945, ibid., fo. 213.
19 Churchill to Halifax, 14 May 1945, ibid., fo. 209.
20 King to Churchill, 27 June 1945, ibid., fo. 199.
21 Cadogan to Churchill, 4 July 1945, ibid., fo. 194 et seq.
22 King to Churchill, 12 July 1945, ibid., fo. 189.
23 Clark-Kerr to Eden, 18 July 1945, ibid., fo. 180.
24 See also Churchill to Eden, 23 July 1945, ibid., fo. 177.
25 Churchill to Eden, 23 July 1945, supra.
26 For a good summary, see Churchill to Attlee, 29 July 1945, PREM 8/109, fo. 33 seq.; Churchill to Hopkins, 27 February 1943, HLH 132.
27 International treatment …, 7 July 1945. PREM 8/116, fo. 277 et seq.
28 Truman, *Memoirs*, vol. I, ibid., pp. 10–11.
29 International treatment …, supra.
30 Churchill, *The Second World War* vol. XII, ibid., p. 274.
31 Conference with President, 6 June 1945. Stimson mss b6–159. Kolko.
32 Churchill, op. cit., p. 274.

33 Truman, op. cit., p. 309.
34 Memo ..., 16 July 1945; conversation with Stalin, 25 July. Stimson mss 422. Kolko.
35 Private meetings Churchill–Stalin, 17 July 1945. PREM 3/430/7, fo. 6 et seq.
36 Private meetings Churchill–Stalin, 17, 18 July 1945, ibid.; also PREM 3/439/6, fo. 45 et seq.
37 Truman, *Memoirs*, vol. I, ibid., p. 346.
38 Memo ..., 16 July 1945 (Stimson), supra.
39 Memo ..., 6 June 1945. Stimson mss b6–159. Kolko.
40 Meeting, 10 August 1945. PREM 8/116, fo. 302 et seq.
41 The atomic bomb, 28 August 1945, ibid., fo. 268 et seq.
42 Supra; see also DFWR to Burke, 29 August 1945, and Attlee to Truman, 25 September, ibid., fos 266, 187 et seq.
43 Dalton diary, 17 October 1945.
44 Kennan to Byrnes, 30 September 1945. FRUS 1945 V, p. 884.
45 Winant to Byrnes, 5 November 1945; Harriman to Byrnes, 27 November, ibid., pp. 914 et seq., 922 et seq.
46 Wallace diary, 1 September 1945. HAW 36.
47 Wallace, supra. See also minutes of Cabinet meetings of 7, 21 September, 26 October in MJC 1, and PREM 8/116, 117, passim.
48 *Sunday Times*, 24 September 1945.

11 CALM BETWEEN STORMS

1 Byrnes to Truman, 13 August 1945. FRUS 1945 VI, p. 603 et seq.
2 Harriman to Byrnes, 23 August 1945, ibid., p. 689 et seq.
3 Harriman to Byrnes, 18 August 1945, ibid., p. 678.
4 Churchill to Peck, 27 August 1945. PREM 8/28.
5 Truman, *Memoirs*, vol. I, ibid., esp. pp. 365–6, 372–85.
6 Grew to Stimson, 28 June 1945 and enclosure. FRUS 1945 VI, p. 556 et seq.
7 Princeton seminars, 1954–5. DA 73.
8 Stettinius to Grew, 19 June 1945. HLH 338.
9 Truman, op. cit., p. 453.
10 CM 35(45), 25 September. CA CAB 128/3.
11 Future of the Italian colonies, 1 September 1945; Disposal ... (Bevin), 10 September. CAB 129/1, 2.
12 Dalton diary, 5 October 1945.
13 Bevin memoranda, CP (45)202, 218. CAB 129/3.
14 Byrnes to Barnes, 24 August 1945. FRUS 1945 IV, pp. 308–9.
15 Balfour to FO, 25 August 1945. FO 371/48129.
16 Barnes to Byrnes, 24 August 1945. FRUS 1945 IV, p. 309 et seq.
17 Houston-Boswell to Bevin, 29 September 1945. FO 371/48131, fo. 121.
18 Melbourne to Byrnes, 21 August 1945. FRUS 1945 V, p. 583.
19 Acheson to Berry, 5 September 1945, ibid., p. 608.
20 Le Rougetel to FO, 4 September 1945; Moscow to FO, 9 September, FO 371/48557, fos 116, 178 et seq.

21 Halifax to FO, 7 November 1945. FO 371/48132, fo. 70.
22 Berry (from Ethridge) to Byrnes, 26 November 1945. FRUS 1945 v, p. 627.
23 Squires to Byrnes, 15 September 1945. FRUS 1945 IV, p. 869 et seq.
24 Schoenfeld to Byrnes, 8 October 1945, ibid., p. 883.
25 Schoenfeld to Byrnes, 17 October 1945, ibid., p. 891.
26 Gascoigne to Bevin, 25 October 1945. FO 371/48471, fo. 29.
27 Budapest to FO, 6 November 1945, ibid., fo. 56 et seq.
28 Gascoigne to FO, 16 November 1945, ibid., fo. 165.
29 Documents in American Foreign Relations, VII, p. 152 et seq.
30 Nelson to Roosevelt, 6 November 1943. FDR/PSF 68.
31 Harriman to Stettinius, 4 January 1945. FRUS 1945(confs), p. 310 et seq.
32 Harriman to Stettinius, 6 January 1945, ibid., p. 313 et seq.
33 Morganthau to Roosevelt, 10 January 1945, ibid., p. 315.
34 Collado memo., 4 January 1945. FRUS 1945 v, p. 938 et seq.
35 Eden to Churchill, 10 July 1945. FO 954/2, fo. 319.
36 CM 35(45), 25 September. CA CAB 128/3.
37 Winant memo., n.d., but ca. February 1945. FRUS 1945 VI, p. 22 et seq.
38 Clayton to Vinson, 25 June 1945. FRUS 1945 VI, p. 54 et seq.
39 CM 50(45), 6 November. CA CAB 128/4.
40 Dalton diary, 7 December 1945.
41 Winant to Byrnes, 14 December 1945. FRUS 1945 VI, p. 196 et seq.
42 Davies to Sinclair, 10 December 1945. THRS 1945.
43 Bohlen, *Witness to History*, ibid., p. 249.
44 Informal meeting ..., 25 December 1945. FRUS 1945 II, p. 781.
45 Harriman to Acting S. of S., 24 December 1945, ibid., p. 760.
46 See, for example, Vandenberg to Dulles, 19 December 1945. Vandenberg mss. Kolko.
47 Vandenberg to Hutchison, 29 December 1945, ibid.
48 Curry, *James F. Byrnes*, ibid., p. 183.
49 Westerfield, *Foreign Policy and Party Politics*, ibid., p. 205.
50 Curry, op. cit., pp. 184–90.
51 Compare Bohlen, op. cit., p. 250.
52 CM 1(46), 1 January. CAB 128/5.

12   1946

1   Berry to Byrnes, 11 July 1946. FRUS 1946 VI, p. 614 et seq.
2   British Embassy to SD14 November 1946, ibid., p. 173 et seq.
3   See Greece ... (Bevin), 30 May 1946. CAB 129/10.
4   Schoenfeld to US Delegation, 22 April 1946. FRUS 1946 VI, p. 282 et seq.
5   Schoenfeld to Byrnes, 6 March 1946, ibid., p. 271 et seq.
6   Schoenfeld to Byrnes, 6 December 1946, ibid., p. 350 et seq.
7   Lane to Byrnes, 16 July 1946, ibid., p. 480; *Ann. Reg.* 1946 p. 240.
8   Lane to Byrnes, 26 July 1946, ibid., p. 484 et seq.
9   Lane to Byrnes, 14 December 1946, ibid., p. 526 et seq.
10 British Embassy to SD, 17 October 1946; Lane to Byrnes 14, 29 December, ibid., pp. 510 et seq., 536 seq., 552 et seq.

11 McNeill memo., 2 December 1946. CAB 129/15.
12 Attlee note, November 1946. PREM 8/222.
13 McNeill memo., supra.
14 Wallace diary, 15 March 1946. HAW 13.
15 Wallace diary, 27 November 1945. HAW 13.
16 Ibid.
17 Hodge to SCAP, 15 September 1946. MacArthur mss RG4. Kolko.
18 Truman, *Memoirs*, vol. II, ibid., pp. 320–2.
19 Bevin: Policy towards Germany, 3 May 1946. CAB 128/9.
20 CM 68(46), 15 July. CAB 128/6.
21 CM 102(46), 2 December. CAB 128/6.
22 Ickes diary, 19 December 1943. HLI 19.
23 Wallace diary, 23 November 1945. HAW 13.
24 See *Times*, 11 February 1946.
25 Winant to Byrnes, 21, 22 February 1946. NA NND 760,050 box 3979.
26 CM 23 (46), 11 March. CAB 128/5.
27 Peterson to FO, 28 May 1946. PREM 8/349.
28 See PREM 8/197, passim.
29 Wallace diary, 12 March 1946. HAW 13.
30 Lane to Byrnes, 17 September 1946. FRUS 1946 VI, p. 494 et seq.
31 Walton, R. J., *Henry Wallace, Harry Truman and the Cold War* (New York: Viking Press, 1976) p. 100 et seq.
32 See also Wallace diary, 10 September 1946. HAW 14.
33 Wallace diary, 18 September 1946. HAW 14.
34 Wallace: Oral history, p. 5013. HAW 33.
35 Walton, op. cit., pp. 114–16.
36 *Ann. Reg.* 1946, p. 209.
37 Wallace diary, 18 September 1946. HAW 14.
38 Curry, op. cit., p. 208 et seq.
39 Cabinet meeting, 31 August 1946. MJC 1.
40 Letter to Attlee, 29 October 1946. FO 371/56764.
41 CM 97(46), 18 November. CAB 128/8.
42 Dalton diary, 29 November 1946.
43 Ibid.
44 Curry, op. cit., p. 198 et seq.
45 Roberts to Warner, 5 June 1946. FO 371/56833.
46 Roberts to Sargent, 9 April 1946, FO 371/56832; Peterson to FO, 28 May, PREM 8/349.
47 Roberts to Warner, 5 June 1946. FO 371/56833.
48 SD Policy and Info. statement, 15 May 1946. CMC 14.
49 Clifford Report, 24 September 1946. HST/MISC 14.
50 Roberts to Warner, 30 July 1946. FO 371/56834.
51 Vandenberg to Luce, 28 May 1946. Vandenberg mss b-166. Kolko.
52 Chipman memo., 23 November 1946, endorsed in Smith to Byrnes, 20 December 1946. FRUS 1946 V, p. 471 et seq., 478 et seq.

13   MOMENT OF TRUTH

1   Scott: Report on Poland, 1 June 1947. Steinhardt mss 55. Kolko.
2   Lane to Marshall, 13 January 1947. Lane mss. Kolko.
3   Oak to Lane, 28 February 1947. Lane mss. Kolko.
4   Impressions of a recent visit ... Silkin, 31 December 1947. CAB 129/22.
5   Andrews memo., 17 November 1947. FRUS 1947 IV, p. 460 et seq.
6   Extinction of human rights ... Bevin, 24 November 1947. CAB 129/22.
7   Crocker to Marshall, 13 January 1948. NA NND 760,050 box 6369.
8   Extinction ..., supra.
9   Horner to Marshall, 22 June 1947. FRUS 1947 IV, p. 164 et seq.
10   Schoenfeld to Marshall, 22, 28 February 1947, ibid., p. 269 et seq., 271.
11   Hickerson to Marshall, 3 June 1947, ibid., p. 1308 et seq.
12   J. M. Dodge bulletin ..., 1 July 1947. Dodge mss. box 6. Kolko.
13   Chapin to Marshall, 14 August 1947(2); McKisson memo., 3 September, ibid., pp. 354 et seq., 356 et seq., 364.
14   Chapin to Marshall, 2 October 1947, ibid., p. 384 et seq.
15   Extinction ..., supra.
16   Steinhardt to Diamond, 27 May 1947. Steinhardt mss. box 84. Kolko.
17   Caffery to Marshall, 31 March 1947. FRUS 1947 III, p. 695 et seq.
18   Dunn to Marshall, 3 May 1947, ibid., p. 889 et seq.
19   Inverchapel to Attlee, 10 March 1947. FO 800/279.
20   WD staff study, n.d. FRUS 1947 II, p. 178 et seq.
21   Exhaustion of the dollar credit, 21 March 1947. CAB 129/17.
22   Norton to Sargent, 7 March 1947. FO 800/276.
23   Acheson to Truman, 15 August 1947. HST/CF 34.
24   Roberts to Sargent, 9 April 1946. FO 371/56832.
25   CM 14(47), 30 January. CAB 128/9.
26   Acheson to Marshall, 27 February 1947. FRUS 1947 V, p. 29 et seq.
27   Truman, *Memoirs*, vol. II, ibid., p. 104.
28   Meeting of 7 March 1947. MJC 1.
29   Truman, supra.
30   Walton, *Henry Wallace, Harry Truman and the Cold War*, ibid., pp. 145–8.
31   Ibid., p. 152.
32   O'Mahoney to Truman, 10 March 1947. Truman mss E.109. Kolko.
33   Dulles to Vandenberg, 21 July 1947. Vandenberg mss. Kolko.
34   Leahy diary, 27 February 1947, cited in Ferrell, R. H., *George C. Marshall*, vol. XV of *The American Secretaries of State and their Diplomacy*, Ferrell, R. H. (ed.) (New York: Cooper Square, 1966) p. 90.
35   The military situation in Greece, 11 October 1947. PREM 8/527.
36   Caffery to Marshall, 31 March 1947. FRUS 1947 III, p. 695 et seq.
37   Caffery to Marshall, 12 May 1947, ibid., p. 709 et seq.
38   Dunn to Marshall, 3 May 1947, ibid., p. 889 et seq.
39   Memo. of conversation, 20 May 1947. FRUS 1947 III, p. 908 et seq.
40   Truman, *Memoirs*, vol. II, ibid., p. 110.
41   Sheppherd to Welles, 7 April 1947, ibid., p. 199 et seq.
42   Kennan to Acheson, 23 May 1947, ibid., p. 223 et seq.
43   European reconstruction ... Bevin, 22 June 1947. CAB 129/19.
44   Douglas to Marshall, 3 July 1947. FRUS 1947 III, p. 306 et seq.

45 Notes ..., July 1947. Dodge mss box 7. Kolko.
46 Steinhardt to Marshall, 10 July 1947, etc. FRUS 1947 III, p. 318 et seq.
47 Notes ..., July 1947, supra.
48 Policy in Germany, Bevin, 5 January 1948. CAB 129/23.
49 Cabinet, 19 December 1947. MJC 1.
50 Bevin, supra.

14 COLD WAR

1   Kennan to Marshall, 24 February 1946. FRUS 1948 I, p. 509 et seq.
2   Kennan to Marshall, 14 March 1948, ibid., p. 531 et seq.
3   Dixon to Sargent, 27 February 1948. FO 800/273.
4   Dockart: Record of conversation ..., 10 March 1948, ibid.
5   Steinhardt to Marshall, 30 April 1948. FRUS 1948 IV, p. 747 et seq.
6   Ibid.
7   Steinhardt to Marshall, supra; Dixon to Sargent, supra.
8   Steinhardt to Marshall, 31 May 1948. FRUS 1948 IV, p. 755 et seq.
9   McNeil to Healey, 9 February 1948. FO 371/72374.
10 *Ann. Reg.* 1948, p. 278; Helm to Bevin, 1 March 1948, FO 371/72375.
11 CM 19(48), 5 March. CAB 128/12.
12 Reading copy 1, 10–11 October 1953. DA 75.
13 Ibid.
14 Policy in Germany, 5 January 1948. CAB 129/23.
15 SD Policy Paper, n.d. FRUS 1948 II, p. 61 et seq.
16 Marshall to Truman, 11 February 1948. HST/PSF 178.
17 CM 22(48), 15 March. CAB 128/12.
18 Marshall to Douglas, 20 February 1948. FRUS 1948 II, p. 71 et seq.
19 Marshall to Douglas, 28 February 1948, ibid., p. 101 et seq.
20 Marshall to Douglas, 20 February 1948, supra.
21 CM 19(48), 7 June. CAB 128/12.
22 Douglas to Marshall, 28 April 1948. FRUS 1948 II, p. 899.
23 Chase to Marshall, 29 April 1948, ibid., p. 900 et seq.
24 Murphy to Marshall, 23 June 1948, ibid., p. 915.
25 Truman 'Memoirs' file, 18 July 1948. HST/Post-Presidential 2.
26 Caffery to Marshall, 24 June 1948. FRUS 1948 II, p. 916 et seq.
27 Policy Planning Staff meeting, 28 September 1948, ibid., p. 1194 et seq.
28 Murphy to Marshall, 26 June 1948, ibid., p. 919 et seq.
29 Marshall to Douglas, 28 June 1948, ibid., p. 930 et seq.
30 Smith to Marshall, 24 July 1948, ibid., p. 984 et seq.
31 Smith to Marshall, 3 August 1948, ibid., p. 984 et seq.
32 CM 43(48), 25 June. CAB 128/13.
33 Truman, *Memoirs*, vol. II, ibid., pp. 124–5.
34 Ibid; CM 54(48), 26 July. CAB 128/13.
35 Truman, op. cit., p. 127.
36 CM 44, 54(48), 28 June, 26 July, CAB 128/13; Marshall to Douglas, 20 July 1948, FRUS 1948 II, P. 971 et seq.
37 Acheson: Princeton seminars, DA 73.
38 Ibid.

39   Cabinet, 2 August 1948. MJC 1.
40   Walter, J. S., *Henry A. Wallace and American Foreign Policy* (Westport & London: Greenwood Press, 1976) p. 171.
41   Smith to Marshall, 9 November 1948. FRUS 1948 IV, p. 931 et seq.
42   Cannon to Marshall, 4 January 1948, ibid., p. 1070 et seq.
43   Reams to Marshall, 18 June 1948, ibid., p. 1073 et seq.
44   See The military situation in Greece (Bevin, Alexander), 11 October 1948. PREM 8/527. Also various documents reprinted in FRUS 1948 IV, p. 1079 et seq.
45   PPS paper, 30 June 1948. FRUS 1948 IV, p. 1079 et seq.
46   'X': The sources of Soviet conduct, *Foreign Affairs*, 25 (July 1947) pp. 566–82; J. L. Gaddis, Containment: a reassessment, *Foreign Affairs*, 55 (July 1977) pp. 873–87.
47   Smith to Marshall, 23 December 1948. FRUS 1948 IV, p. 943 et seq.

15   THE LESSONS

1   Stalin to Ivanov, 12 February 1938, reported in *Pravda*, 14 February. Translation taken from FRUS (SU 1933–39), p. 524.
2   See Douglas, R., *The Advent of War 1939–40* (London: Macmillan, 1978) p. 34 et. seq.
3   Churchill to Eden, 16 January 1944. PREM 3/399/6, fo. 81.
4   *Life*, XXV, 30 August 1948. Quoted in Farnworth, B., *William C. Bullitt and the Soviet Union* (Bloomington & London: Indiana U.P., 1967).
5   Mikolajczyk to Roosevelt, 18 March 1944. FDR/PSF 66.

Index